A KITCHEN IN CORFU

A KITCHEN IN CORFU

James Chatto and W. L. Martin

NEW AMSTERDAM
New York

For Audria
For Rosalind

Copyright © 1987 James Chatto and W.L. Martin

All rights reserved.
First American edition published 1988 by
NEW AMSTERDAM BOOKS, 171 Madison Avenue,
New York, N.Y. 10016.

Published by arrangement with George Weidenfeld and Nicolson Limited, London.

Series Editor: Vicky Hayward
Map and line drawing by
Joy FitzSimmons

Library of Congress Cataloging-in-Publication Data

Chatto, James.
　A kitchen in Corfu.

　Includes index.
　1. Cookery, Greek. 2. Cookery — Greece — Corfu
Island. 3. Corfu Island (Greece) — Social life
and customs. I. Martin, W.L. II. Title.
TX723.5.G8C42 1987　　　641.59495'5　　　87-38323
ISBN 0-941533-17-4

🍇 CONTENTS

ACKNOWLEDGEMENTS

This book began in the kitchen of our friend, mentor and *koubaros*, Philip Parginos. Without his continuing generosity and advice it could not have been written.

We should also like to thank our many other friends in Loutses and Peritheia for their help, in particular Koula Parginou, Maria Parginou, Vasiliki Sarakinou, Paradisi Parginou, Michelle Parginou, Billi Rosen, and all the others whose names are mentioned in this book. Mr Andreas Papadatos of the Corfu Reading Society, Mrs Georgopoulou of the Corfu Radio Station and Mr Vasilakis of the Union of Agricultural Co-operatives of Corfu were kind enough to assist with our research, and Deborah Sanderson and Audria Tracey gave invaluable assistance in preparing many of the Loutsiot recipes in England and Canada.

Lastly we must thank our editors Vicky Hayward, Barbara Mellor and Kate Ferry for their unfailing patience, encouragement and guidance.

When first *o koubaros mou* asked me to help him write this book, my reaction was that I may be a good bartender, or seaman or dairy technician, but I am not a writer. Later, though, I began to think how books bring people, cultures and civilizations together: I hope this one will help to do this.

Philip Parginos

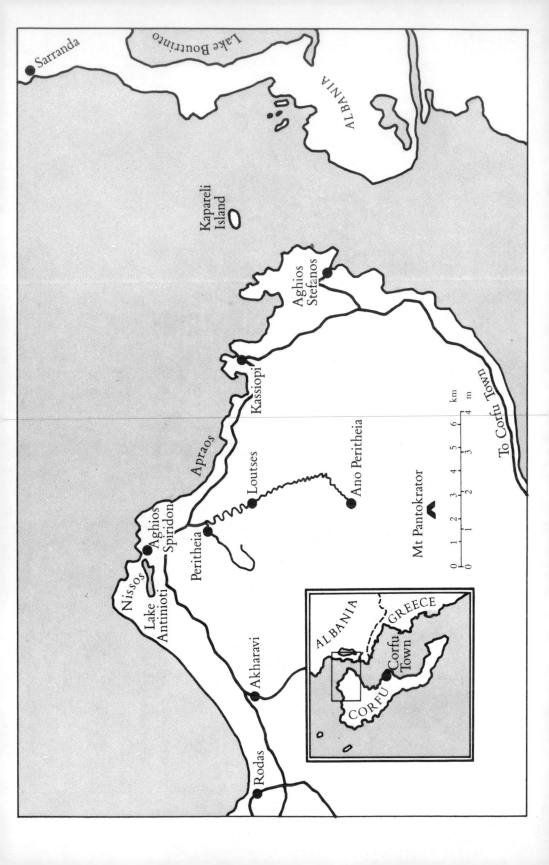

🍇 INTRODUCTION

The road to Loutses begins by the sea, winding up into the great bulk of mountains that form the north-eastern corner of the island of Corfu. Two miles inland and eight hundred feet up, it enters a valley shaped like a shallow bowl, backed by a looming escarpment of the mountains and sheltered on the northern, seaward side by a low, crenellated ridge called Zervou.

The view from Zervou is spectacular. Northwards lies a great arc of the open sea, dazzling under the cloudless sky. To the west the mountains draw back from it, creating a narrow, fertile plain that stretches into the Ionian in a series of bays and promontories. Out beyond the furthest cape stand three small islands, reaching over the horizon towards the heel of Italy, forty miles away. To the east, across two miles of water, soar the jagged peaks of Albania, barren ranges clambering further and further back into the Balkan mainland until they are lost in a blue haze.

Behind Zervou sprawls the village of Loutses. As it climbs gently upwards, the valley floor crumples into combes and outcrops, and upon the steepest of them stands a small pink church. Below it, hugging the road, is a scattering of houses and bungalows, two shops, two tavernas and a bar.

These are the central buildings of the village, but Loutses is a great deal larger. Every few hundred yards along the road small lanes twist away among the trees to isolated groups of houses. Perched upon a rise or tucked away in some fold of the land, each of these communities within the community has its own name and history. Around them are sheds and ramshackle chicken coops; and even further away, some of them a twenty minute walk from the main road, lie the outlying farms of the village, visible only as a scattering of ochre-tiled rooftops protruding from the olive trees.

Loutses is an olive-farming community, historically self-sufficient, and in its heyday, fifty years ago, it was the centre of the isolated hamlets and farms in the wooded hills of the north-east. We first came here by chance, as tourists, but after two hedonistic summers we succumbed to temptation, bought a ruined house with a fine view, and moved here for good.

Corfu changes in the winter. The island is shaken by storms and soaked by interminable rain. The coastal resorts are dark and shuttered, the restaurants closed and the few shops that remain open have little to offer when compared with the abundance of summer. The proscriptions of the season are firm, and during our first winter we could find no way round them. Circumstances forced us to eat what the Loutsiotes eat, and to learn to cook as they cook, for friends in the village found our foreign recipes strange and unpalatable.

As we became more involved in the life of the village, our patterns of eating changed too. The Loutsiotes do not have breakfast, but they eat a substantial, usually cold 'elevenses' before a late lunch, followed in the summer by a two-hour siesta. They eat their evening meal at various times, depending on the season. In the winter, when work in the olive groves is at its most demanding, the family has dinner at eight or nine o'clock – or even later if the man of the house has lingered up at the bar. In the summer when the social life of the village is more active everyone, including the children, eats at some time between ten o'clock and midnight, depending on their mood. Most households cook only one substantial meal in a day, either in the afternoon or evening; the other will be lighter, for example a simple dish of pasta or vegetables.

During our first, educative winter on the island we learned that there is more to Corfiot cooking than we had ever imagined from our experiences as tourists. Friends, acquaintances and even total strangers were our teachers, for the people of Loutses take a keen interest in food and are delighted by any opportunity to talk about it. Often our conversations began with a reaffirmation of a series of loyalties. It was necessary first to understand that the cooking in question was indisputably Greek. Having agreed upon that we could explore the reasons why it was nevertheless uniquely Corfiot. Once that was established we learned what differentiated a rural recipe from the same dish when it was made in the island's capital, Corfu Town. When this point was grasped we were able to progress to the curious nuances of seasoning preferred in neighbouring villages or even households.

It is a truism that any regional cuisine is the result of that area's history and geography, but where Corfiot cooking is concerned these influences have often been contradictory. Corfu has had two histories – that of the town and that of the countryside – and for the last thousand years the fashions of one and the environmental demands of the other have been pulling the islanders' culinary tastes in different directions. Through it all, though, certain precepts have remained the same and they can be traced back to the very beginning of Corfu's history.

To Homer the island was a place on the shadowy frontier of geography, lying just over the horizon of Mycenaean consciousness – a real island with a powerful navy, but *terra incognita* to his audience. Nowhere could have better suited his poetic purposes as a halfway-house on Odysseus's journey back from the lands of fantastic monsters to the domestic reality of his home on Ithaca. Luxurious, urbane, devout without being obsequious, the civilization he sketches is extraordinary in its perfected embodiment of the ordinary.

Scholars have always been wary of taking Homer literally, but it is difficult to avoid it when so many of the details of daily life he offers correspond so precisely to present-day Corfu. Homeric raisins for example, are dried on wooden boards exactly as they used to be twenty years ago in Loutses, Odysseus is given 'many little dainties' to eat with his bread and wine – a menu that should surely be translated as *mezethes* – and on the following day is feasted with spit-roasted meat.

Homer's descriptions of the wealth and naval strength of the island proved prophetic. By classical times it had very definitely pulled itself into the world as one of the richest and most powerful states in the Mediterranean. Xenophon recalls that the local troops lived so well off the land that they would only drink wines with a good bouquet. But their salad days came to an end with the Peloponnesian war and the subsequent civil struggles that ruined the island. In 229 BC, unable to defend themselves from pirates and barbarians, the islanders voluntarily surrendered to the protection of Rome, becoming the Republic's first Greek possession.

Corfu flourished under Rome. Forests were destroyed for timber for the shipyards, but vineyards and wheat production were encouraged, and cities like Kassiopi became very rich indeed from tourism.

For the next two thousand years the island drifted in a curiously repetitive tide of events, prospering, often for many centuries at a time, as a favoured corner of some mighty empire, then plummetting into ruin as the influence of her rulers declined, only to rise again on the back of a different Leviathan. Her strategic position made sure of her inclusion in any grand schemes for the Mediterranean, and her natural wealth gave her the means for rejuvenation over and over again, provided someone was guaranteeing her military protection.

Throughout these vicissitudes, the traditions of classical Greek cooking remained intact. The Romans' obsessive interest in Greek culture had led them to adopt Greek cuisine in its entirety, and Greek chefs in the entourages of Roman gentlemen carried their skills and theories to the ends of the empire, thus laying the same Greek foundations for all the subsequent edifices of northern Mediterranean cuisine.

When the Roman empire split into east and west in AD 395, Corfu was included in the eastern, Byzantine half. Two hundred years of barbarian raids and harrassment were to pass, however, before the influence of Byzantium grew powerful enough to reach the Ionian. By the seventh century Corfu had become one of the principal western ports of the empire, with a population of 100,000, only a little smaller than it is today. The ancient culinary traditions had been safely preserved by the cooks of Byzantium, but as the centuries passed, the fringes of the Orthodox empire grew increasingly tattered. In the Middle Ages Corfu was both the victim and envied possession of Norman adventurers, Genoese pirates, Byzantine despots and, for a hundred years, the Angevin kings of Naples.

Corfu has a habit of obliterating the endeavours of men: entire cities have disappeared utterly from the face of the tiny island. Each of this long succession of foreign rulers left only the faintest of impressions on Corfu. Partly because the governing powers were only really interested in the island for its strategic position, partly because the Greek sense of national and religious identity is so strong, Corfu remained an indisputably Greek island.

When the Angevins no longer had the ability to protect the island from their enemies, the citizens took it upon themselves to offer

Corfu to Venice in return for her protection. The fleet arrived in 1386 and sixteen years later the Most Serene Republic made the occupation legal by officially buying the island from Ladislaus of Naples for thirty thousand ducats. The Venetians were to hold Corfu for the next four hundred years and it was from this time that the history of the island and the identity of its cuisine really began to diverge from that of the mainland.

Today Corfiots returning from Athens and points east continually report that the food there is too oily and over-spiced; even the cooking of the north-western parts of the mainland can seem unpalatably rich. The islanders blame this on the influence the Turks had on mainland tastes. When they overran Constantinople, the Turks adopted the sophisticated Greek cuisine of Byzantium and in the opinion of the Corfiots they coarsened it considerably with their Eastern love of spices and heavy textures. During the centuries in which they occupied Greece, these preferences were assimilated by the native population. But the Turks never conquered Corfu. There the ancient traditions were influenced more by the Venetians, at least among the upper classes of Corfu Town, whose education and career prospects depended upon Venetian patronage.

The islanders are adamant about this disparity, and proud of it but it would be misleading to claim, as many guidebooks do, that the Venetian influence on Corfiot gastronomy was as obvious and profound as it was on more concrete aspects of life, such as the island's architecture. A better analogy might be drawn with the Corfiot dialect: the people speak Greek of course, but with a distinct Italianate lilt and every now and then a pure Italian word will have slipped in to replace a Greek one. On Corfu the cooking is definitely Greek, but the use of spices is uncommon and though olive oil is inescapable it is used less heavily than it is on the mainland. The Italian influence is clear-cut in the islanders' love of pasta, but this is one of a few isolated examples rather than a typical illustration of a general rule.

In the countryside, particularly in the remote northern villages, the Italian influence is even less apparent. The rural population of the island had always led very different lives from the citizens of the town. Depriving the peasantry of education and civil rights had always made economic sense to the landowning aristocracy and the Venetians made no attempt to reform the feudal system they inherited. Even the security of the island beyond the walls of the town was essentially incidental to the safety of the citadel and the harbour.

When the Turks laid waste to the countryside and took 20,000 of its inhabitants into slavery in 1537 the Venetians were still able to claim a victory since the citadel had not fallen. While the culture of the town became increasingly Italianate, the rural population was continually reinforced by refugees from the mainland, and their tastes were more relevant within the community than those of the urban aristocracy.

In 1797 Venice fell to Napoleon and the old Venetian territories in the Ionian passed into the hands of the Republican French. They, however, were soon ousted by an alliance of the Russians and Turks, who in 1800 set up a technically independent republic of the seven Ionian islands, headed by Corfu; it lasted seven years, until the French returned, this time as an Imperial power. After the abdication of Napoleon, the Septinsular Republic was re-established, but under the protection of a British governor and occupying garrison. In 1864, Britain ceded the island to the newly formed kingdom of Greece.

For the next century, life in the villages of Corfu remained entirely static, held in place by rigid ties. Culinary traditions were constantly reinforced by the strictures of an unchanging landscape and economy. The links to Byzantium were still strong because of the Church, and the influence of ancient Rome was still felt in the technology of the olive industry. The supremacy of olive oil in all culinary matters continued to show the direct influence of classical Greek tastes.

The structure of family life also helped to bolster tradition. In the past, when a woman married, she went to live in her husband's house. Her husband's parents lived there too and the new wife was expected to obey her mother-in-law and to suggest no innovations to the way the household was run. Because the wife spent much of the year working in the olive groves, her mother-in-law was largely responsible for bringing up the children; passing on her own culinary knowledge to her granddaughters she thereby ensured a strong conservatism in all matters relating to the kitchen.

More important and more ancient than any other influence on local cooking, however, were the economic and ecological facts of rural life. The poverty and isolated location of Loutses led to an almost total self-sufficiency, and the wild plants and creatures of the mountains and seashore became an important part of the local diet. The lack of any arable land limited the village's resources further but, at the same time, the climate and natural fertility of the island meant that what could be grown locally was of a consistently high quality.

All these factors, combined with the culinary traditionalism that is a mark of any poor rural community, gave rise to a conscious simplicity in village cooking, especially where meat and fish were concerned. The Loutsiotes have always preferred recipes that reveal the virtues of both wild and cultivated produce rather than those that disguise them.

In the last twenty years a new invasion has swept the island. Since the end of the 1960s, Corfu has been the goal of millions of tourists, and the affluence and employment this has brought have touched everyone. But the old differences between town and countryside have not completely disappeared. Instead they have been transmuted into a new dichotomy between the inland regions and the beaches. Every summer the population of Corfu doubles as a girdle of tourism squeezes round the coast. All but a very few of the visitors stand resolutely facing out to sea, as indifferent to the interior of the island as any Roman admiral or Byzantine despot.

As ever, this dichotomy is reflected in the island's cooking. The tavernas where the tourists eat have their own traditions and they have their money to make in a competitive market and they cater their menus to the proven tastes of their international clientele, be it for curry and chips or frozen pizza. The people of Loutses are not snobs. Some of the men eat in some of the same places the tourists do and they actually like what the waiter brings them. Nevertheless, they would always choose more familiar food at home and there is no danger that traditional cooking will disappear. The tourists are, after all, a seasonal phenomenon. In the winter it is as if they had never been here at all.

🍇 COOK'S NOTES

The people of Loutses do not use written recipes. They cook from memory, correcting the seasoning of a dish by frequent tasting and, except when they bake cakes or biscuits, measuring their ingredients by eye. For the purposes of this book, we measured the amounts they used while we watched them cooking, but the resulting quantities are not intended to be immutable law. Without distorting the spirit of a particular dish, the villagers often change the relationship of its ingredients – or even leave some out altogether – according to their mood.

The quantities given in this book are in metric and standard amounts, and liquid measurements are also given in US cups. Our tablespoon is equivalent to three teaspoons. Unless otherwise stated, each recipe should make enough for four hungry people.

The provenance and quality of their ingredients is just as important to the cooks of Loutses as the way in which they are subsequently prepared. We have tried to reflect this in the arrangement of the chapters in this book, grouping the recipes according to the source of their principal ingredient. We have also tried to suggest alternatives to some foodstuffs that are difficult to find outside Greece.

The oil we mention is of course always olive oil – the pure, mellow-flavoured, golden oil of Corfu. The Loutsiotes occasionally press a thick green oil from unripe olives, but they consider its flavour too strong for anything but salads. Corfu oil (recognizable by the word Kerkyra, the Greek name for the island) can occasionally be found in Greek emporia in other countries; otherwise, any good quality Greek table oil will have to do.

The Corfiots cook with fresh garlic bulbs which have an exquisite, deep flavour but none of the heat of dried garlic. Where herbs are concerned, dried *rigani* is increasingly available in Greek shops and so are the more esoteric flavourings such as *mahlepi*, a spice used in certain cakes. Fresh *selino* is not often found, but a finely-chopped stick of celery is an adequate substitute. It is worth seeking out fresh Mediterranean parsley, though since its flavour in North America and Europe is noticeably more vague than it is in Greece, it may be necessary to use a little more than we suggest. The same is true of Greek tomato paste, which seems much more strongly flavoured than its equivalents elsewhere.

For the American Reader

European names are given in the text for some of the vegetables used in Corfiot cooking. We list them here, with their American equivalents:

aubergine — eggplant;
courgette — young firm zucchini, usually less than five inches long, often with the blossom still attached;
dried haricots — kidney beans;
mangetouts — edible-podded peas;
vegetable marrow — zucchini, either the long or the oval variety.

OLIVES

Indolent beyond belief, the Corfiot peasant is satisfied with the food which Providence affords him off the neighbouring olive-tree; and which he patiently waits to see drop on to the ground. The kindly berry, added to a piece of bread and some salt fish, forms his daily sustenance; its oil gives him light, and its wood supplies his fuel.

Henry Jervis-White Jervis
A History of Corfu, 1852

The olive groves of Loutses are solitary places in the motionless heat of a July afternoon. Beneath the trees, a carpet of orange-coloured leaves muffles every sound but the murmur of insects; the dark green canopy of foliage refracts the glare of the sun into a blur of light and shadow. A stranger can lose himself for hours along the paths that twist away through the avenues of gnarled old trunks – up over steep ridges, down into gullies where a dried-up stream bed disappears into a tangle of briar and bracken.

Unpruned, tall and occasionally magnificent, the trees seem petrified by the heat of summer, but in the winter they come to life. From Zervou ridge, one can see the patterns of the wind gust up from the distant sea, bending the high branches and turning the leaves in waves of green and silver-grey. On wet mornings the village wakes up to fog and no journey is made that is not absolutely necessary, but the women are working out in the groves. Passing the olive press on the road down to the coast, the damp air is heavy with the tangy smell of crushed berries and men are busy loading shiny metal drums of oil into the back of a truck.

In winter, the light under the dripping trees is dim and the air cold. In all directions the ground is covered by black plastic nets which the villagers laid the previous November, cutting them to fit around the twisted, pitted trunks and sewing them together with nails or supple twigs threaded through the fine mesh. The nets are there to catch the olives, for the percentage of oil in an olive increases as it ripens, turning from green to mottled purple to black, and to take advantage of the fact that the farmers of Corfu let their olives ripen until they fall. In all other countries and in most of the rest of Greece the berries are either picked by hand or beaten from the trees, but the Corfiots, according to the proverb, beat neither their olive trees nor their women.

The families who first settled the valley nearly two hundred years ago came here to farm the trees and their descendants do so still. Throughout the winter and spring the principal work of the women is to gather and collect the fallen olives before they begin to rot. It is a back-breaking and solitary job that numbs the fingers and the mind, but it has to be done once a month beneath every tree during the long olive season or the berries will begin to decay and the quality of their oil will deteriorate.

The money from their oil remains the basis of the villagers' income. In the last two decades tourism has brought a new affluence to the island: the men of Loutses build houses and hotels down on the coast and their sons find jobs in the restaurants, but the trees have not disappeared. Every year from November to June the villagers must work among them as their great-great-grandparents did, for whatever else a family does for a living, it is still bound to the calendar of the olive.

There have been olives on Corfu since the Bronze Age. Homer mentions them in his description of King Alkinoos's garden, but no one knows how or when they first came to the island. The tree itself, *olea europaea*, was almost certainly cultivated from the wild olive or oleaster, a thorny shrub with dry hard berries, and it seems likely that this happened about five thousand years ago. Greek historians credit the achievement to the Cretans; Middle Eastern experts claim that the pioneers were a Semitic tribe living in Syria, but the most persuasive theory is that both civilizations created the olive simultaneously and independently of one another.

Olive trees could have reached Corfu from either place. They were introduced into Greece from Minoan Crete, but Corfu was not yet a part of the Greek world. The Utopian civilization that Homer describes in the *Odyssey* may well have been Phoenician rather than Mycenaean, in which case olive tree cuttings could have been brought here from the Levant.

Salted and spiced, olives are often mentioned as food in the *Iliad* and the *Odyssey*, but it seems as if in Homeric times olive oil had not yet become a commonplace of the kitchen. It is repeatedly referred to, but as an unguent, golden and precious – an indispensible cosmetic to the aristocrat, to be smoothed over the body after bathing.

During the classical period, however, the extraordinary versatility of olive oil raised it to a position of unique importance in the Greek world. It became the best possible medium for cooking, for rich and poor alike, and it was a valuable and abundant trading commodity that was often treated as actual currency. It was both a simple lubricant and a part of the most esoteric religious mysteries; it was the prize awarded to the greatest athletes and the basic lamp oil of the humblest household.

The history of the olive groves of Loutses begins eighteen hundred years later, in 1386, when the Venetians first sailed into the harbour of Corfu Town. Olive oil was still a fundamental of Corfiot daily life, though it had long since ceased to be an important economic commodity. A Venetian inventory of the island's taxable produce taken in 1386 contains no reference to the olive. The Venetians wanted Corfu for its strategic position on the trade routes, but as responsible book-keepers they also looked for a way of making their new colony pay for itself. They decided to develop the olive oil industry and for the next two hundred years tried to impose this wish on the landowning nobility, but with indifferent results. An English visitor to the island in 1596 records the 'fruits, corn, wines [and] currants' he saw but there is still no word of oil. Finally, laws and ordinances having failed, the Venetians turned to bribery, offering a bounty of 36 drachmas for every ten olive trees planted. The idea was a good one. By the end of the seventeenth century there were two million trees on the island, exporting a biannual total of 60,000 barrels of oil.

Every metre of available land was put under olives, including, eventually, the inaccessible slopes and valleys of the north-east, but the Venetians found it harder to encourage the growth of the work-force needed to pick and press them into oil. In 1499 the population of the island had been 37,075; a hundred years later it had dropped to 17,500 and the decline had occurred largely among the rural areas as a result of raids by the Turks, who controlled all of mainland Greece except for a handful of Venetian enclaves down the coast of Epirus. Of these the most important was Parga, a tiny promontory two miles wide and six miles long, protected from land attack by daunting mountains. It was events there that were to lead to the settling of Loutses.

The Parganauts must have been extraordinarily accomplished dip-lomats. After Venice fell, their town passed into the hands of the Republican French, then the Russians, then the Imperial French and finally the British. Each of these powers agreed to give Parga to Ali Pasha of Iannina, the local Turkish leader, but on each occasion the Parganauts managed to persuade them not to. By 1817, however, Ali Pasha's patience had run out and he demanded that Britain, now in control of Corfu and the Ionian islands, should give him Parga at last. The British were bound by treaty to comply, but they invited the Parganauts to move *en masse* to Corfu. Two thousand seven hundred of them, all but two families, accepted the offer.

Henry Jervis-White Jervis, an artillery officer with the British garrison on Corfu, noted their arrival with approval: 'To the Ionian islands and Corfu in particular, the accession of the Parguinotes became excessively beneficial; and they now form one of the most industrious portions of the community.' The British gave those who wanted them rent-free houses in the suburb of Corfu Town called Mandouki, but others, families who had been farmers in Parga, soon moved out into the countryside, taking the surname Parginos in memory of their heritage.

With the active support of the British, many new settlements were founded on the island at this time, and many small ones began to grow into sizeable communities. The impoverished and mountain-ous north-east was particularly underpopulated, so the exiles from Parga were encouraged to apply for land to the local administration of the ancient town of Peritheia (now called Ano Peritheia), high in a secluded valley in the mountains. From there three of the Parginos families were brought north to a valley called Loutses, halfway down the mountains towards the sea.

The name Loutses means 'holes in the ground where water collects' – an apt enough description in the winter, but possessed of a certain irony in the summer months, for there is not and never has been water in the valley. Nevertheless, there were already several olive farmers living there, some of them smallholders, some of them the tenants of absentee landlords. Parts of the valley belonged to the Church, including the bare ridge known as Zervou, the bequest of a nobleman called Zervos from the south of the island. The soil on the ridge was too poor to support even olives, so the Church was pleased to mortgage it to the three immigrant families as a place where they could build their houses.

In this way, as a scattering of farms all over the valley, the village of Loutses began to grow. Not surprisingly, life was centred around the olive. A family's wealth was measured by the number of trees it owned, and land was valued and even referred to in terms of the trees it supported. Olive trees became the currency of dowries and bequests and those who wished to remember the Church in their will left it one or two, named after their favourite saint. Today the Church owns about two thousand trees in the area, many of them scattered about somebody else's grove. The devout believe that the olives they bear belong to God and so year after year the berries rot upon the ground, ungathered and unpressed.

The settlers in Loutses had little choice about their future employment and no opportunity at all to improve upon the techniques of their work. During the nineteenth century and for the first half of the twentieth, Greece was too poor a country to invest in agricultural reforms or new technology. So from Roman times until the 1960s olive farming scarcely changed at all.

Philip Parginos is descended from the Parganaut families who came to live on Zervou. As a child in the 1950s he grew up helping his parents in the olive groves. By this time, Loutses had grown into a large and influential community with a population of more than five hundred, a number that was doubled during the olive season by the itinerant pickers who came to help with the harvest. There were no nets in those days and a large workforce was needed to collect the fallen berries from the ground, picking them out from between rocks, raking through leaves and grass and rescuing strays from gullies and ditches. Philip's family owned five hundred trees and during the season they would employ between one and ten pickers, depending on the size of the crop, for a total of about a hundred and fifty days.

The wages paid to these casual workers were low even by the standards of a severely impoverished Greece: 12 drachmas a day – the equivalent, perhaps, of 6p or 10 cents – or alternatively the workers could take their payment in oil. They were mainly women, some from other villages, some travelling gypsies, and they sang all day as they worked. Many of the songs were simple, traditional chants such as 'Good Luck to the Olive', with its cheerful refrain of 'Good luck to the olives that make the oil; And bring my darling to offer us oil', designed to alleviate some of the backache of the labour and to flatter the owner who was to pay them. Others, particularly those for the end of the season, were more sophisticated laments. Philip can remember one that women sang when the olives were finally gathered in:

I want to be alone to sing of my passions.
How can I find an end of them,
When I'm crying so hard?
Neither God nor man knows how
For I weep for two lands now.
I will wet my eyes with poisoned tears
But the sea has ears to hear my weeping –
If I told you my love
The wild sea would destroy the world –
If I told you my love under the moon and sun
They would both be blown into darkness.

In those days the olives were still pressed in the village. There were twelve *litrouvia*, olive presses, operating in Loutses and one of the three up on Zervou belonged to Philip's family. It consisted of three pieces of machinery sunk deep into the floor of a room in the house and secured to the ceiling by massive beams. Taking up half the space was the mill, a circular bowl of dressed stone about ten feet in diameter, and as high as a man's waist. From the centre rose a spindle made from a single cypress trunk, and attached to this by axels were three enormous querns of imported millstone grit, chiselled into perfect wheels by skilled men a hundred years ago. Turned by a tethered horse, the stones crushed the olives as they were poured in by the farmers. Then the pulp was shovelled into pouches of knitted rope which were drenched with hot water to loosen the oil and carried to the press itself in the centre of the room.

Here the full pouches were stacked on to a metal plate while four or five men levered a second plate down on top of them, straining in the noisy, overheated room, their mouths full of the acrid smell of the pulp. When they were no longer able to budge the lever they removed it and fastened a rope from the screw to the third and simplest machine in the building, a wooden capstan with the girth of a tree-trunk.

Beside the press was a deep pit into which a barrel was put to catch the oil and water that oozed out of the rope pouches. The pure oil eventually rose to the surface and was ladled off into clean barrels; the water was thrown away. The pulp from the pouches, which is called *liosta*, was sold as fuel. It looks and feels like greasy, dark brown peat but it burns well and is still used in bakeries with traditional stone ovens.

By modern standards the system was far from efficient – five men and a horse working a hard ten-hour day could crush 800 kilos of olives – but it had always been good enough to produce the family's small income. Then, at the beginning of the '60s, the rural economy which had barely recovered from the long years of war and Civil War, finally collapsed altogether. Olive farming ceased to be economically viable and there was neither money nor work to be found in the countryside. The itinerant pickers moved away for good and half the population of Loutses left to seek their fortunes elsewhere, in Athens or Thessaloniki, in West Germany or in the merchant navy.

Philip's father Leonidas had sold some of their land in 1961 to finance the bar he was opening in the village, but they still had far too many olives for the family to gather unaided, even if the price they could get for their oil had made the effort worthwhile.

It was at this time that nets were introduced to the island, changing the economics of olive farming suddenly and completely. Now one or two people could do the work of ten, no olives need be lost or wasted in the undergrowth, and the quality of the oil itself improved since the berries were no longer bruised when they fell to the ground. Almost simultaneously, the first modern electrically-driven olive press reached the area. It was now possible to press eleven times as much oil in a day, and with hardly any effort at all.

Nearly all of Corfu's 3,000,000 olive trees are of an ancient and unadulterated stock called *lianolia*, producing slim, almost pointed oval berries that at their biggest are no more than two centimetres long. *Lianolia* olives linger naturally on the tree far longer than most varieties, and the olive season on the island lasts well into the summer. In Kalamata in the Peloponnese, where the best olives in the world are grown, the trees are bare of berries by February; on Corfu the first of them ripen and fall in December, but the last berries from the same tree will not be ready until the beginning of June.

The best Corfu oil is unique. Because it is made from ripe olives it is golden yellow, without a trace of green, but it is heavy and resists blending with oil from other sources. Its flavour is clean and fresh, less peppery and pungent than oils pressed from younger berries. Elsewhere, oil made from berries picked early from the trees is generally thought to be superior to oil pressed from very ripe olives, but the proportion of oleic acids in the mature, golden oil from the island can still be lower than 1 per cent, which qualifies it, by the standards of Italy, Spain and France, as 'extra-virgin'.

To the connoisseur and the merchant alike, it is the acidity of olive oil which largely determines its quality and price. The level can vary from a toxic 10 per cent to the extraordinarily pure oil made in Kalamata which has an acidity of 0.05 per cent. On Corfu, the poorest grade rarely tops 3.5 per cent.

When the villagers have gathered their olives and had them pressed into oil, its acidity must be assessed by either the State board or by the Corfu Agricultural Union, the two bodies who price and buy the farmers' oil. Philip and his father now own 350 trees and they were able to sell their oil last year at the top rate of 270 drachmas (£1.40 or $2.50) a kilo. It was a good year for their trees and they made 700,000 drachmas after tax, about £3,500.

Until very recently more than 90 per cent of all fats in the rural Corfiot diet came from their oil. The average family still gets through almost 300 kilos of it in a year, and there is not a man, woman or child in the village who does not consume a certain amount of it every day of their lives.

Like wine, olive oil is alive. Because heat or direct sunlight can affect its chemical properties and therefore its flavour, the family's annual supply is kept in the *apothiki*, the special outhouse or room which serves as toolshed, storeroom, larder and barn. Somewhere in the cool darkness, among the wine barrels and tins of *feta* cheese, stands an enormous metal or plastic drum, the modern equivalent of the *kapases*, the old earthenware oil-jars. From it the kitchen bottle is filled with a ladle and funnel. In the winter when the temperature in the *apothiki* drops very low, the oil begins to solidify. It is no longer wholly translucent, and star-shaped, primrose-coloured flecks hang suspended in the bottle of golden liquid that is brought into the kitchen. As it warms up on the table they gradually melt away.

The Loutsiotes use their oil for deep as well as shallow frying. Food that is deep-fried in olive oil tastes marvellous, but heating the oil to the necessarily high temperature changes its chemistry and flavour so it is never used more than once. Some households pour this tainted oil into a special drum kept for the purpose, heedless of the morsels of batter or fish that go in with it. At certain times during the year a man from Corfu Town discreetly visits the villages and buys it all. He works for a company which makes a famous brand of soap.

Olive oil is the soul of all cooking on the island. With the exception of a handful of specific dishes in which butter is used, it is the one and only medium for virtually all savoury dishes, and as central a flavouring as salt. That this ubiquity is deliberate seems to surprise some foreigners. Waiters in the tavernas are continually informed by their customers that they can 'taste the oil the food was cooked in'. To a local, of course, this is the point. Greeks love the flavour of olive oil and use it as a condiment just as much as they do when actually cooking. In a Loutsiot household the family oil bottle stands on the table at mealtimes so that the golden liquid can be poured over anything from boiled greens or *feta* cheese to a plate of fish stew. It is one of the virtues of good olive oil that it can be added cold at the table to food that is warm. The heat releases dormant depths of flavour in the oil which in turn seem to liberate and enhance the true flavour of the food, especially of vegetables or pulses.

Oil is central to the villagers' cooking, but it does not occupy the position unopposed. At the heart of nearly every savoury dish it is confronted by salt and by an acid, either wine, lemon juice or vinegar, or in the form of tomatoes, whether fresh or tinned as paste. The cooks of Loutses balance the equation instinctively. In Philip's recipe for *taramasalata* (p. 86), for instance, the fish roe, the lemon juice and the oil blend into a delicate and perfect unison. At its most violent, in the battle waged by a glass of lemon juice and a glass of oil over the glittering golden body of a smoked and salted Dutch herring, the combatants disarm each other. None of the three could be eaten on their own; together they form a delicious, if breathtaking combination. In reproducing the recipes in this book the cook must bear in mind this confrontation between salt, oil and acid, and send generous reinforcements wherever they are needed.

In keeping with its history as a cornerstone of Greek culture, olive oil is still used outside the kitchen in an extraordinary variety of ways. Babies are christened with it in the Orthodox Church. Fishermen working in calm shallows dribble some on to the water when they need to see the bottom even more clearly, and a spoonful of oil will seal a corkless bottle of wine – it floats on top and prevents the wine coming into contact with the air. Also, according to the older generation of Loutses' master-builders, the best possible white-wash can be simply and cheaply made from ten litres of water, two kilos of lime and half a litre of olive oil, all stirred together with a stick. Two coats cover any blemish on a plaster wall, and if you brush against it when it is dry it won't leave a white mark on your clothes.

Until the 1930s and the arrival of paraffin the homes of the Lout-siotes were lit by olive oil lamps, and the tiny red glass lamps that burn all night in the homes of the devout are still fuelled by it. So are the lamps in the church and those in the roadside shrines. The one on the road up to Loutses is modern and made of wrought iron, painted white – the gift of a man who survived an accident at one of the hairpin bends. Through the glass window of the box the weary traveller can see an icon of the Virgin Mary, and should he wish to light his spiritual way home there is a lamp, a box of matches, and an old brandy bottle of oil.

Kittens and puppies are weaned on bread soaked in olive oil, and it is also the medium for a specific against scorpion venom that can be found in a number of old-fashioned households in the village.

Elsewhere in the world, the extraordinary medical virtues of olive oil are only now being fully investigated but the wisewomen of Loutses have always known its value as an aid to digestion, blocked ears, and skin problems. It is also an important ingredient of an embrocation used in the villages to combat rheumatism. Kleopatra Vitali-Vlahou, who lives at the end of Zervou in a part of the village called Koulouri, knows the recipe. She puts a handful of oleander leaves and a chilli pepper into white paraffin, seals it in a glass jar, and leaves it in the sun for two or three months. After this time, she stirs in a little olive oil and a tablespoon of iodine and the mixture is ready to be rubbed on to the skin when the damp cold of winter brings on aches and pains.

Halfway through the long olive season, in April, when the hard-working trees are laden both with the previous winter's crop and the tiny green-white blossom of spring, the people of Loutses gather the olives they will eat during the coming year. Every household has its own favourite way of preserving them, and many of the villagers are as vociferously proud of their method as they are of their family wine.

Olives for eating are picked from the tree rather than from the nets, since they should not be over-ripe. Some families take them when they are already black; others when they are still purple, but they must all be kept in salt for a while to leech out the bitter water in their juice. There are essentially two ways of doing this but the olives must first be soaked in fresh water for anything from two days to a week, changing the water every day. They are then either packed between layers of salt in a barrel, or more usually these days in a rectangular tin called a *teneki*, or else they are put into brine of a salinity of about 15 per cent for one or two months. One man who lives on the coast, his powers of invention sparked, it is said, by extreme laziness, combines the soaking and salting by filling a wicker basket with olives and hanging it in the sea.

Olives packed in salt will emerge slightly shrunken and wrinkled from the ordeal; those kept in brine will retain their sleek proportions, but in both cases the berries must now be thoroughly washed in fresh water. Some families eat them without further ado, enjoying the true flavour of the olives; others nick each berry twice with a razor blade or a very sharp knife and put them into a mixture of oil, home-made wine vinegar, *rigani* (the dried flower-heads of oregano) and a little salt for a day, a week or even one or two months, depending on the degree of pungency they seek.

These olives are one of the principal household delicacies and are treated with respect. They are often offered to guests as a *meze* – a little something to eat when one is drinking – and an unadorned plate of the home olives is a favourite hors-d'œuvre. With a couple of thick slices of bread they can also form the basis of a *marenda*, a frugal snack for people working away from home.

Olives are such an integral part of village society that it is surprising how little the berries themselves are used in cooking. The only dish known in Loutses in which olives are actually a cooked ingredient is *soutsoukakia* (p. 192), the small, soft sausages originally from Smyrna on what is now the Turkish mainland; and even then, some of those who prepare *soutsoukakia* leave the olives out. One reason for this might be the rather disappointing loss of flavour that afflicts an olive when it is cooked.

Corfu olives are prized all over Greece as a garnish for salads, but there is one of which they are a principal ingredient – a particularly delicious combination that the villagers make as a snack rather than as part of a meal. It consists of one or two sweet, juicy oranges which are peeled with a knife to leave a thin skin of white pith, and which are then sliced on to a plate. To this the cook adds finely sliced onion rings and a generous handful of her olives and the whole thing is dressed with plenty of oil and a sprinkling of mild paprika. It looks magnificent and the wildly disparate flavours are linked by the oil into a masterpiece of sensual surprises.

🍇 HERBS AND HORTA

Just below Zervou, where the road from the coast skirts a steep hillside, is the spot where a Loutses man was pursued by a cypress tree. For four nights in a row as he trotted up from Peritheia on his horse, the tree lay in wait to chase him, but on the fifth night he carried a burning cloth wrapped around a stick. The cypress tree was scared away but horses still shy when they pass the place.

The relationship between the Loutsiotes and their environment is broad; at one end of the scale is a vague and rarely articulated sense of an alien nature that gives rise to such stories as that of the phantom cypress; at the other end is their entirely pragmatic attitude to their olive trees, which for all their beauty are seen as a cash crop and nothing more. The villagers are countrymen and their feelings for their surroundings are necessarily exploitative; they are also Greeks, and at the risk of indulging in nationalistic generalization, that seems to mean that they care more about people than about place, and more about the present than about the future or the past. Environmental concern is not something the villagers think about. That anyone should object to the use of potent herbicides or the decimation of birds and animals, or even to their casual habit of burning rubbish by the roadside or dropping it over a convenient cliff, appears foolishly romantic to most of the people of Loutses.

Foreigners, entranced by the beauty of the island, are continually dismayed by such nonchalance, but though the emotional gap between the landscape and its population is wide, the two are closely linked in other ways. Historically isolated and impoverished, the villagers have always valued the natural offerings of the land.

Corfu is a green island. Its long summers are mild by Greek standards, and its annual rainfall, though crowded into a few wet months, equals that of southern England. As a result, the island supports an extraordinary abundance and variety of wild plants, including many that are not found in the rest of Greece. By the same token, some herbs that are an integral part of mainland cooking are completely ignored by the villagers or else do not grow here at all. Thyme, for example, is unknown in Loutses, and sage, though common, is used only to make a bitter but restorative tea.

Their place in the Corfiot kitchen is taken by *rigani*, the dried flower-heads of oregano, *oreganum vulgare*. This distinction between the parts of the plant is important to Greeks, for the idea of eating the leaves does not appeal to them: they are too bitter and they lack the fragrance and heat of the flower-heads. Every family in the village gathers their *rigani* in early June, just as the tiny white flowers are opening. The plant is ubiquitous among the olive groves, by the roadside and up in the bare mountains, its thin tough stalks growing about sixty centimetres high. They are cut close to the ground, well below the first leaf stipules, and are tied into tight bunches with string, rinsed once in cold water to get rid of dust and insects and then strung up to dry in the shade, for direct exposure to sunlight turns the flower-heads brown and impairs their flavour. After ten days the bunch is dry enough to hang in the kitchen, often inside a plastic bag to catch any flower-heads that might fall, though many people prefer to rub them off and keep them in a jar or a bowl.

Bay, *daphni*, is also gathered in the early summer. The villagers pick sprigs of it from the tough, small trees that grow wild in the mountains above Loutses and take them home to hang in the kitchen. The dark glossy leaves turn a marvellous bronze colour, but they keep their flavour well for a year.

Thiosmos, ayiosmos and *ithikos* are all names for the wild mint that grows everywhere around Loutses. There are many different species of mint in the area, some good for cooking, some too bitter, and their fragrance underfoot is glorious in the spring and autumn. Whenever Philip is up in the hills he picks a handful of the best varieties and dries them by wrapping the sprigs in newspaper and leaving them in his fridge for a week or two. In this way they keep their colour, and their flavour is miraculously resurrected when added to a sauce. *Ayiosmos* is also used by the priest in a ceremony to mark the beginning of term in the Loutses school. On the first day, the children in their dark blue uniforms standing stiffly in line behind him, he dips a bunch of mint into holy water and shakes it at the building three times, blessing the school and the incipient endeavours of its inmates.

Of the other herbs that are gathered for cooking the most treasured is *selino*, the wild celery that grows down by the coast. With its flaccid, dark green leaves it looks a little like Mediterranean parsley but its flavour is distinctively that of celery, though more pungent than the cultivated variety. It is an important ingredient in all vegetable soups and some sauces and is always used while it is fresh. In recipes where the flavour is needed, a stick of celery is a perfectly good substitute.

Selino needs to grow in the sandy soil of the coast, but there are many other herbs that the villagers grow in their small gardens. When the settling families first came to Loutses they had to create vegetable gardens to feed themselves, but the soil in places like Zervou was too thin and poor to grow enough. Their solution was to enclose sheltered plots with low walls and to fill them with olive leaves gathered from the ground under the trees. Within a year or two the leaves decomposed to a rich, fertile loam. Families unwilling to buy a lorry-load of earth from elsewhere on the island still create or rejuvenate a garden in this way. Invariably some corner of it will be set aside for those herbs that are best used while they are fresh.

Of these the most ubiquitous is certainly *maithano*, Mediterranean parsley, which is called *petroselino* on Corfu – rock-celery. Its flavour is strong and sweet and the villagers use it a great deal in cooking. *Dendrolivano*, rosemary, is another. Although it grows wild in the hills, many villagers prefer to transplant roots to their garden where they can be sure of finding it when they need it. Corfiots do not cook with rosemary very much, using it only in two or three specific recipes such as *marinato* (p. 83), but it is used when they do the laundry for freshening linen and clothing, boiled in the water for the final rinse.

Sweet basil plants, *vasilikos*, are to be found everywhere on the island, bought very cheaply at the beginning of the year, planted four or five together in a pot, and kept on window sills or ledges outside in the sun. If watered every evening they grow into a glorious ball of tiny leaves with minute white flowers. Passers-by habitually brush them lightly with the palm of their hand to release their clean, peppery fragrance, which clears the head and, it is said, keeps flies and other unpopular wildlife away.

The last two of the variety of herbs that the villagers use regularly in their cooking are fennel and dill weed, and they grow together all over Loutses. Fennel, known in Greece as *marathro* but on Corfu as *malathro* is picked and dried in the early summer before it seeds, though the villagers prefer to use the fine leaves fresh whenever possible, adding them to everything they cook in the springtime. Failing that, the flavour of the herb is also present in the dried yellow flowers, but fennel seed is considered too bitter and indigestible. Fresh *anitho*, dill weed, is also a favourite ingredient in the spring, and is carried, discreetly, by the very superstitious as a specific against witches.

The relationship between plants and the supernatural is of course ancient and universal, but there are some beliefs that seem peculiar to the village. Pregnant women, for example, are encouraged to eat black-eyed peas to ensure that they will be able to breast-feed their babies, but if their milk should fail they must rub their breasts with lemon juice. A wild onion placed on the window-sill in the new year is said to be just as good as garlic at warding off vampires.

Even the most pragmatic villager believes in the evil eye, visited upon an individual by a curse, or upon a child simply by spoiling it, but it can be detected and averted with the help of nine cloves. The person who suspects herself of being afflicted mounts the cloves on pins and divides them into piles of three. If the first three shatter when lit with a match the evil eye was indeed upon her, but now is gone; if they just blacken, she tries again with the other two sets of three. To find out who laid the curse, the victim drops grains of charcoal into a glass of water and suggests names. The charcoal will sink when she guesses correctly.

Given such parameters as these, the somewhat esoteric medical qualities that the villagers attribute to their herbs hardly seem strange at all. Historically, the isolated position of Loutses necessitated self-sufficiency in medical matters and even today the villagers share an enthusiastic fascination with matters of health. This can look like the most rampant hypochondria until one remembers how recently diseases such as malaria and pellagra were endemic in the region. A tradition of home medicine based on herbal remedies still flourishes in the more remote villages, passed on from grandmother to grand-daughter.

Perhaps the most complete pharmacopoeia in Loutses belongs to Kleopatra Vitali-Vlahou, who lives with her husband Kosta in an old house in Koulouri, a quiet valley tucked away behind Zervou ridge.

Kleopatra has a repertoire of infusions and decoctions to cure a wide variety of problems. The most commonplace of her many teas is made with chamomile. The flowers, like large, open-faced daisies, carpet the hillsides in May when they are picked and dried. Boiled for three minutes, strained and mixed with a little sugar, the resulting tea is usually the first thing a newborn baby is given, and a digestive bottle of it becomes a daily routine for its first six months of life. Brewed stronger, it is also a very popular drink with the village women, mildly soporific and easing stomach pain, while a cool decoction applied on cotton wool helps to clear up eye irritations, rashes and allergic skin reactions. For stomach and chest problems it can also be applied externally by crumbling the dried flowers and leaves in a pan of olive oil and warming it over the fire. The patient rubs the mixture on to the tender area and then lays a warm, damp cloth on top.

Tisanes of mint, sage or marjoram, or of the leaves of a tree known as Louisa are generally good for colds and upset stomachs, and quince tea flavoured with an infusion of geranium flowers is a useful pick-me-up, but Kleopatra's favourite is a tea made from *linarosporos*, a species of blue-flowered flax, boiled with a teaspoonful of sugar and a cinnamon stick for flavour.

For urinary problems Kleopatra recommends an infusion of either couchgrass or scaly spleenwood, called *skorpithi* in Greek, perhaps because it grows in cracks in rock walls where scorpions live. For bronchitis an infusion of stinging nettles is best for adults, while children with coughs can be relieved if they sleep on a small pillow stuffed with seaweed.

Kleopatra always keeps some eucalyptus leaves in her kitchen. In the winter, when her house is heated by the woodstove, the air can get too stuffy, so she puts a pot of water on top of the stove, throws in a handful of leaves and lets their pungent scent pervade the house for an hour or two.

For most of its long climb up from the sea, the road to Loutses is shadowed by olive trees. Even after it enters the village it is still

not free of them, but as it passes the last house at the head of the
valley it breaks suddenly into the sun, for Loutses lies on the treeline
– the level of altitude beyond which the olive will not grow.

Above that abrupt delineation, the road deteriorates quickly into
a rugged track, carved from the flank of a hillside. On one side is
a precipitous drop on to the narrowing valley floor; on the other,
above the exposed slabs of white limestone marble and veins of dark
red soil, the land rises steeply beneath its aboriginal undergrowth
of stunted myrtle and bay, ilex and arbutus, a dense and prickly
groundcover beloved of snakes and scorpions. This is an older Corfu
– the island as it was a thousand years ago, when the road was first
made and when the olive was not ubiquitous – a wild landscape
that lies parched and shimmering in the remorseless heat of summer,
and in the winter is shrouded in fog and rain.

The high peaks are inhospitable places, but they have their part
to play in the lives of the villagers. All year round, the people of
Loutses make expeditions into the mountains, sometimes to gather
herbs or to cut forage for donkeys and goats, and sometimes to look
for *horta*, the general name for dozens of varieties of edible wild
greens.

Whether the Greek taste for *horta* is primitive or rather sophisticated is a moot point but it is certainly very ancient. *Horta*, and
also olives, honey and nuts, as well as mallow and the roots of asphodel, were cited by numerous puritanical authors in classical and Hellenistic times as the original and proper food for heroes. Today the
Loutsiotes go to considerable lengths to rid their land of asphodel,
but like all Greeks they prize their *horta* greatly. The citizens of Corfu
Town buy any that comes into the market and the country people
eat it throughout the autumn and spring, usually as a light supper.
The children of Loutses learn to recognize the different plants, and
men and women alike take pleasure in gathering them wherever they
are to be found, by the roadside and in those orchards and olive
groves where the undergrowth is still cut rather than sprayed with
herbicides, as well as in the hills. People with gardens encourage
any kind of *horta* that seeds itself there: English passers-by have been
heard to make disparaging remarks about the number of weeds in
what they take to be a poorly-kept lawn.

The *horta* season begins on Corfu in October, when the first good
rainfall of the autumn rejuvenates the island. Within a week delicate
leaves are growing deep among the dried yellow vegetation; the dust
of summer is washed away, colours are suddenly vivid again and

among the olive groves, newly cleared, a green bloom seems to glow under the trees.

From then until May, when the plants flower and then wither in the burgeoning heat of summer, Philip's father Leonidas often goes out early in the morning with a plastic bag and a small table knife, heading for certain familiar hillsides above the olive tree line. He is not looking for any one type of *horta* in particular, but will pick whatever takes his fancy until his bag is full, collecting enough to provide dinner for himself and Philip for several nights to come. Perhaps he will come across some *sinapi*, a wild mustard plant that is a little indigestible but very good to eat, having all the flavour of mustard without its fire. There may be some *reposinapi*, another species of mustard, or some *zahoulia*, a small bitter plant at its best while its yellow flowers are budding. *Lapsana* is bitter but still good if boiled in enough water, and so is *psalithaki*, a bitter weed with milky sap. *Skortholithes* are Neapolitan garlic: small plants with tiny white flowers in May and a delicate garlic flavour. *Vorvorlithia*, grape hyacinth, are bluebell-like flowers that are boiled up with other horta; *zohios* has yellow flowers, though only the stem and big broad leaves are eaten.

Not all the varieties are so esoteric. There is *rathiki*, the dandelion, which is eaten in the spring when the plants are sweet and tender and especially, in some households, over Easter as an alternative to the more popular lettuce or curly endives. There is *pikralithia*, dwarf chicory, and *lappato*, burdock, whose wide, slightly bitter leaves are often baked into *horta* pie, and a type of charlock called *vrouva*.

The people of Corfu always cook their *horta*; they do not eat them as a cold salad as Greeks in other parts of the country sometimes do, though a hunter out in the fields might pick a few leaves to chew on if he feels hungry. As a rule the leaves, stems or flowers are washed, boiled briefly in plenty of salted water, drained and then anointed with a great deal of oil at the table, to be eaten with some salty delicacy such as *feta* cheese, salted sardines or anchovies, a dish full of olives, and plenty of fresh white bread. Some elderly people drink the liquid the *horta* was boiled in once it has cooled: mixed with lemon juice it is considered very healthy.

Among the local *hortas* are some, like *politrixous*, maiden-hair, that have a particularly sweet and delicate flavour. They are known as *tsigarolahano*, a term which describes vegetables that are to be fried lightly, and which includes other, more easily recognized plants such as spinach and leeks and beetroot leaves, picked very young before the stalks of the plants have turned purple. A dish of *horta tsigari* is a favourite dinner among the Loutsiotes, served with bread and *feta* and accompanied by a bottle of the home wine.

 To cook **Horta tsigari** (fried wild greens) for four, you will need a kilo (2 lbs 2 oz) of any sweet tender greens such as beetroot tops, rapini, escarole or curly endives, 50 ml (1½ fl oz, ¼ cup) of oil, 2 medium-sized onions, 3 fresh bulb garlic or 1 large clove of garlic, a three-fingered pinch of *rigani*, the same amount of fresh chopped parsley, a little chopped mint, salt and mild paprika, and either 2 ripe tomatoes or a generous tablespoon of tomato paste.
Boil a very large pan of unsalted water and tip the greens into it for five minutes. Meanwhile chop the onions and garlic very finely and fry them gently in the oil until they yellow. Stir in the herbs, salt and paprika, and the peeled and chopped tomatoes or tomato paste. Let this sauce cook for a minute before adding the well-drained greens. Pour on enough water to cover everything and let the mixture simmer for a further ten minutes until the water has evaporated.

The villagers vary this recipe slightly when cooking **Spanaki tsigari** (spinach *tsigari*) to complement the slightly stronger flavour of fresh spinach. Philip, who likes to cook with lemon juice at every opportunity, substitutes the juice of a large ripe lemon for the tomatoes, adding it at the last minute and then letting the food stand covered, away from the heat, for five minutes before he serves it, so that the flavours blend together.
Alternatively, some cooks add a cup or two of rice to the mixture at the same time as the spinach, covering everything with just enough water to cook the rice and leaving it to simmer for twenty minutes. The result is something like a moist pilaf, but it is important not to drown the vegetables with rice.

To the villagers the most precious of all the *tsigarolahana* is undoubtedly wild asparagus. The hills above Loutses are one of the few places on Corfu where it is found and though it is known and loved on the island (and also, they say, on Crete) it is not often remembered on the mainland. Six or seven inches long, dark green and very slender, it grows hidden amongst other grasses, and Leonidas's trips into the hills for it are undertaken with a devoted concentration.

Its season is short, lasting from March until the middle of April, though in certain rainswept years it has been found growing in

October, in places where a bush fire had burned the previous summer. Leonidas looks for asparagus which is long and straight, without a lot of foliage at the base, and he only picks young soft shoots, for the older plants are tough, with a strong, bitter taste.

Once he has brought it home to their spacious new kitchen, he and Philip trim off the already discoloured bases and rinse the stalks under the tap. Then they boil a great deal of water – half a kilo of wild asparagus needs at least three litres of water to dissipate any bitterness – and plunge the asparagus into it for fifteen minutes.

Strained, it is now ready to eat, once a dressing of oil and lemon juice has been dribbled over it. Alternatively, Philip sometimes goes on to fry it, heating a little oil in a frying pan, stirring in a teaspoon of salt and then adding the asparagus which he allows to cook slowly for ten minutes, removing the lid of the pan from time to time and gently moving the asparagus around to stop it sticking. Then he lifts it out on to the plate, pours the oil from the pan all over it and squeezes on plenty of lemon juice.

He has also been known to bake it, wrapping the boiled asparagus in aluminium foil with the juice of half a lemon, three or four table-spoons of oil and some salt and black pepper. The foil package is put into a hot oven for half an hour.

However Philip cooks it, but particularly when he serves it simply boiled, the flavour of wild asparagus is unique. Underlying the familiar alkaline tang of cultivated asparagus is a piquancy that may be merely the taste of chlorophyll but which the startled imagination interprets as the very flavour of the colour green.

Ask the villagers why they go out into the hills to look for asparagus or *horta* and they answer that it tastes so good – far better, one suspects, than if it had been picked by anyone else. Added to this is a predeliction for freshness in the things they eat. But herb and *horta* gathering also exemplifies more subliminal attitudes. Part of the heritage of an impoverished past is a pride in living off the land and the villagers take pleasure in all activities that prove their self-sufficiency whether as farmers, fishermen or hunters. It is with a hunter's faith in his instincts and experience that Leonidas sets out for asparagus. *Horta*, on the other hand, is gathered in a spirit of opportunism, with the mind and the carrier-bag open for whatever may be available. This too illustrates something of the way the villagers think about food: an almost casual acceptance of whatever turns up. It is only when it reaches the kitchen table that the unconscious discipline of tradition takes over. A Loutsiot cook will welcome any unexpected bounty, but once it is in her kitchen she will prepare it exactly as she has always done.

Kleopatra's kitchen is typical of the more old-fashioned households in the village, though this has more to do with economics than any conscious affection for the past. She and her husband spent much of their married lives in Athens and so they never restored their old home in Loutses as many of their friends did during the 1970s, when the money from tourism made such things possible. Now they have returned to the village, but the house still reflects an earlier lifestyle, the way the villagers lived in the less affluent decades between the end of the nineteenth century and the middle of the twentieth.

The kitchen is in its original state, dark and flagged with smooth stone, occupying the whole ground floor of the building. Against the rear wall stands the woodstove: its long steel stovepipe disappears high up into the wall to give extra heat in winter. On a table is the Calor gas ring upon which Kleopatra cooks in the summer. The sink has no plumbing except for its drain, but a flat-backed water container with a tiny plastic tap in its base is nailed to the wall above it. One modern concession is an enormous old Italian refrigerator, but Kleopatra prefers to keep her eggs and fruit and vegetables in bowls on the shelves and in cupboards. An old dresser holds her crockery and cutlery.

In contrast to her formidable supply of herbs, Kleopatra keeps few spices in her kitchen. The cooks of Loutses use only cloves, cinnamon and red, black and white pepper with any regularity. Other flavourings such as *mahlepi*, the dried kernels of a type of cherry tree, will be bought when they are needed for specific recipes, but in general the villagers prefer to use only those herbs that they gather themselves. Imported spices are considered bad for the '*stomaki*', a word which refers to all internal human organs and is illustrated with a scowl and a chopping gesture to the waist.

Even salt is thought of as suspect unless it is demonstrably pure and from the sea. Because of the small amount of meat in the traditional rural diet, the villagers cook with a lot of salt, and salting was always the most widely used method of preserving food. When the Venetians owned Corfu, one of the products they derived from the colony was salt, dried in sea-pans near Corfu Town and in the far south of the island. It was a valuable commodity and a Corfiot found taking some for his own use received a heavy prison sentence.

The pans are no longer worked, and neither are most of the others all over Greece. As a result, Greece was forced some years ago into the embarrassing step of importing salt from Turkey, though the public outcry became so hysterical that the practice quickly stopped.

Like the rest of the villagers, Kleopatra has few utensils. She uses a sharp little table knife for all her cooking and cutting, preferring a plate to a board for fine chopping, or more often just holding what needs to be cut in one hand and the knife in the other, expertly slicing an onion or a tomato straight into the pan. She has no spatulas or whisks, no wooden or perforated spoons; her only other equipment is a sieve and a variety of ladles.

In a deep cupboard close to the sink are Kleopatra's *kasserolia*, her pots and pans. The *rihia* is the principal Corfiot cooking utensil, a circular, flat-bottomed casserole with vertical sides about ten centimetres deep, and Kleopatra has several of them. They come in many sizes but they all have fitted lids and two small, looped metal handles. Made of thin aluminium, they are equally suitable for the oven or hot-plate of a woodstove, or for today's Calor gas cookers, and are used for frying, stewing and baking; a low heat and plenty of oil prevents the food from sticking. Kleopatra also has a variety of saucepans, a heavy aluminium deep-fryer, a small frying-pan for eggs, and a *tapsi*, the rectangular baking tray with sides a little lower than a *rihia*, in which she bakes her pies.

The kitchen has always been the principal room of a rural Corfiot house. Until the mid-eighteenth century it was also often the only one for the families who worked the land for their feudal lords. There were wealthy villages, like Ano Peritheia in its mountain fastness, safe from pirates and the malarial mosquitoes that infested the coast, where the farmers built elegant stone houses, fronted by charming balconies and arched doorways of careful masonry, but the 'folk' as the peasantry were called, inhabited low crofts, rented from the landowner and consisting of a single room that they shared with their livestock.

During the last decades of Venetian rule, and then under the British dominion in the first half of the nineteenth century, the houses became more comfortable. A second storey was added, often on to the original building, and these upstairs rooms, with their floors of seasoned cypress wood, became the bedrooms for the family. The animals were moved into outhouses, and the downstairs area became the kitchen. In the summer, the families socialized outside, lingering on the doorstep, talking well into the evening and until late at night, but in the winter they sat inside around the fire – the only source of heat in the house – before going up early to the cold damp bedrooms to sleep.

As conditions improved, open fires were replaced in many houses by monumental charcoal ranges and by large ovens built into the outer wall of the kitchen. One of these can still be seen in a ruined house in Koulouri, its arched mouth opening on to the now roofless porch. The family would fire and seal the oven in the afternoon when they returned from the day's work in the olive groves, scraping out the ashes an hour or two later. A covered *rihia* containing the meal for the following evening would be slipped inside, the opening sealed again, and two hours later the food would be ready. The back of the oven protruded into the kitchen inside, heating the room; food that had been prepared the evening before could be warmed up on the top of the brickwork.

The great disadvantage of the system was that in the summer an interior oven or charcoal brazier raised the temperature in the house to an unbearable degree. To get around the problem, many families built ovens outside, domed beehive constructions of brick and fireclay: only one survives in Loutses today, used by a family as a sheltered barbecue.

The old ovens undoubtedly did much to influence the way the people of rural Corfu did their cooking. Slowly baking a casserole of vegetables, meat or fish and then gently reheating it the following evening brings out the flavour of the ingredients superbly, especially with the addition of a generous stream of fresh oil and a little lemon juice for piquancy. Cooking in the oven was also responsible for the still-prevalent habit of using only one pan whenever possible, and of centering everyday meals around a single cooked dish, accompanied by a variety of salads, *feta* cheese and bread, sometimes preceded by a cold hors-d'œuvre. More formal meals follow the same pattern, but with the addition of a 'first plate' between the hors-d'œuvre and the meat or fish, consisting usually of a cooked vegetable, potatoes or pasta.

In the late nineteenth century, cast-iron woodstoves were introduced into the village. Over the next fifty years they replaced the old brick ovens and indoor charcoal ranges and they are still widely used today. They have done little to change the old cooking habits of the villagers. A woodstove's oven supplies the same low, even heat and the plates on top are no more versatile than a well-managed charcoal brazier. Woodstoves are also seasonal, moved into the kitchen in the autumn as much for heating as for cooking, and stored out in the *apothiki* again every spring. Calor gas rings have been in use in the village for many years for frying and boiling, but full-sized Calor gas cookers are still rare. Their ovens are expensive to run and as a result stews that would once have been baked are increasingly simmered on top of the stove.

Cooking over charcoal, however, was too central a part of Greek cuisine to have disappeared altogether. The modern *psistarias*, the 'grill-room' restaurants so popular with both tourists and local people, preserve the tradition, and in the summer-time most families cook much of their meat or fish outside on a barbecue.

To supply their own needs, some of the villagers still burn their own charcoal, using olive wood from their groves. The method Philip uses is typical. First he stacks the wood as compactly as possible, then he builds a stone wall around the pile, leaving an opening at both ends. He covers the top of the wood with *vrahlo*, bracken, then packs the whole thing with earth, sealing any little gaps along the sides of the pile, but leaving a large hole at each end. He kindles a fire in a bundle of sticks and pushes it into the wood pile, then gouges a small hole in either side of the construction, near the open end. When smoke comes out of these holes he seals them up and opens two more further along. When smoke comes out of these, he seals them too and so on all along the pile, finally closing the other end as soon as the smoke and flames reach it. Now he seals the whole thing with earth and leaves it to smoulder on for two hours without air. To douse the fire, he rakes the earth away and pours water over the charcoal beneath it.

Maria Parginou, whose husband Stamati runs one of the shops in Loutses, gets up every morning at dawn to take her sheep out to pasture. Often on her way home she pauses to pick whatever *horta* she should chance to see. Her favourite is *seskolo*, a rustic cousin of Swiss chard. In springtime, when the plants are young, she takes a pin and splits open the stems, removing the sweet insides and boiling them; later in the season she turns the large, spear-shaped leaves with their firm white stems into a pie: *hortopitta*.

Pittes have an important place in the repertoire of the village cooks. In the more traditional households one will be baked at least once a week, to be eaten either warm or cold, as a light dinner or part of a larger meal, as something to take into the olive groves for lunch, or just when somebody feels hungry and happens to be passing the kitchen. A variety of foods are used as a filling – *feta* cheese, spinach, *horta* or other vegetables, and less frequently chicken or fish – but *hortopitta* is Maria's speciality. It is made with the pastry called *fyllo*, a word which means leaf in Greek but which in this case should surely refer to the gold leaf of illuminators rather than anything botanical.

Fyllo pastry has a somewhat daunting reputation as being extremely difficult to make and troublesome to use. The first of these caveats is certainly true. The ingredients could scarcely be simpler – flour and water and a little baking powder – but it takes years of practice to stretch balls of this paste into unbroken sheets as thin as tissue paper. Experts perform the feat by throwing the dough from hand to hand and at the same time manipulating it into a flat disc. Then they spin and toss it some more until it is as thin and flaccid as a crêpe, held in shape by its own momentum through the air, and finally let it fall on to a round perfectly flat table. Now it is stretched and rolled around the slimmest and longest of rolling pins until it is almost translucent – some say the test for good *fyllo* is to see if you can read newsprint through it – then it is finally trimmed and set aside for use.

Fyllo has never been as popular on Corfu as it is in the rest of Greece, but even on the mainland few amateur cooks bother to make their own these days. Some *pâtisseries* in the largest cities sell it by weight, but on Corfu everyone, including commercial bakeries, prefers to buy it frozen in packets that come from Athens. Using frozen *fyllo* is enjoyable and easy, provided the cook bears in mind that its thinness makes it dangerously prone to dehydration. It must first be allowed to thaw in the unopened packet for three hours before carefully unwrapping the folded leaves. They will dry out and become brittle and useless in a minute once the air reaches them, so keep a moist cloth over them, removing it only to separate each individual leaf. Unused *fyllo* cannot be refrozen, but it will stay fresh for a week if it is properly wrapped in plastic and kept in the fridge.

Seskolo is the principal *horta* in Maria's *hortopitta*, but she usually combines it with other *hortas* for variety. In reproducing her recipe one might use Swiss chard for the *seskolo* and an equal amount of a mixture of dandelion or rapini, escarole, beetroot tops or even brussel tops, spring greens, or fresh young spinach (never frozen).

To make a **Hortopitta** (*horta* pie) big enough for at least six hungry people, you will need 750 g (1 lb 10 oz) of various *hortas* (see above), 1 generous tablespoon each of fresh fennel leaves, dill weed and parsley, 3 bulb onions, 100 ml (3½ fl oz, ½ cup) of oil, 250 g (9 oz) of *feta* cheese, 3 eggs, 100 ml (3½ fl oz, ½ cup) of milk, 2 tablespoons of uncooked rice, salt and pepper, and 8 sheets (200 g or 7 oz) of *fyllo* pastry. Boil three litres (five pints or 14 cups) of water in a very large saucepan with two tablespoons of salt. When the water is bubbling fiercely put in the spinach and *horta* and let it boil for two or three minutes. Drain it for fifteen minutes and then chop it finely. Chop the fennel leaves, dill weed, parsley and onions finely and fry them gently in half the oil until the onions yellow. Add them to the chopped greens with the rice and all but two tablespoons of the milk. Beat two of the eggs with the white of the third egg and add them to the vegetables. Mix everything together thoroughly. Take a rectangular baking tray, sized about 28 cm by 35 cm, with sides at least 8 cm deep, and moisten it with oil. Lie a leaf of *fyllo* over the bottom of the tray and brush it with oil. Grate the *feta* or chop it very finely and divide it into eight small heaps. Scatter one heap of *feta* over the *fyllo*. Lay three more leaves of *fyllo* on top, brushing each one with oil and sprinkling each with cheese, then smooth the vegetable mixture on top of everything. The *fyllo* leaves are larger than the pan: oil the protruding sides of each leaf and fold them in over the *horta*, sprinkling on a little cheese between the pastry. Lay a new leaf of *fyllo* over everything, brush it with oil, sprinkle it with cheese and repeat the procedure twice more. Lay on the last *fyllo* leaf and brush it with a mixture of the remaining milk and the last egg yolk. Score the top few layers of the *fyllo* with a sharp knife, making four parallel incisions from side to side of the tray. Bake it in a moderate oven for forty minutes – until the pastry is golden. Let it cool for five minutes before cutting the pie into rectangular slices.

Before *fyllo* became available in frozen packets, the rural population of Corfu used a different kind of pastry, known locally as *petouro*, for their pies, and in comparatively isolated communities like Loutses it is still the most popular piecrust. Maria Parginou makes a marvellous spinach and *feta* cheese pie using *petouro*. She serves it as a snack and often gives slices away to friends who call at her shop, lured by the smell of baking. Greeks approve of the combination of *feta* cheese and fish, so this pie is also frequently offered as a first course before fish.

 To make **Petouro** pastry, you will need 400 g (14 oz) of plain flour, 150 ml (¼ pint, ⅔ cup) of milk, 1 egg, 2 tablespoons of oil, 1 heaped teaspoon (5 g) of dried yeast and ½ teaspoon of sugar (or 8 g of fresh yeast and no sugar), 50 ml (1½ fl oz, ¼ cup) of hand-hot water, and 1 level teaspoon of salt. If using fresh yeast, dissolve it in the water, if using dried yeast, dissolve the sugar in the water and then sprinkle on the dried yeast and let it stand for ten minutes until it foams. Meanwhile, combine the flour and salt in a mixing bowl. In a separate bowl, beat the egg and stir in the oil and milk. Stir in the yeast when it is ready and pour everything into the flour. Mix them together and then tip the dough out on to a clean, dry surface and knead it for about five minutes until it is no longer sticky. Put it into a clean bowl, cover it with a damp cloth and set it in a warm place for 30 to 45 minutes until the dough has doubled in size, then roll it out. *Petouro* is strong and pliant and bakes into a hard crust like pizza dough so roll it very thinly. Rub a little oil over the bottom of the same baking tray described in the recipe for *hortopitta* and lay the *petouro* into it, bringing up the sides to a height of about an inch and a half. For Maria's *spanakopitta* you will also need a topcrust of *petouro*, rolled as thinly as possible.

To make the filling for a **Spanakopitta** you will need 750 g (1 lb 10 oz) of fresh spinach, 2 large fresh bulb onions or 200 g (7 oz) of spring onions, 75 ml (2½ fl oz, ⅓ cup) of oil, 250 g (9 oz) of *feta* cheese, 2 tablespoons of rice, 2 tablespoons each of fresh chopped parsley and fennel leaves, a little salt and black or white pepper.

Wash the spinach thoroughly and pick out any damaged leaves. Boil two litres (9 cups) of water in a large pan and put the spinach into it. By the time the water comes back to the boil the spinach is ready. Drain it well, chop it finely and leave it in a colander for five minutes. Meanwhile chop the onions finely and fry them in the oil over a low heat until they being to yellow. Mix in the spinach and let it fry for a further seven or eight minutes, then tip it into a bowl. Mix in the herbs and the finely crumbled *feta* (it is always best to taste *feta* before using it – if it is too salty, rinse it under the cold tap for a moment). Scatter the uncooked rice evenly over the *petouro* in its baking tray then spread the vegetable mixture evenly over it. Lay the *petouro* top crust over the top and pinch it into the protruding sides of the bottom crust. Trim any excess dough with a sharp knife. Sprinkle a few drops of water on to the pastry then put the pie into a moderate oven for fifty minutes until the crust is golden brown. *Spanakopitta* is at its best when eaten warm.

Another of Maria's best *pittas* is *kolokithopitta*, a firm pie made from vegetable marrow and baked without a top crust so that it emerges from the oven looking like a quiche. Its flavour is subtle and sweet, especially if evaporated milk has been used, and some cooks in the village make it even sweeter by adding a handful of raisins to the mixture. Others add small pieces of dried, salted cod, reconstituted by an overnight soak in water.

Courgettes are often substituted for the marrow and so are pumpkins during the winter. Cut from their vine in September when they are ripe, pumpkins will keep until the following spring if they are stored in a cool, airy place like the family *apothiki*.

To make **Kolokithopitta** (marrow pie) for a large family, you will need a marrow or marrows of about 750 g (1 lb 10 oz), 2 tablespoons of rice, 2 eggs, 50 ml (1½ fl oz, ¼ cup) of milk, either evaporated or fresh (Maria uses milk from her sheep), plenty of black or white pepper, 2 small onions, salt and 3 tablespoons of oil. You will also need the ingredients of *petouro* pastry, as described in the previous recipe.

Make *petouro* and lay it as the base for the pie in an oiled baking tray. Scatter the uncooked rice over the pastry. Peel and grate the marrow and chop the onions finely; mix them together and smooth them evenly over the rice. Beat the eggs and milk with salt and pepper and pour the mixture carefully over the marrow. Dribble the oil on top and put the pie into a moderate oven for an hour.

A variation of this recipe suggests a sauce instead of the egg and milk; 2 chopped onions, 3 ripe, peeled and chopped tomatoes, some parsley, dill weed, fennel leaves and a little mint, salt and pepper are stewed over a very low heat with 75 ml (2½ fl oz, ¾ cup) of oil and 100 ml (3½ fl oz, ½ cup) of water for fifteen minutes. The grated marrow is laid on to the pastry without the addition of the other onions and the sauce is poured on top. The pie is baked in the way described above.

🍇 THE GARDEN

Tomas Vlahos is the second oldest person in Loutses. He was born sometime in the early autumn of 1890 and he can still remember his childhood with precision. Sometime during the 1820s the Vlahos family moved to Loutses from Preveza on the mainland. The British-held island offered a great deal more security than was available on the mainland under Turkish rule. So they realized what they could on their property and took ship for Corfu, settling finally in Koulouri, the small valley that lies to the east of Zervou.

Koulouri was not perhaps the ideal place to begin a new life: the wind blew straight across the sea from the snow-covered mountains of Albania in the winter, and much of the steep hillside was bare rock, but the olives that grew there were tough old trees and with hard labour they could bring in enough money for the family to survive.

There was, however, one intractable problem facing the Vlahoses, the same question that had plagued the people of Loutses since the valley was first settled: how to grow food in a place that had no water. The vegetable gardens that the earlier immigrants had worked so hard to create had been only partially successful. In the warm, wet spring they produced an abundance of vegetables, but the summers continued to desiccate the earth. The Vlahos family *sterna*, the enormous underground cistern where the winter rain was collected, was situated half a mile from Koulouri on another property they owned, and though they were prepared to carry water back to Koulouri for themselves and for their livestock, it was too precious to be poured on to the ground.

No direct solution was ever found. But the family, like the rest of the community, adapted to the problem. The abolition of the feudal fiefs by the British had given the people the right to own their land; the rigorous traditions of dowry and inheritance and the fact that there was no alternative wealth made sure that it was land that was passed on to sons and given away with daughters. Women from the coast who married Loutses men brought with them the title to plots more fertile than those in the mountains – orchards in the moist valleys around lower Peritheia or meadows on the watered plain between Nissos and Akharavi – and these small properties became the real summer gardens of the Loutsiotes.

So, by the end of the nineteenth century, the Vlahoses had come to own several acres of good farmland on the coast near Aghios Spiridon, and every June, when the exhausting eight-month cycle of the olives was finally over, they would turn their attention to vegetables. Down in their carefully tended holdings they grew everything they needed – most importantly an annual crop of beans and pulses to be dried in the sun and stored for the coming winter, but also melons, cucumbers and marrows, courgettes and tomatoes, onions and oranges... even tobacco, which the men dried and cut and stored in pouches with a lemon leaf to keep it moist and fragrant.

The work was hard, but it was easier and more interesting than the awful monotony of olive-picking. Tomas helped his parents with both, joining them full-time when he left the village school at fourteen. He gave up when he was eighty – seven decades of crouching had left him with aching knees.

Only two events have interrupted the relationship of Tomas and many other Corfiots with their land: the Turkish war of 1921 and the Second World War. In the first Tomas was a soldier, stationed on the disputed borderland of eastern Thrace. Coming from Corfu, he did not share his countrymen's deep-rooted loathing of the Turks, and he confesses to a certain fondness for the people he met so long ago. They were friendly, he recalls, and there was work to be had. It was an adventure for a young man alone and far from home. He might even have considered settling there if the food had not been so strange.

The Second World War was a very different experience. That some calamity was imminent became clear to the *savants* of Loutses in the late summer of 1940. One hot afternoon a great cloud of butterflies rose from the barren peaks behind the village – so many that they cast a shadow upon the houses before the wind dispersed them. The old women, familiar with the lore of omens, began to wait for some appalling disaster, and three months later the Italians began their invasion of Greece, bombing Corfu as they moved south from Albania.

Tomas remembers the day well. As the bombs began to fall the villagers evacuated Loutses and hurried into the mountains, heading for an enormous cave, as cool and dark as a cathedral, that opens into the bottom of a densely vegetated crater on a peak behind the village. Shepherds sometimes sheltered there with their flocks and the boys from the village had always played there, hunting for dead fledgling crows that had fallen from their nests on the sheer sides of the crater.

The Italians, however, were driven back and it was not until April 1941 that Greece fell, after German divisions were diverted to the attack. Corfu and the other western islands were given to Mussolini. The Loutsiotes watched from Zervou as the four ships that carried the new Italian garrison steamed out of Sarranda on the Albanian mainland, heading for Corfu Town. Within days Italian troops entered the village and occupied the police station on Zervou.

The invaders had orders to try their best to win the acceptance and support of the islanders. Part of the Fascist scheme for the Ionian was the re-establishment of an independent republic in the islands, with its own coinage and an Italian military administration, and this was initiated at once, with Corfu Town as the republic's capital. The practical effect of this on the villages was minimal. A far more tangible intrusion was the platoon in the police station, cutting down olive trees for firewood, commandeering food and indulging in rowdy behaviour in the bar.

Another profound impression left on the village, and more especially on the children, was the appetite the Italian soldiers displayed for the wild tortoises of the area, animals which amuse the Greeks and which they are usually unwilling to molest. That the Italians should bake and eat them shocked them greatly.

The villagers each have their own memories of the war and the years of poverty that followed it. One remembers watching a British commando with a radio set sitting on top of a hill above Loutses and targetting enemy shipping for Allied bombers. Another speaks with awe about the durability of the shoes people wore. Those who were children during the 1940s shudder at the memory of the food they had to eat.

The produce of their coastal properties was difficult to hide and it was taken as soon as it ripened. After a while the villagers stopped working their land down there. Even more seriously, there was no longer any flour to make bread. Tomas and a few others tried to sow wild wheat as discreetly as possible up in the valley around Ano Peritheia, but the crop failed in the withering heat of summer. Instead they made *babota*, a substitute for bread made from bran and ground maize, remembered with horror. But men and women of Tomas's generation point out that no one in the village actually starved. Households eked out what they had and dried beans, always a winter staple, now became the only regular source of nutrition. There is a saying: '*Fassoulatha essose tin Elatha*', 'Bean soup saved Greece'. It certainly saved the people of Loutses during the bitter years of the war.

Despite its association with those times *fassoulatha* is still eaten a great deal. Tomas sometimes prepares it himself on those afternoons when his daughter-in-law Maria is away working in the olive groves. The recipe he uses is the one he learned from his grandmother eighty years ago.

Simple, filling, and delicious, Tomas's recipe for **Fassoulatha** involves soaking half a kilo of dried white haricot beans overnight in warm water and then boiling them in salted water with a glass of oil, a little pepper, and 5 or 6 whole cloves of garlic. It is ready when the skin of a bean that has been lifted out of the saucepan on a spoon breaks as it meets the air. In Loutses this means about an hour and a half of gentle simmering; elsewhere it takes longer, depending on the water.

The local opinion is that rainwater from the *sterna* cooks beans quickly and well, but anything else may not work at all. In town, for instance, where the water comes from springs and is harder, beans will never soften. You could stew them for days without success unless you add a pinch of bicarbonate of soda to the boiling water and delay adding the salt for an hour.

Another recipe for **Fassoulatha** (bean soup) comes from Philip. To make it you will need 500 g (1 lb 1 oz) of dried haricot beans, 2 big onions, 200 ml (7 fl oz, a generous ¾ cup) of oil, 2 sticks of celery and 2 large carrots, salt and red pepper, *rigani*, 1 tablespoon of tomato paste or 2 ripe tomatoes, and water.

Soak the beans overnight in plenty of warm water. Next day drain them and put them into three litres (5¼ pints, 12 ½ cups) of fresh, boiling water until they are soft. Drain the beans again to avoid any danger of indigestion and tip them into another litre of already boiling water. Chop the onions, celery and carrots finely and put them in with the beans. Stir in the tomato paste or peel and mash the fresh tomatoes and add them too. Pour in the oil, add pepper, salt and *rigani* to taste, and let everything stew for fifteen minutes more.

In 1943 Italy surrendered to the Allies and the Italian troops on Corfu found themselves in an unenviable position. Mainland Greece was still in the hands of the Axis and a large German force immediately moved up through Epirus to occupy the islands. The Italian commander asked that he be allowed to evacuate his men back to Italy, but the Germans refused to negotiate. The Italians decided to resist. For twelve days German planes dropped incendiaries on the town and then on the villages. For the second time Loutses was bombed. Finally the Italians surrendered and the Germans moved on to the island. Almost their first act was to massacre five thousand of the eleven thousand Italian garrison, throwing some from the battlements of the old Venetian fort in Corfu Town and drowning the rest in the Straits, their hands bound and sacks tied over their heads. Many more died when a ship that was finally permitted to evacuate them was accidentally hit by Allied bombs. In the end only two thousand survived, scattered about the countryside.

The humanity of the villagers prevented them from giving these men up to the Germans, despite the threats of the new Kommandant. So they hid them and fed them with the little they had, and tried whenever possible to smuggle them across to Albania where resistance groups could help them back to Italy. They were not always successful. Some died of malaria, others were found dead in caves in the mountains, victims of exposure and malnutrition.

The German occupation dispensed with conciliatory gestures. The coast was more heavily fortified, with a garrison near the beach at

Aghios Spiridon and another in Kassiopi. Gunboats patrolled continually between the two and food was taken systematically from the villages. Soon there was so little left in Loutses that some of the men from Zervou decided to try their hand at smuggling. As ever, the only commodity they had to trade was olive oil and so, on moonless nights, barrels of it were taken down to Kalamaki beach and loaded into fishing boats. Between patrols, and with the gunwales only inches above the water, the men rowed silently across the Straits to the Albanian mainland. There they bartered the oil for sacks of flour, sometimes waiting days until a signal fire at Apraos told them it was safe to return. They were never caught.

Despite the success of this *contrabatta* conditions did not substantially improve until the German withdrawal from Greece in October 1944. When the villagers watched the soldiers embark from Aghios Spiridon they descended on the fort to salvage the food that had been left behind as soon as they were out of sight. Minutes later the place blew up. It had been mined by the departing garrison and three men were killed.

Tomas has no complaints about the diet he grew up on. He calculates that for the first seventy years of his life he probably ate beans or *horta* five days in every week. That, a regular bowl of yoghurt and a daily glass of warmed goat's milk, sweetened these days with sugar and thickened with a little crumbled bread, have kept him fit, for though he has given up picking olives he still, at ninety-six, carries the family's wood up from the land during the winter, milks the goat and helps his widowed daughter-in-law Maria with her garden.

Tomas no longer lives in Koulouri. After the war the family dispersed, some to the mainland, most to other parts of Loutses, and the old house stood empty, the downstairs an *apothiki* useful for storing sacks of wool and almonds, the upper rooms open to the rain and nesting swallows. Tomas followed the Greek tradition and went to live in his son's house next to the taverna on the main street of the village; when they built a new bungalow across the road he moved with them.

The garden that surrounds the bungalow is the finest in the village, and at the back of the house Tomas and Maria cultivate their vegetable plot, the source of much of the family's food during the first part of the year. Here they grow lettuces and beans, artichokes, onions and herbs, and also the one vegetable that Tomas will not eat: broad beans.

Apart from their taste for tortoise, the eating habit of the Italian garrison that most intrigued the people of Loutses was their penchant for *koukia*, uncooked, young broad beans. Many villagers grow them and eat them greedily, but not without considerable care in their cooking, for in Greece they are believed to be poisonous. They are never given to children or the elderly and every family has stories of an aunt or uncle who nearly died from *koukia*, driven to their bed for days, passing blood and running a terrible fever.

The origin of these tales caution may lie in the violent allergic reaction some people have to the flowers of the broad bean plant, or even in some vague memory of the ancient Greek belief that the souls of the unborn reside in the beans. Whatever the reason, *koukia* are approached with circumspection. To this day Greek merchant shipping companies forbid their presence on board ship. And yet they are relished by many who condemn them. They simply cook them by boiling them twice in fresh water to clean out the poison. Maria either bakes them with onions, tomatoes, fennel leaves, *rigani*, garlic and oil, or else fries them whole in their pods – though for this they must be picked in their infancy, before the beans have matured and become dangerous.

 To make **Koukia freska me lathi** (fresh broad beans in oil) you will need 1 kilo (2 lbs 2 oz) of very fresh, very young broad beans in their pods, 4 green onions (or 16 spring onions), 120 ml (4 fl oz, ½ cup) of oil, salt and pepper, 1 tablespoon of chopped fennel leaves, 1 tablespoon of chopped parsley, and either the juice of 1 large lemon or a bowl of plain, unstrained yoghurt.
Top and tail the bean pods and pull off any tough string from their sides. Wash them well. Chop the onions, fry them in the oil in a large shallow pan until they yellow, and then remove them. Put in the bean pods and fry them very gently for five to ten minutes, until their colour changes to a brighter, more vivid green; then return the onions to the pan, cover it and fry the vegetables for a further seven or eight minutes over a low heat, occasionally shaking the pan to prevent sticking. Add the fennel leaves, parsley, salt and pepper and just enough water to cover everything. Let it stew gently for half an hour, until nearly all the water has boiled away. If you prefer lemon juice, now remove the pan from the heat, pour the juice over the beans and move them about so that

the juice coats every one; if using yoghurt, leave out the lemon and spoon a little yoghurt over the beans on each plate after you have served them.

Young broad beans cooked this way are delicious, like rather vigorous mangetouts (which could be used in their place). Some people add one or two chopped fresh bulb garlic with the herbs, and like all bean recipes, *koukia* are prepared for the afternoon meal as they are considered too heavy to be eaten at night.

When Philip was growing up his family also had a vegetable garden on the coast, just above Apraos. Here they grew beans and whatever else they needed, and also chickpeas that were particularly good – their green shells salty from their proximity to the sea, the insides tender and sweet. They also cultivated lentils and Philip's father still cooks them, expertly, into a wonderfully aromatic stew reminiscent of a *dahl* in Indian cooking. The oil and vinegar loosen the thick consistency and draw out the full magnificence of the garlic.

 To stew half a kilo (1 lb 1 oz) of lentils or **Fakes**, Leonidas uses pepper, 3 or 4 bay leaves, a whole head of garlic (some people prefer only 3 or 4 cloves), a pinch of *rigani*, ½ level tablespoon of salt, oil and vinegar. The lentils are not soaked but are boiled for an hour in a little more than a litre (about 2 pints or 4 ½ cups) of water, with the peeled garlic cloves, salt, pepper, *rigani* and bay. When they are soft, Leonidas takes them off the heat and pours about 100 ml (6 or 7 tablespoons) of oil over them. Everyone adds their own vinegar at the table.

The vegetable gardens on the coast were one of the first casualties of the great boom in local employment that tourism brought to the north-east of the island. Now that there is money coming in and many more shops where they can spend it, the villagers no longer need to cultivate pulses and vegetables and dry them for the winter, and so the old summer chores have faded away and the coastal plots, with only one or two exceptions, have been sold or built upon or put under olives.

Up in Loutses, however, the allotments and gardens have not disappeared, and in the springtime, before the sun turns them again to patches of dry earth, they come gloriously into their own.

There is a sense of satisfaction and even a quiet excitement in the air as the first spring vegetables ripen. In the past this was due to the change of diet they brought after the winter months; these days, even though the market in Corfu Town is full of produce from more sheltered parts of the island weeks before anything is ready in Loutses, the villagers await their own harvest with a special anticipation. Vegetables are taken seriously in Greece. They are regarded as a food in their own right, not as an inferior companion to a piece of meat or fish. When buying them the women scrutinize each small courgette, each gleaming aubergine, questioning their provenance and comparing them with the produce of other weeks or years. When growing them, they do so with passion and concentration.

The vegetables reach their peak in April when the mountains are green and the olive groves carpeted with lush grass and a hundred varieties of wild flowers, from tiny white chamomile daisies and violet-blue Venus Looking-Glass to enormous flag irises, whose exotic purple and golden heads nod in the breeze and saturate the air with the heaviest, sweetest perfume. In the gardens, among the wild *horta*, fresh bulb onions are ready to be pulled, green and white and juicy. These are the most prized of all onions to the villagers, better than the great purple balls of summer or the more delicate cream-coloured salad onions of September – better even than the tiny baby onions of the autumn, whose subtle sweetness is a principal flavour of a *stifatho*. Beside the green onions grow fresh garlic, like potent shallots, the size and shape of our spring onions but with a faint mauve blush towards the bulb. Their flavour is exquisite and the Loutsiotes would cook with them all year round if they could. There are also lettuces and radishes and beets, new potatoes and baby carrots, early peas and *koukia*.

In every garden, towering over the other plants as they do in the minds of the villagers, are artichokes, the vernal nonpareil. Nothing excites the palates of the Loutsiotes in the way artichokes do, except perhaps the wild asparagus they gather in the hills, or the first glass of the year's new wine. The artichoke is an ancient hybrid of the cardoon and thistle and has retained its ancestors' habit of virulent growth. The plants outdistance everything else in the garden. By April, when their brief, four-week season begins, they are more than a metre high, the heavy sage-green leaves sagging inelegantly around the stalk, the flower buds thrusting out stiffly, tight and glossy and still an immature purple colour. That is how the villagers like them, small and tender, before the fibrous heart has developed, and they pick them when they are no more than ten centimetres long.

Philip's friends know that no vegetable is as precious to him. Maria Vlahou sometimes brings him a carrier-bagful of them from her garden, and then he leaves his father to look after the bar and goes off to his kitchen to prepare them.

The work is in the trimming. First, with a small sharp knife, he cuts off the stalks, which he peels of their stringy outer layer and puts into a bowl. Then he pares off at least half the leaves from each globe until he is left with a pile of tight bulbs, pale green at the base, turning purple halfway up, and each the size of a large egg. Working quickly now, before the stiff petals discolour, he makes a deep, diagonal cut halfway up the bulb so that the tip of his knife emerges just below the pointed crown, on the opposite side. Then he cuts all the way round, removing all traces of purple, slices off the remaining tip and trims any last leaf bases at the bottom.

Now he cuts a couple of lemons in half and, holding one over the bowl containing the stalks, pushes each artichoke into the middle of the lemon and twists it. The lemon juice will prevent the artichokes from discolouring and also draws out their flavour a little. Philip puts the artichokes in with the peeled stalks, squeezes the lemons over them and covers them with water, weighing them under with a plate and leaving them to soak for two hours while he goes back to the bar. When he returns he throws away the liquid and begins to cook.

Philip usually prepares artichokes by stewing them with herbs, fresh garlic bulbs and bulb onions, and a great deal of lemon juice, but there are many additions and changes to the basic recipe that he makes from time to time. His favourite includes potatoes and carrots and is finished with a delicate *avgolemono* sauce. This is also popular with restaurants, for one needs fewer artichokes than for most of the variations of the recipe. Their generous flavour spreads into the other vegetables with extraordinarily delicious results. In a restaurant they are offered as a 'first plate', but anything subsequent is inevitably an anticlimax; Philip just makes a lot and serves them as a meal in themselves.

To make **Anginares avgolemono** as Philip does, you will need 16 very young globe artichokes – more mature ones will not do – ½ kilo (1 lb 1 oz) of fresh bulb onions (or spring onions), 4 fresh garlic bulbs, 3 large potatoes, 3 carrots, 3 lemons, 150 ml (¼ pint, ⅔ cup) of oil, white pepper and salt, a pinch each of *rigani*, parsley, and mint and at least 1 tablespoon of fresh chopped fennel leaves, and 1 egg.

Trim, soak and drain the artichokes and their stalks as described above, using two of the lemons. Roughly chop the onions, garlic and herbs and soften them for a minute or two in the oil. Add the artichokes, salt and pepper, and the carrots, chopped into pieces, and cover everything with water. Let them simmer for an hour and a half, until most of the liquid has boiled away. Peel and cut the potatoes into large pieces and stir them into the pot with enough water to just cover everything once again. Simmer on for a further thirty to forty minutes, stirring as little as possible so as not to break up the artichokes. By now there should be about half a litre (about 1 pint, 2¼ cups) of liquid left. Take the pot off the heat and drain half the liquid into a bowl; let it cool for a few minutes. Meanwhile beat the egg and make an *avgolemono* sauce by squeezing the juice of a lemon into it with five or six tablespoons of the liquid from the bowl, added one at a time. Beat well and then pour the sauce into the rest of the liquid in the bowl and beat them well together. Pour the sauce back over the vegetables and return them to the heat until the sauce begins to thicken but does not quite boil. Eat immediately.

To the villagers this is the best of all ways to eat artichokes, but they know many others. A stew of lamb and vegetables can also be added to half a dozen artichokes, as can nuggets of soft salt cod or other spring vegetables such as broad beans or peas. In January, when the new artichoke plants are no more than a pair of tiny leaves sticking out of the mud of the garden, some people take the white shoots, breaking them off below ground level so that the plant will recover, and boil them briefly to eat with oil and lemon juice. *Anginara koulouga*, as they are called, are as tender as braised lettuce and already have the flavour of the mature vegetable in their pale cells.

Peas are another vegetable with a special place in the cook's heart. That the character of the pea has been carefully considered is borne out by the fact that they are one of the very few savoury foods that the Loutsiotes cook in butter, a precious commodity. Even in its heyday, before tourism severely damaged the dairy industry on Corfu, butter was a very limited food, eaten only on a slice of bread as if it were some kind of preserve. That *arakas voutirou*, peas in butter, calls for actual dairy butter, brands it therefore as an obviously imported recipe, perhaps from the northern interior of the country around Iannina, where sheep's butter was a traditional cooking medium.

To make **Arakas voutirou** you will need 1 kilo (2 lbs 2 oz) of fresh peas in the pod (dried or frozen peas will not do), 3 large green onions, 150 g (5 oz) of unsalted butter, parsley, fennel leaves, salt, white pepper and water.

Shell and rinse the peas, then put them into enough boiling water to cover them. Let them stew slowly for twenty minutes. Melt the butter gently in a pan and add the chopped onions. Let them soften but not brown. Drain the peas and add them to the onions with the chopped herbs, salt and pepper and 150 ml (¼ pint, ⅔ cup) more water. Let them simmer until the water has evaporated and then serve them immediately, unaccompanied.

A variation of this is known as **Arakas sautée**. Instead of the butter, 150 ml (¼ pint, ⅔ cup) of oil is used to fry the onions, and 2 medium-sized tomatoes, peeled and chopped, are added to them in the pan.

A more local recipe for cooking peas is **Arakas latheros,** (peas stewed in oil). The flavour of the fresh garden peas of Loutses stands out even against the other ingredients, which are 2 or 3 large carrots, 3 bulb onions, 2 fresh garlic bulbs, parsley, 1 tablespoon of chopped fennel leaves, a pinch of fresh mint, a little mild paprika, 1 tablespoon of tomato paste, 200 ml (7 fl oz, a generous ¾ cup) of oil, salt and water. Shell and rinse 1 kilo (2 lb 2 oz) of fresh peas. Roughly chop the onions, garlic and carrots and fry them in the oil until they soften, adding the chopped parsley, fennel leaves and mint after the first minute. Add the peas, paprika to taste and 300 ml (10½ fl oz, 1¼ cups) of water and let everything stew gently for half an hour. Then stir in the tomato paste and salt and simmer it for ten minutes more.

This recipe is equally good with fresh green beans. The Loutsiotes eat it with plenty of fresh white bread as a light dinner, or as the first dish of a more formal meal.

A final recipe for peas uses them more casually as one of the many optional ingredients in a vegetable soup. Corfiots love soups and cook them often throughout the year, improvising them creatively from whatever is available, boiled up with stock or if possible a raw beef bone, and usually eating them for the evening meal with half a loaf of the day's bread and perhaps a little *feta*. The best of them all is a *hortosoupa* made from fresh spring vegetables from the garden.

 To make **Hortosoupa** (vegetable soup) you will need 1½ kilos (3¼ lbs) of mixed spring vegetables (Philip's ideal choice would be a couple of fresh garlic bulbs, 2 bulb onions, a green pepper, some carrots, potatoes and the celery-like herb *selino*), 100 g (3½ oz) of semolina, white pepper and salt, 100 ml (3½ fl oz, ½ cup) of oil, the juice of 1 lemon or 1 tablespoon of tomato paste, and 2 litres (3½ pints, 8¼ cups) of stock, or water if you have some raw beef or lamb bones. A stick of celery could be used if you have no *selino*.
Dice the potatoes and chop all the vegetables finely. Put all the ingredients into a large saucepan, cover it and simmer slowly for at least an hour and a half.

It is difficult to imagine the cooking of Mediterranean Europe without tomatoes but the ancient Greeks, who devised the notion of *haute cuisine* and whose writers described its precepts and achievements fifteen hundred years before the first tomato crossed the Atlantic, managed to do very well without them.

The Venetians introduced the tomato to Corfu, but no record survives of the event to indicate whether the *pomodoro* reached the island as an exotic food or as one already familiar to the Italians and integrated into their cuisine. The climate suits it so well, however, that it must surely have taken a fast hold, at least among the urban population who were always eager to mimic the tastes of their rulers. In the villages it was quickly recognized as a vegetable and treated as such. Greeks rarely mix fruit into their savoury recipes so it was probably the palatable acidity of tomatoes that appealed to them.

Greek tomatoes are big and ugly. Unforced, grown in the open air and available from May until November if the autumn is mild, they have a flavour that can startle a northern palate – tangy and rich all summer, becoming much sweeter as winter sets in. Western Europeans on Corfu seem to choose them when they are firm and bright orange in colour; the locals prefer the riper fruit, crimson, soft and often split by the sun.

When the old vegetable gardens on the coast were still cultivated every household in Loutses grew its own tomatoes and preserved them, with the beans and pulses, for the winter. Because sugar was impossibly expensive, the women would squeeze out the seeds and dry the tomatoes in the sun, to be reconstituted as they were needed. But they never assumed the invaluable status they enjoyed in other parts of the Mediterranean because of the lemons that were a part of cooking here long before the tomato and still grow so well in the sheltered valleys around Peritheia. They are both still in very active competition with each other. Many recipes described by the villagers present an alternative between the two: tomatoes cooked into a dish early on, or lemon juice added later, to provide that necessary balance with the oil. During the spring and early summer when both are available, it becomes a matter of taste which is used.

Nobody in Loutses preserves tomatoes any more or makes their own tomato paste. Those that are grown locally are eaten as they ripen, cooked or sliced as a salad. Tomato paste is bought in tins from the shops. It is used liberally in the kitchen and also serves as an effective siccative for burns: a tablespoon of tomato paste smeared over the burn dries to a crust, preventing contact with the air and letting the skin heal more effectively than a fat like butter; a further application keeps the first from flaking off.

One of the favourite ways to cook large ripe tomatoes is to stuff them. In restaurants the standard filling is a mixture of minced meat, rice and herbs, but many of the village cooks prefer a vegetarian stuffing both for reasons of economy and because it has a more subtle blend of flavours without the meat. The following recipe comes from Maria Parginou, whose husband Stamati keeps the shop in Loutses. Their daughter-in-law Michelle is English and some of the foods that her friends bring out from England have found their way into Maria's cooking, particularly Bovril. Maria loves its flavour and uses it often as an alternative to home-made stock or stock cubes.

 To make Maria's **Domates yemistes** (stuffed tomatoes) you will need 4 large ripe tomatoes, 1 large onion, 1 tablespoon of chopped parsley, a sprig of *selino* or a small stick of celery, 2 teaspoons of chopped fennel leaves, 1 tablespoon of Bovril, black or white pepper, salt, 2 teaspoons of tomato paste, 150 g (5½ oz) of rice, a litre (2 pints, 4½ cups) of water and 100 ml (3½ fl oz, ½ cup) of oil.

Cut a small hole around the stalk of each tomato and scoop out the insides, taking care not to cut the flesh around the sides. Chop the onion and fry it in the oil until it is soft, then add the herbs and any seedless flesh from the scooped-out part of the tomatoes and fry for a further two minutes. Stir in the Bovril (previously mixed with a little of the water), the pepper, salt and tomato paste. Stir everything well then pour in the water and the rice. Let it simmer for ten minutes, until the rice is partially cooked. Remove it from the heat and with a teaspoon fill each tomato three-quarters full of the mixture. Stand the tomatoes in a greased dish and pour any of the mixture that is left around them. Put the pan into a hot oven for thirty minutes, adding water to the loose mixture if it threatens to dry out.

Maria also uses this recipe to stuff other vegetables, particularly green peppers. When she and her family sit down to eat them there is always a plate of her home-made *feta* cheese on the table.

By the middle of June the vegetable gardens of Loutses are drying up. The hills above the olive tree line are turning yellow as the more delicate plants flower and wither. For weeks to come not a breath of wind will stir the gathering heat, and across the straits Albania recedes into a blue haze. Meanwhile, the airport has turned into a monstrous Black Hole of Calcutta as the charter flights come and go, day and night, and every morning the ferries from Italy disgorge new crowds of backpackers and an endless line of German and Italian family saloons. By July the population of Corfu has more than doubled.

To cater for the tourists, and for those families in Loutses who own no car and have no particular reason to leave the village, a few enterprising farmers make regular journeys up into the mountains. Their land is down on the coast around and beyond Akharavi, and they have always taken their produce to the hills to sell it. Twenty years ago they would come on scooters with a crate or two of vegetables lashed to the pillion; now they arrive on smart tractors, pulling a trailer full of courgettes, leeks, lettuces and tomatoes – whatever was ripe and ready to be cut that morning.

Two or three times a week Dmitri the travelling greengrocer also puts in an appearance, in the evenings after a long day selling to tourists in their rented villas on the coast. His open truck winds up Zervou and the other roads leading to the more distant parts of the village, halting at strategic points. Dmitri climbs out, swings his scales free of the van and waits for the women and their daughters. The fruit and vegetables he sells are always of a quality good enough for even their expert scrutiny and the brief gatherings around his truck are an occasion for gossip and news as well as shopping. Six o'clock is the social hour in Loutses, the hour for formal visits and for strolling up the main street. Everyone is out and about and awake after the afternoon siesta, and Dmitri does good business. The only problem for the housewives up on Zervou is that by the time he gets there, he will probably have sold out of anything especially popular – his crate of beetroot is empty; there is no *selino* left, no parsley or baby carrots.

Because the Loutsiotes buy their summer vegetables these days, some dishes have become increasingly rare. Courgettes are still common, but marrows, once an inevitability in every coastal vegetable garden, are not: the time they need to grow deters today's commercially minded farmers. Should one or two reach Loutses on Dmitri's truck, however, they are pounced upon.

The cooks of Loutses have two ways of dealing with a vegetable marrow: they turn it into *kolokithopitta*, or they bake it in the oven, calling it *kolokithia briyam*.

 For **Kolokithia** (or **Kolokithakia**, if using courgettes) **Briyam**, you will need a vegetable marrow of about 1 kilo (2 lbs 2 oz), 2 medium-sized onions, 1 kilo (2 lbs 2 oz) of ripe tomatoes, 1 or 2 green peppers, a sprig of parsley, a pinch of fennel leaves and mint, a pinch of *rigani*, black pepper, sea salt and 150 ml (¼ pint, ⅔ cup) of oil.

Cut the marrow into slices about 1½ cm (0.5 in) thick – if the marrow is small, cut them askance so that the slices are larger. Put half the oil into a baking pan and lay the marrow slices in it, turning them so that they are wet with oil. Sprinkle them with sea salt, pepper and the herbs, then cut the green peppers into thin rings and lay them on top. Cut the onions into rings and lay them on top of the peppers. Slice the tomatoes and lay them on top of the rest, pour the remaining oil over everything, cover the dish with tin foil and bake it in a hot oven for an hour and a half. Then remove the foil and put the pan back into the oven for a further thirty to forty minutes until the surface of the vegetables is dry and beginning to brown.

Kolokithakia briyam is a fine dish, but it has sometimes failed to please visitors to the island who are familiar with French cooking. The trouble is that it is just too close to a *ratatouille*, as if the cook had tried to prepare one without aubergines or garlic and with no instinct for texture. The comparison is unfair and irrelevant, but it persists, and it also raises the question of why *ratatouille* is unknown on Corfu. The ingredients are all there, side by side on Dmitri's van, and it would be hard to conceive of a dish more likely to appeal to the Greek palate or of one so appropriate in style to the traditions of Corfiot cooking.

The answer lies with the aubergine. Somehow, aubergines have never been fully assimilated into the island's cuisine. It is as if the vegetable arrived on Corfu bringing with it a handful of eastern, mainland recipes from which no one has managed to free it for any wider use. With the exception of a few sophisticates like Philip, the cooks of Loutses have a rigidly traditional attitude to food, and the presence of an aubergine in the kitchen conjures up these recipes and no others.

Most demonstrably of the mainland are *papoutsakia*, a name which means 'little shoes', for there is something of the slipper about the final appearance of this dish, which has remained the same since immigrants brought it to Corfu from the east. If the aubergines are well enough cooked in the initial stages it turns out to be one of the most delicious of all Greek vegetable dishes, so perhaps the recipe has remained inviolate because no one can work out a way to improve it.

 To make **Papoutsakia** you will need 8 small, long aubergines, which should add up to between 1 and 1¼ kilos (about 2½ lbs) in weight, 1 large onion, 4 cloves of garlic, 2 large tomatoes, 100 ml (3½ fl oz, ½ cup) of oil and more oil to fry the aubergines, parsley, 2 tablespoons of fresh dill weed, sugar, salt and black pepper, 100 g (3½ oz) of *kephalotyri* cheese (or of Parmesan), and about 250 ml (9 fl oz, 1 cup) of béchamel sauce, for which you need 50 g (1¾ oz) of butter, 2 heaped tablespoons of plain flour, an egg, 250 ml (9 fl oz, 1 cup) of milk, salt, white pepper and a little grated nutmeg.

First cut the stems off the aubergines and then cut a long thin slice from the side of each one. Take a teaspoon and gouge out a little of the exposed insides, making a hollow as long and deep as a man's finger. Then, with a small, sharp knife, score the inside of the vegetables deeply in a criss-cross pattern, taking great care not to puncture the skin. Shallow fry the aubergines very gently in a centimetre of oil, turning them once, until the skin has wrinkled and darkened. It is very important to fry them enough at this stage: their insides should be as soft as mashed potato. Drain away some of the oil by laying them with their open sides down in a colander. Now slice the onion into rings and fry them briefly in the 100 ml (3½ fl oz, ½ cup) of new oil. Chop the garlic, peel and chop the tomatoes and add both to the onions with a little salt, pepper and four or five tablespoons of water. Let them stew on a very low heat for twenty minutes, then stir in the finely chopped parsley and dill weed and remove the pan from the heat. Lay the cool aubergines, cut side up, in a shallow dish. Into each one sprinkle a pinch of sugar and two teaspoons of finely grated cheese. Carefully spoon a little of the onion mixture into each aubergine. Now make a béchamel sauce by melting the butter in a saucepan and frying the flour in it for a minute or two, stirring continuously, until it begins to brown: this takes away the flavour of the flour. Beat the egg with the milk and slowly stir the mixture into the pan until the texture is smooth. Add salt, pepper and a hint of nutmeg. As the béchamel begins to seethe and thicken, remove it from the heat and allow it to cool for a while, then lay a tablespoon or two of it along the top of each aubergine, concealing the stuffing. Put the pan into a moderate oven for forty-five minutes, until the béchamel is golden brown.

Because of the time and effort involved the Loutsiotes tend to cook *papoutsakia* for special occasions. More frequently prepared is *melitzanosalata*, aubergine salad. This is made in two ways in Loutses, the first being another mainland recipe, the second coming specifically from north-western Greece and favoured in September when the almonds are ready to eat.

 To make **Melitzanosalata** you will need about 750 g (1 lb 10 oz) of aubergines – either 3 or 4 small ones or 1 large one – 3 cloves of garlic, 1 small onion, 1 small ripe tomato, 100 ml (3½ fl oz, ½ cup) of oil, 1 tablespoon of wine vinegar or 2 tablespoons of lemon juice, salt and a little mild paprika.

Cut the stems from the aubergines, rub their skins with a little oil, and bake them in a hot oven, on an oiled metal plate or better still a piece of aluminium foil since they tend to secrete a dark sticky juice. They bake in the same amount of time as a potato of similar size – a single large aubergine is ready in forty-five minutes – but test them by squeezing: you should be able to squeeze the two sides together. Let the aubergines cool, then cut them open and scrape out the insides. If using a very large aubergine, first scrape out the bitter seeds and throw them away. Then throw away the skins. Now grate the onion and crush the cloves of garlic; peel the tomato and either sieve or mash it. Mash the augergine with a fork and add all the other ingredients, mixing them together into a soft paste. Garnish it with olives and rings of green pepper and eat it with fresh bread.

 To make **Melitzanosalata** as they do in the north-west you will need the same weight of aubergines, baked and scraped in the same way, 2 hard-boiled eggs, the juice of 1 lemon, about 100 ml (3½ fl oz, ½ cup) of oil, and 100 g (3½ oz) of blanched almonds.

Pound the almonds to a paste in a pestle and mortar or a blender. Mash the hard-boiled eggs or chop them finely if you prefer, then mix all the ingredients together with a fork and garnish them with parsley.

The first of these recipes produces a *melitzanosalata* that is cool and tangy, with a flavour like a very mild *gaspacho* soup underlying that of the aubergine. The northern variation is altogether different, cleaner and more subtle, a pale delicacy rarely found in restaurants. Each is an extremely good hors-d'œuvre and they deserve to emerge from the shadows cast by their great rivals, *taramasalata* and *tsatsiki*.

In Greece, however, no other aubergine recipe can hope to compete with *moussaka*. Over the years *moussaka* has acquired the reputation of being the national dish, and yet at the same time has contributed to the disdain for Greek cooking that is sometimes encountered abroad. The reason for this is that it is easy to cook *moussaka* badly and even easier to spoil a good one, as many restaurants do, by reheating or by leaving it too long on a hot plate. The béchamel crown is particularly vulnerable to such neglect.

Recipes for *moussaka* differ all over Greece. No one really knows when or by whom *moussaka* was invented, but it is certainly a mainland Greek dish and, like *papoutsakia*, reached Corfu with immigrants from the east. At the risk of generalization one can say that it is spicier and more oily in the east, while in Athens more attention is given to the meat; on Corfu it is considered very much an aubergine dish. Philip believes that bearing this in mind leads to a successful *moussaka*: the vegetable needs the care and the meat looks after itself.

On the mainland, *moussaka* was originally made with minced lamb, but on Corfu, and increasingly in the rest of Greece, beef is now used. Any kind of aubergine is appropriate and it is cooked in different ways, depending on its size. Small ones are fried whole, turned in the shallow oil until their skins are wrinkled and dark and their insides as soft as butter; large ones are sliced, soaked in acidulated and salted water to draw out any bitterness, drained, brushed with oil, and then laid on a tray and baked in a hot oven until they are brown. Both methods prevent the aubergines becoming merely sodden with oil as they will if simply sliced and fried.

 To make **Moussaka** for six people you will need 1½ kilos (3¼ lbs) of aubergine, ½ kilo (1 lb 1 oz) of minced lamb or beef, 1 large onion, 80 ml (2½ fl oz, ⅓ cup) of oil and more to fry the aubergines, 80 ml (2½ fl oz, ⅓ cup) of a dryish white wine, 3 medium-sized ripe tomatoes, 1 very large ripe tomato, some parsley and dill weed, salt, sugar, pepper, 100 g (3½ oz) of grated *kephalotyri* cheese (or Parmesan); and for the béchamel sauce, 130 g (4½ oz) of butter, 6 tablespoons of flour, 500 ml (18 fl oz, 2 cups) of milk, 1 egg, salt, pepper, ¼ teaspoon of grated nutmeg and 4 tablespoons of grated *kephalotyri* or Parmesan.

First prepare the aubergines in the manner described above. Put the minced meat into a dry, heavy casserole on a very low heat, spreading it around a little with a wooden spoon. Let it fry undisturbed until the underside is brown and then turn it. At first it will stick a little to the casserole, but this stops after a while and the mince is left in dry grains, the best texture for nearly all Greek minced meat recipes. As it begins to stick again, and before it can burn, add the oil, the finely chopped onion, the three smaller tomatoes, also chopped finely, the chopped herbs, salt and pepper, and after three or four minutes, the wine. Let all this stew slowly for twenty minutes.

Take a large (28 by 35 cm), flat-bottomed baking pan with sides at least 10 cm deep. Slice the aubergines and cover the bottom of the pan with half of them. Peel and finely slice the large tomato and press half of the slices gently on to the aubergines. Sprinkle on a teaspoon of sugar (to bring out the sweetness of the tomatoes) and a quarter of the cheese. Smooth half the meat mixture in a layer on top of this, sprinkle on a pinch of salt and another quarter of the grated cheese. Repeat all these layers, starting with a second layer of aubergines. Make a béchamel using the method described in the recipe for *papoutsakia* (p. 55) but adding the grated cheese to the egg and milk mixture. Pour the sauce over the top of the *moussaka* – it should be about three centimetres (one inch) deep – and spread it evenly to the sides of the pan. Bake it in a moderate oven for at least an hour, until the top of the béchamel is golden and patched with darker brown. Allow it to cool for ten minutes before cutting it into rectangular slices and serving: piping hot, the full flavour of the *moussaka* will not yet have emerged.

Sometimes, especially in restaurants eager to economize on more expensive ingredients, cooks put a layer of fried courgettes or even fried potatoes at the base of a *moussaka*, though the latter causes dismay among purists.

The introduction of the potato to Greece is a familiar story in the village, largely because it demonstrates the wisdom of a Corfiot, Count John Kapodistrias, an international statesman and Greece's president from 1828 to 1831. In the early part of the nineteenth century Kapodistrias had been a diplomat in Russia, where he had seen the value of potatoes as a cheap, nutritious food for the poor. When he came to power in the embryonic nation of Greece he decided to bring the potato to his own people, so he purchased a shipful abroad, brought them to Nafplion, the Greek capital at the time, and had them unloaded on the docks. But the locals, though hungry, were wary of the strange vegetables and it looked as if the load would rot on the quayside, when Kapodistrias hit upon a plan. He let it be known that the potatoes were not for the Greeks at all, but destined for Russia as food for soldiers; by the following morning the Greeks had stolen the lot, cooked them and found them good.

The story is based on an identical ruse Parmentier used to tempt Parisians into accepting the potato a hundred years earlier, though whether it was Kapodistrias or the story-tellers who borrowed the idea is uncertain. In any event potatoes quickly established themselves throughout Greece. On Corfu they became as important a staple as bread and pasta, and the three have remained equal in status ever since, with rice a close fourth.

Undoubtedly the most popular way to cook potatoes on the island is to fry them. The Greeks were eating chips long before the English tourists came to Corfu, and egg and chips is as much a favourite dinner in Loutses as it is in London. Often at important events such as wedding banquets both chips and rice are served on the same plate to accompany the main meat course, the two together implying a certain affluence. Potatoes are also perfectly suited to the Greek taste for baking poultry or meat in oil, emerging half roasted, half casseroled in the gravy and entirely delicious.

 In the past, when meat was scarce, potatoes were made into **Patatas lemonatas** and were cooked in this way on their own, peeled and cut into long pieces, sprinkled with *rigani*, salt and black pepper, and baked in a pan in half a centimetre of oil and a little water. After forty-five minutes in a hot oven, the juice of two lemons was squeezed over the potatoes and they were returned to the oven for another quarter of an hour. The lemon juice both toughened and flavoured the potato skins. In their day, these *patatas lemonatas* were often eaten hot but were far more popular as a cold *meze* with ouzo or brandy, or as lunch for workers in the olive groves.

Another favourite way of cooking potatoes is to turn them into *patatas keftedes* or croquettes. This is a recipe that could have reached the island from a number of sources, one of which was through the large Jewish population of Corfu Town which thrived for centuries until the Fascist occupation during the Second World War. *Patatas keftedes* have been popular in Loutses for a long time and, as ever in the village cuisine, tradition has made certain accompanying foods mandatory – in this case beetroot salad and *skorthalia*.

 To make **Patatas keftedes** you will need a kilo (2 lbs 2 oz) of potatoes, 2 eggs, about 80 g (3 oz) of grated *kephalotyri* (or Parmesan) cheese, a generous pinch each of parsley and either fennel leaves or dill weed, 2 bulb or small white onions, white pepper, salt, flour and (olive) oil for frying.
Boil, peel and mash the potatoes. Chop the onions and herbs very finely, beat the eggs, and mix them all together with the potato,

cheese, salt and pepper. Let the mixture cool in the fridge and then form it into rounds about the size of golf balls. Roll them in flour and shallow fry them in very hot oil until they are golden brown. Inevitably they will absorb a little of the oil, so be sure to use good olive oil for the frying.

Skorthalia, the regular partner of *patatas keftedes*, is one of the simplest and most memorable of all Greek sauces, and Koula Parginou makes it superbly. On days when their husbands are working she often asks her sister-in-law over for lunch, especially when she has cooked one of her specialities – salt cod and potatoes.

 To make **Skorthalia** Koula soaks the dried fish overnight and next day puts it on to boil with a little salt and 6 potatoes, peeled and cut into bite-sized pieces. When the potatoes are soft she removes eight or nine of the pieces and puts them in a saucer. Then she takes two large heads of garlic, breaks them up into cloves, peels them, and mashes them to a pulp with her pestle and mortar.

With the scent of the garlic and the fish mingling tantalizingly in the kitchen, Koula makes her *skorthalia*, dropping the potato bit by bit into the mortar as she continues to pound, and dribbling in a little of her best olive oil at frequent intervals. The process takes ten minutes, for Koula is thorough, and uses about 80 ml (3 fl oz, ⅓ cup) of oil, but at the end she is left with a bowl of warm, creamy sauce, pungently hot from the garlic. The fish and remaining potatoes are drained and served up beside a heap of fresh green beans, with three or four tablespoons of *skorthalia* between them on each plate, and as a last touch she and her sister-in-law dribble a little more oil over everything. Half a loaf of soft white bread completes the meal.

A potato sauce over potatoes might seem like too much of a good thing, but it is undeniably successful, and besides, in a good *skorthalia* the identity of the potatoes vanishes during the long pulverization. When Koula makes it for her stewed cod, some of the flavour of the fish inevitably finds its way into the sauce, though it is barely detectable beneath the overpowering heat of the garlic. When it is made to accompany *patatas keftedes*, some of the mashed potato from the original recipe is used.

As the autumn deepens towards winter and the people of Loutses return to the olive groves to lay their nets, the variety of vegetables available shrinks. The last tourists have left the island now and Dmitri no longer visits the village with his truck. Down in the minimarket in Peritheia Spiro has replaced his stock of imported luxuries with more familiar produce – things that the locals are willing to buy. Sacks of potatoes and onions crowd the tables where the old men of the village spend their days playing cards and sipping coffee or ouzo, and ranged along the wall are crates of carrots and cabbages, the year's last tomatoes, and occasionally a box of locally grown cauliflowers.

Ask a cook from Loutses what to do with a cauliflower and the answer will be the same as it is in most of Europe and North America: cook it *au gratin*. This is certainly the most popular cauliflower recipe, but there are others, notably *kounoupithi tiganita*, in which the cauliflower florets are dipped in batter and deep-fried. The resulting crisp, golden coloured nuggets are eaten immediately, very hot.

 To make **Kounoupithi tiganita**, (deep-fried cauliflower) you will need a big head of cauliflower, salt and pepper, 100 ml (3½ fl oz, ½ cup) of milk, 50 g (1¾ oz) of butter, about 90 g (3¼ oz) of plain flour, 2 eggs and oil for frying. Remove the leaves and tough stalk from the cauliflower and cut it into bite-sized florets. Boil them in a lot of salted water for five minutes, then drain them well in a colander. Beat the eggs and melt the butter gently in a pan. Mix them both in a bowl with the flour, milk, salt and pepper. Heat the oil and then dip the cauliflower florets into the batter and deep fry them until they are golden.

Cauliflower is also eaten as a *salata*, boiled until it is soft and served warm with a little oil and lemon juice poured over it at the table, but for some reason it has never been a vegetable of any great importance in the minds of local cooks. Looming a great deal larger is the cabbage.

Corfu cabbages are hard and white with big, tightly wrapped leaves, and during the winter they are the indispensable ingredient of nearly every salad, for their nutty flavour merges superbly with a dressing of oil and lemon juice.

They are also made into *lahanodolmathes*, stuffed cabbage leaves, one of the perennial dishes of all the Balkan countries, and into the more unusual *lahano kokinisto*, or cabbage in red sauce. Philip makes this often as a first course before fried or grilled fish, but with its thin but well-flavoured sauce it is equally good as a vegetable to accompany meat.

 To make **Lahano kokinisto** you will need a small head of cabbage, 2 onions, a sprig of parsley, a generous pinch of dill weed, 1 teaspoon of mild paprika, 1 tablespoon of tomato paste, 2 teaspoons of salt, 75 ml (2½ fl oz, ⅓ cup) of oil and 500 ml (18 fl oz, 2 cups) of water.
Remove any damaged leaves from the cabbage and shred it very finely. Finely chop the onions, dill weed and parsley. Put the cabbage and onions into a saucepan with the oil and fry them for seven or eight minutes on a low heat, stirring them from time to time. Add the other ingredients and let everything stew for forty minutes, until the water has almost evaporated. Remove it from the heat, stir everything once more and serve.

An important feature of this recipe is the way the cabbage is shredded. Grating produces an unsatisfactory result, as do the chopping blades on some food processors; Philip uses a large, razor-sharp knife, first quartering the cabbage and then slicing across the lie of the leaves, working expertly and very close to the fingertips of his other hand, shaving off a slice at a time, each one no more than a couple of millimetres thick.

This is also how he prepares a cabbage salad, adding a little grated carrot and some salt and then pouring on a well-beaten dressing of three parts oil and one part of either lemon juice or *skorthostoupi*, wine vinegar in which a broken-up head of garlic has been steeped for a month or two. He leaves the dressing to soak in for ten minutes and then, cupping the salad in his hands, squeezes out the liquid and returns the vegetables to a clean bowl. He garnishes them with very thin rings of green pepper and a lot of black olives, and sometimes a little finely sliced onion. The resulting *lahanosalata* is moist and piquant and especially good with a heavily flavoured main course such as *mayiritsa* (p. 169).

The word *salata* embraces such a variety of foods that it is difficult to find an adequate definition of the term. It could be argued, however, that to call a dish a *salata* is to suggest that it has been prepared in the way most likely to exploit the natural virtues of the particular subject.

Some of the simplest *salatas* involve a single vegetable, lightly dressed for the table. During the summer, for example, a large percentage of a family's meals will include a *domatasalata*, a dish of sliced tomatoes, soused in oil and sprinkled with *rigani* or basil. In the spring, when they are plentiful, lettuces are chopped very finely by rolling up the soft leaves like a cigar and shredding them with a sharp knife, and are served with a little lemon juice squeezed over them. Baby courgettes are another favourite, cleaned and plunged into boiling water for a minute or two, then drained and served warm with an oil and lemon dressing, four parts oil to one part lemon juice beaten well with a fork. Boiled green beans are eaten hot or cold with oil and vinegar, and so are sliced, boiled beetroot, the latter with a plentiful scattering of roughly chopped garlic.

Other *salatas* call for a little more preparation. Philip's recipe for a white bean salad begins the night before it is needed when he soaks half a kilo of haricot beans in warm water. Next morning he boils them in fresh salted water until they are soft, drains them and leaves them to cool. Then he slices two fresh bulb onions and finely chops three fresh garlic bulbs, a little parsley and some fresh fennel leaves and mixes them in with the beans. His dressing for this is oil, lemon juice, paprika and a little salt, beaten together and poured over the top just as he serves it.

These are a few of the *salatas* Corfiots prepare regularly, but it is unlikely that a tourist will encounter many of them, for of all the omissions and deceits practised by the restaurateurs of the island none is more curious than their treatment of vegetables. On the menus of the resort tavernas one might see two or three vegetable dishes, listed among the hors-d'œuvres or in the section reserved for items cooked in oil, but on the rare occasions when they are available they are as likely as not to be tinned. In the grand hotel restaurants cultural snobbery forces an imitation of a supposed French cuisine and vegetables appear, grudgingly, as a garnish to a piece of meat. As for salads, the tourist will find only three: tomato salad, cucumber salad, and the famous *horiatiki*, the village salad, which has come to mean either lettuce or cabbage mixed with tomatoes, onion, olives and a few scattered morsels of *feta* cheese.

It is hardly surprising that visitors leave the island ignorant of the love and reverence Greeks have for their vegetables, but though they may never taste them, they can at least see what they're missing.

Corfu Town vegetable market sprawls picturesquely up the old fosse of the New Fortress, an awesome bastion built by the Venetians in the seventeenth century. Here, every morning except Sundays, the small-holders and market-gardeners who farm the marvellously fertile land of the Ropa valley and the plains in the south of the island bring their produce. Some of the stalls consist of nothing more than a chair and a basket or a spread-out newspaper on which to display whatever is fresh and newly grown, others are permanent shops from which the greengrocers shout out the day's bargains to the milling crowds and draw their attention to the glistening piles of colour and fragrance on their barrows and trestle tables. In May the scene is one of white and mauve and a hundred shades of green, sacks of beans and pulses, towering heaps of spinach, *horta*, and beet-root tops, leeks a yard long and as thick as a child's arm, green onions and small bundles of fresh garlic. In the summer the colours change – among the greens the imperial purple of aubergines gleams in the sun, and crimson tomatoes and the livid yellow and orange of courgette flowers brighten the deep shade of the stalls where the old ladies lurk among their bunches of herbs.

The market is a venerable institution and nowadays many of the Loutsiotes shop there – certainly those who, like Philip, have business that brings them regularly to town. Given such abundance it is difficult to remember how little the villages of the north had, as recently as forty years ago. In those days the town was a far more distant place, and to men and women of old Tomas's generation it remains a great deal further away in the imagination than the hour it takes his grandchildren to drive there.

🍇 THE SEA

When Philip was a boy, his family still lived in their old stone house up on Zervou, on the northern, seaward side of the ridge that shelters Loutses. From his window, on hot summer mornings, he could look down the tumbling, olive-covered slopes to the sea, sky-blue in the distance where Albania blurs into the horizon, sparkling clear and turquoise below him in the broad bay of Apraos. The view was a constant temptation to truancy and Philip was happy to succumb. Using paths that skipped long loops of the dusty road he could be on the beach in fifteen minutes, spend half an hour swimming and diving for sea urchins and be home and dried again almost before he was missed.

Long before tourism turned the coast into Corfu's principal asset, the people of the villages enjoyed a special relationship with the sea. Twenty-five years ago the roads that now link Rodas and Kassiopi with the town were unmade tracks, and any commerce between Loutses and the capital was necessarily by boat. Individuals could make the long hike over the mountain tracks, but the area's exports, oil and lambs, had to be taken down to the beaches at Apraos or Aghios Spiridon for transportation, the lambs crowded into small boats and rowed to waiting caïques, the oil barrels floated out over the sand banks in the shallows. Families with land on the coast also spent much of the summer down there, as did those who fished, either for a living or for sport. The rocky promontories between Aghios Spiridon and Kassiopi were as much a part of the life of Loutses as the hills above the village.

The same is true today, though the nature of the relationship has changed. Land near the sea has become valuable, worth three or four times as much as the equivalent *stremata* in the hills, and the enterprising can turn a half acre of scrub-covered rock into a major source of income by building a rentable villa on the site. In other parts of the island this has resulted in hideous over-development (during the time of the Colonels all restrictions on such activities were lifted) but in the less accessible north-east, exploitation has been slower. Even Kalamaki, the beautiful white-sand beach that fringes half the bay of Apraos, has managed to preserve its old identity, largely because it can only be reached by boat or down a precipitous path from the road high above. Until three years ago the path was unmarked and invisible among the olive trees, a casual secret of the villagers – for the Greeks enjoy their beaches too, a fact which seems to surprise some tourists.

The people of Loutses go down to Kalamaki and Aghios Spiridon in July and August, when the children are home from school and the sea is so warm that even the most careful hypochondriac feels safe from double pneumonia. On Sundays, when the men and their trucks are available, the whole family descends to picnic and sleep in the shade of the olive trees above the beach, venturing occasionally on to the sun-scorched beach to swim in the sea. On weekdays, the morning bus carries mothers and children to the top of the path, picking them up again at four. It is still a notable excursion and the habit remains to count the summer's trips carefully: the housewife with fewer visits finds compensation in a martyred righteousness. For the rest of the year, and in the evenings and early mornings when Kalamaki is at its most beautiful, the beach is deserted except for an occasional fisherman and the swallows swooping suddenly over the water.

The same is true of Aghios Spiridon: packed tightly in summer it is empty from October to May. Before the new complex of villas was built there, the only buildings visible from the shore were an old house on a distant promontory and the small pink chapel on the beach itself. It seems a strange and lonely place for a church, but it was erected for their own special protection by the fishermen who once used the bay. As in the principal church to the island's saint in Corfu Town, seamen gave thanks for narrow escapes and looked for continuing good luck by leaving tokens around Saint Spiridon's image – tiny paintings or photographs of their boats, or small models of a caïque stamped from a sheet of silver.

A more important link between the Church and the sea concerns the complicated rules of the Lenten fast. In theory, these strict laws of abstinence exist to cause a real hunger and physical exhaustion in the congregation during Lent, thereby leading to a consciousness of their dependence on God; in practice matters are much more relaxed. The bewildering daily changes in the list of prohibited foods has been reduced to an observance of *xerophagy* on Wednesdays and Fridays, a word that means 'dry eating' and describes abstinence from meat, fish with backbones, all dairy products, and – the real sacrifice – from olive oil and alcohol. Other vegetable oils and octopus, squid and shellfish are permitted.

Leading up to the seven week period of Lent is Carnival week and then Cheese week, which derives its name from the fact that dairy products may be eaten although meat is forbidden. Cheese week culminates in a second weekend of carnival, the last party before Easter Sunday, and still an occasion in certain villages, such as Avliotes on the north-western coast, where a straw guy is burned on a bonfire; and the fun goes on well into the following day. Those Loutsiotes who have friends or relatives there sometimes drive over for the celebrations; others, like Philip, head for Corfu Town. There the main streets have been hung with lights and during the afternoon there is a parade and a competition for local brass bands; the children stroll around in fancy dress, just as they do in Venice, buying toys and sweets from stalls along the pavement, and the families eat out in the evening. Even some of the night clubs and discothèques, built for summer tourists, have opened especially for the fortnight, and the bouzouki-bars take over when they leave off, reaching a fortissimo of music and noise at about midnight and sustaining it until dawn.

The next day, the first day of Lent, is called Clean Monday and is a public holiday for everyone except the two bakers down in Kassiopi. They have been working since four in the morning baking *lagana*, the special loaves for the day, flat and rectangular with sesame seeds on top, pierced with a nail to prevent their rising, and made from a finer, sweeter dough than usual. There will be queues all morning as customers wait to buy two or three loaves fresh from the oven.

The Church decrees that this should be a day of total fast, or at least of *xerophagy*, and most people make a gesture in this direction, at the same time taking advantage of the tradition to enjoy themselves. If the day is fine, many families from Loutses go down to the coast to spend the cool spring morning looking for *horta*, sitting about on the rocks or picking their way along the water's edge, collecting shellfish. Even if the sky is overcast the men will be there, in T-shirts, trunks and sandals, or, in a few cases, longjohns, combing the jagged peninsulars between Apraos and Kassiopi for limpets, winkles and the rarer murex whelks. Some of these are eaten on the spot, pulled out of their shells, the intestinal tract pinched out and discarded, the succulent white flesh washed in the sea and then swallowed; others are dropped into a bag and taken home to cook into either a pilaf or a *rizatha*, a thick but delicately flavoured soup.

At other times of the year, the Loutsiotes make a *rizatha* with game birds, and on the mainland, though not on Corfu, snails are also used. During Lent however, only shellfish are considered appropriate, the most popular species for the recipe being the Mediterranean limpet, *patella coerulea*. In the rest of Greece they are known as *petalitha*; on Corfu, where Italianate words have infiltrated the vocabulary, as *patalis*.

To make a **Rizatha patalis** (rice and limpet soup) you will need 300 g (10½ oz) of shelled *patalis* (mussels or clams, preferably fresh, will do), 1 small onion, 2 heaped tablespoons of finely chopped fresh parsley, 1 heaped tablespoon of finely chopped fennel leaves, 4 cloves, a pinch of *rigani*, 150 ml (¼ pint, ⅔ cup) of oil, 1 tablespoon of tomato paste, salt and white pepper, 2 litres (3½ pints, 8¼ cups) of water, and 175 g (6 oz) of short-grain rice.
If the limpets are fresh, pinch out their stomachs leaving only the white flesh, then wash them in salt water before cutting them into small pieces. Chop the onion. Heat the oil in an ovenproof casserole and briefly soften the limpets and onions in it before adding the herbs, cloves, salt and pepper, and the tomato paste. Fry them for a few minutes longer, then add the water and the rice. Stir it well and let it simmer over a low heat for an hour. There should be a good six cups of broth left after an hour, so more water may be needed.

Down among the shellfish hunters on the shore this Lenten morning are several other men armed with slender bamboo poles up to four metres long, cut from the thickets behind Kalamaki beach. With the water still too cold for swimming, they are out after octopus. In the end of the bamboo pole has been set a barbed hook around which the hunter has tied a small fluttering white rag as a lure, or else some of the pale flaccid leaves and splayed yellow flowers of a shrub called Jerusalem Sage, or *asvaka*. This bait is pulled through the water outside the holes and small caves where the octopus live. The creature emerges to investigate and wraps itself around the lure, the fishermen jerks the hook into it and hoists the whole dripping apparatus out of the sea and on to the rock beside him.

The technique seems strangely prehistoric. Perhaps the earliest immigrants to Corfu, whose palaeolithic remains have been found at various places along the northern coast, practised it in much the same way and with similar equipment. It relies on a detailed knowledge of octopus habitats and is favoured by the elderly – for most of the young men prefer to wait a month or two before they go after octopus, with a mask and snorkel and a spear-gun.

Philip's favourite summer sport is octopus hunting. He goes out often between May and October, two or three times a week or even daily if he can get away from the bar. The best weather for it is when the *siroko* is blowing from the south-east, bringing cloud and humidity and a threat of rain up the Ionian and a peculiar calm to the waters between Apraos and Kassiopi. When the wind comes from the north, driving the sea down through the straits, the octopus tend to leave their holes and go deeper, down among the weed which hides their traces utterly.

Philip leaves his orange van upon the road near a cove called Siki and climbs down to the water's edge to make his final preparations. As well as his trunks, spear-gun and snorkelling gear, he puts on a T-shirt and flippers and a canvas-backed net bag that straps around his waist. He ties his sandals behind him with a piece of wire. Sometimes, if he feels like it, he also takes a carrier bag to gather certain of the sea-urchins that form the shoreline's densest population. The black ones are inedible, but those with pink or purple spines, *sphaerechinus granularis*, he spikes on his trident as he swims and then knocks into his bag, to be eaten in a cleft in some secluded rocks, or back at home. Athenian gourmets enjoy the tiny yellow roe of sea-urchins, but Philip prefers to eat the whole thing, enlarging the mouth aperture with a knife, squeezing in a little lemon juice and a dribble of oil, stirring, and then eating the whole thing by dipping pieces of bread into it, as if it were a soft-boiled egg.

But octopus is his main prey, particularly since the waters here now hold few large fish. He paddles slowly away from the rocks, diving frequently to explore the holes that experience reminds him have held octopus in the past, and looking especially for the remains of any crab, the principal food of the octopus. Five metres down he sees a broken orange shell and dives to investigate. A nearby hole is occupied, an octopus lurking inside, relying on its camouflage. Philip can bring the spear-gun to within inches of it before he fires.

The spear is left sticking out of the hole. Philip rises to breathe and to wait for the wounded octopus to emerge. Any attempt to pull it out will merely tear out the spear while the animal is wedged into its den. Eventually a long tentacle appears, whipping the space in front of the hole, another uncurls and then suddenly the whole octopus billows out and Philip dives again to lift it above the surface. Treading water, he pulls out the harpoon and quickly turns the octopus's head inside out, pulling off the ink-sac and the entrails. The creature has wrapped itself around his forearm; he pulls it off with a noise like tearing velcro. Amazingly it is still alive, but only half so, and it can no longer co-ordinate a defence. Philip puts it into his pouch and swims off again, looking for more. Sometimes, depending on the weather, he will find four or five mature octopus, each weighing a kilo or more, in the hours he spends in the water; at other times he finds only one. At night the chances of success are greater: the beam of his underwater torch illuminates a far more active world.

When he has had enough, or when experience tells him that it is not worth the effort of continuing, Philip comes out of the water and sets about killing the octopus he has caught. He does this by repeatedly hurling it against a flat rock, as many as forty times if the creature is a large one, and then rubbing it against a convenient slab as if it were a handful of rag. The animal is dead when its tentacles hang long and loose; it is tender when pulling two of them apart tears the flesh between.

Some men eat their octopus there and then, raw and superlatively fresh: the meat is surprisingly sweet. Philip, however, puts them back in his bag, unties his sandals, and climbs up to the road to walk back to his van. At home he finishes cleaning each octopus by cutting out its tough beak and also its eyes, which contain a hard beadlike lens. Then whatever the recipe he intends to use, he must first seethe the octopus.

This is done by putting it whole into a covered saucepan with two tablespoons of water, and setting it over a very low heat for twenty minutes. A strange, marine odour pervades the kitchen, while in the pan the octopus sweats a salty crimson juice and braises itself, contracting into a curious, almost floral shape. The juice is discarded and the octopus removed.

At this point it is already essentially cooked. Sometimes Philip eats it as it is, dressed only in a little olive oil and lemon juice. Or else he cuts it into pieces, rolls it in flour and deep fries it very quickly in very hot oil. More often, though, he stews it.

To make **Htapothi yahni** (octopus stew) in the way preferred by Philip you will need 1 octopus of between 1 and 1½ kilos (2 lbs 2 oz and 3¾ lbs), or 2 smaller ones, 100 ml (3½ fl oz, ½ cup) of oil, 2 large onions, 2 cloves of garlic, 1 or 2 tablespoons of tomato paste, black or red pepper, 2 large potatoes, *rigani* and water. First tenderize the octopus, either by persistent beating or by freezing it for at least twenty-four hours. Test for tenderness by pulling two tentacles apart: if the flesh between them tears, the octopus is tender. Then seethe it by the method described above and cut it into bite-sized pieces. Chop the onions and garlic and soften them in the oil in a heavy pan or casserole. Add the tomato paste and the pepper and fry them for one minute, stirring well. Peel the potatoes and cut them into large pieces and add them with the octopus to the onions. Add a pinch or two of *rigani*, cover everything with water, stir and simmer, covered, until the potatoes are soft – for perhaps half an hour.
The resulting stew has a thick pungent gravy of a startling colour, a sort of dark Venetian red, and is eaten with a great deal of fresh white bread, usually as the afternoon meal since it is considered indigestibly rich before bedtime. A light salad of cucumber and green pepper is an excellent accompaniment.

If Philip has caught a lot of octopus, or if he feels like a new flavour, he sometimes pickles them. This is a famous hors-d'œuvre and *meze* in Greece and is one of the few preserved foods still regularly prepared in Loutses. Its success depends upon using the very best wine vinegar – though it might be interesting to try English cider vinegar for a change.

To make **Htapothi toursi** (pickled octopus) you should seethe the octopus longer than usual, removing the lid from the pan and allowing the juices to evaporate (washing the pan immediately saves it from being stained too badly). Then cut the octopus into small pieces. To see how much vinegar he will need, Philip puts the octopus into the container he has chosen (it should fill it loosely) and pours the vinegar in, right up to the brim. He then pours the vinegar out again into a pan, with a tablespoon or two more to allow for evaporation, and brings it to the boil with two or three bay leaves and a pinch of both *rigani* and mint. For a hotter pickle he occasionally adds a teaspoon of red pepper or a couple of dried chillies. After three minutes of vigorous boiling he removes the pan from the heat and lets the vinegar get quite cold before pouring it back over the octopus in the jar. The vinegar and herbs must cover the octopus completely and should fill the jar so that as little air as possible is left under the lid. It is ready to serve in three days, drained and arranged on a small plate, with plenty of bread and oil.

Octopus is an important seafood in Greece. During Lent it is the most versatile permissible meat and for the rest of the year it enjoys a status somewhere between that of the ubiquitous squid and the rare extravagance of a lobster. Its flavour also lies between the two and properly prepared its legendary rubbery texture becomes as tender as a crawfish's tail.

In the summer on Corfu octopus can be hard to find in the restaurants, except pickled, as a *meze*. With a clientele of tourists who seem disconcerted by the very name of the creature, let alone the sight of suckered tentacles on their fork, the restaurateurs are unwilling to go to the trouble of making a stew that they may end up eating themselves. Squid, however, are available on every menu – appealing to the tourist because of the featureless anonymity of their flesh and to the chefs because they can be prepared in minutes, with a minimum of effort.

Ptodarodes sagittatus, the sagittal squid, is abundant all year round, inexpensive and easily caught at night when they rise to the surface by the offshore fishing fleet. The people of Loutses can buy them fresh in Corfu Town, or frozen in the shops in Peritheia. They freeze very well and their flavour is unimpaired. Alternatively, Stamati stocks tins of baby California squid in his shop in Loutses. They are expensive and tiresome to clean and when fried taste exactly like bacon – which may be part of their appeal.

Fresh squid, however, have a subtle flavour of their own and a 'lightness' in terms of both digestion and texture that endears them to Corfiots. At home, as in the restaurants, they are usually fried and are welcomed as a main course, an hors-d'œuvre or a *meze*.

Cleaning squid is a simple but time-consuming job. Very little of the creature is inedible: really just the transparent cartilage and the eyes, which tend to explode if they reach the hot oil (Corfiots say '*Vlastimane*' – 'the eyes are blaspheming'). First pull off the head of the squid and either pinch out the eyes or, if the squid is large, cut the head in two just above them. Keep the part with the tentacles and throw away the part with the eyes. The cartilage runs the length of the fish and is lightly secured at the tip of the tail. If it does not come out easily, massage the tail a little, then pull it out. The viscera are also usually discarded, though there is no harm in eating them. Smaller squid may have an amount of roe towards the tail; this is delicious and should be included in the recipe. Now wash the long cylindrical bodies and the tentacles and let them drain thoroughly in a colander.

To make fried squid, **Kalamaria tiganita**, as a main course you will need 1 kilo (2 lb 2 oz) of fresh or frozen squid, plain flour, salt, red pepper, a pinch of *rigani*, oil for deep frying, and 2 or 3 lemons to squeeze over the finished article.

Clean the squid, and while they are draining make a seasoned flour using a little salt, *rigani* and half a teaspoon of red pepper. Cut the bodies of the squid into rings one or two centimetres wide and coat both them and the tentacles with the flour. Deep fry them in very hot oil, timing one piece first: they cook quickly and are tough if overcooked or underdone. Ideally they should be golden brown and crisp on the outside, still moist within. It is very important to serve them immediately as they quickly toughen as they cool. On Corfu, mayonnaise is usually prepared only for very important seafood such as lobster, but it is very good with squid, especially with the addition of two teaspoons of chopped capers, an innovation of which Philip approves. Otherwise they should be served on their own or with a simple green salad.

Less frequently found on Corfu, though it is well-known in the rest of Greece, is **Kalamaria Yemista**, (stuffed squid). This is definitely a main course and the flavour of the tender, golden squid emerges even more deliciously than when they are fried. To make it you will need a kilo (2 lb 2 oz) of medium-sized squid, 2 medium-sized onions, 30 g (1 oz) of raisins, a little salt, 100 g (3½ oz) of long-grain rice, 120 ml (4 fl oz, ½ cup) of oil, a little parsley, mint and *rigani*, black or white pepper, 500 ml (17½ fl oz, 2 cups) of dry white wine, 1 ripe tomato and a little coarse sea salt for cleaning the squid. Clean the squid as described above, but do not cut their bodies. Instead, rub them with sea salt, wash them thoroughly and leave them to drain. Put half the oil in a frying-pan and fry the chopped onion until it begins to yellow. Chop the parsley and mint and add it to the onions with a pinch of *rigani*, the uncooked rice, raisins, pepper and salt. Fry all this for one minute, stirring well, then remove it from the heat. At this point the squid can be stuffed, sewn shut with a chef's needle and sautéd further, but Philip finds this too time-consuming and, more importantly, liable to toughen the squid. Instead he briefly fries the bodies of the squid in the remaining oil, just for a minute, so that they stiffen and open, making them easier to stuff. Then he removes them from the oil, fills each one half-full with the rice mixture and packs them tightly in an oven-proof casserole in pairs with the openings pressed together. The tentacles are scattered on top. Into the oil left in the frying pan, put the peeled and finely chopped tomato, another pinch of salt and the wine. Just as this sauce begins to boil, pour it carefully over the squid. Cover the pot and put it into a moderate oven for an hour. It is ready when the sauce has thickened and the stuffing has swelled to fill the squid, but if the sauce threatens to evaporate before this can happen, add a little water. Let the pot stand, covered, for at least five minutes before serving. The sauce in this recipe is not its important feature. Its role is to cook and flavour the rice and to leave the squid themselves succulent and tender. *Kalamaria yemista* should be moist but not swimming in sauce. They are very good with a green salad.

Philip is not a devout man – he has conducted a determined campaign against the Church for years through the letters pages of the national newspapers – but some of his father's friends are. For them he has devised a special pilaf for Lent, using a combination of permitted foods such as squid, prawns and shellfish.

Greeks have been eating rice since classical times and the pilaf (rice boiled in a mixture of stock and oil, flavoured with bay, cinnamon, salt, pepper and lemon) is one of the most basic ways in which they cook it, serving it as a meal in itself, often with grated cheese and tomato sauce or as a garnishing vegetable with octopus, lobster or fried liver. The inclusion of seafood in a *pilaffi* is particularly popular both because it allows the flavour of fish and shellfish to stand out against a relatively muted background, and because it stretches a small catch into a meal for the whole family.

 To make **Phillipakis pilaffi Sarakostino** (Philip's Lenten pilaf) for six people you will need about 1½ kilos (3¼ lbs) of seafood – for example 600 g (1 lb 5 oz) of squid, 400 g (14 oz) of raw prawns of any size and 500 g (1 lb 1 oz) of shelled shellfish such as limpets, clams or mussels – 500 g (1 lb 1 oz) of long-grain rice, 1½ litres (2½ pints, 6¼ cups) of water or better still, fish stock, about 4 tablespoons of oil, half a whole lemon, 3 bay leaves, 2 cloves of garlic, a small onion, salt and white pepper.

Clean the squid and cut them into small pieces. Clean the shellfish as described in the recipe for *rizatha patalis* and cut them into small pieces too. Peel the prawns, but leave the heads and tails on (this is done for flavour and colour – the heads and tails are not eaten). Chop the onion and garlic. Bring the water to the boil and add all the ingredients except the rice. Simmer it very slowly for forty-five minutes then add more water, if it is needed, to make up six cups of liquid again. Remove the half lemon, add the rice and put the pan into a moderate oven for thirty to forty minutes, until the liquid has been absorbed. The lemon and the bay are wonderful together in this pilaf, and the prawns give a pale pink colour to the rice. Philip sometimes serves it by moving everything into a clay pot before putting it into the oven and then carefully upending the pot over a plate so that the emergent *pilaffi* stands unaided in a glistening dome. A garnish of sliced salad vegetables and fresh parsley completes the picture.

Corfu is renowned as one of the few places in Greece where the spiny lobster, *palinurus elephas*, can be found. Lacking claws, it is really a crawfish and the edible meat is all in the tail, which is also the animal's main defensive weapon. Many a waiter lifting his customer's chosen dinner from a tank has had his fingers lacerated by a sudden contraction of razored armour.

The creatures are found on the western coast of Corfu, where the sea is colder and rougher than in the Straits, and several tavernas at Palaeokastritsa have made themselves famous by the practical gimmick of a lobster pot larder in the sea itself. The lobsters are cooked very simply, dipped briefly in boiling water to kill them, split down the middle with a cleaver, and then grilled over charcoal or on a searingly hot metal plate. In an attempt to justify the extraordinary price of these 'first among fish', they are served with dishes of homemade mayonnaise and a garnish of the best vegetables the restaurant has to offer.

Lobster can also be found on the eastern coast of the island in the restaurants of a tiny, picturesque bay called Aghios Stefanos. Four miles from the main road down a partially made-up track, it is the nearest settlement on Corfu to the Albanian mainland, only a mile away across the sea. Many of the Loutsiotes drive down there on summer evenings, but not for the lobster. The speciality of Aghios Stefanos is *ghonos*, a word that means the fry of any fish, but when whispered discreetly to the waiter here refers to the hatchlings of the *gavros*, a type of anchovy.

The secrecy is necessary because it is illegal in Greece to fish for these tiny things, or even to own nets with mesh small enough to catch them, though such nets, called *aghonodikto*, are made by most fishing equipment firms. *Ghonos*, accordingly, never appear on the menu, but word gets out and the gourmets gather, amongst them, it is said at this particular bay, even cabinet ministers. The *ghonos* can be cooked as a *bianco*, or baked in the oven with tomatoes, but more commonly they are deep fried like whitebait – dusted with flour and lowered briefly into very hot oil. Their notoriety has much to do with their appeal, but there is something unique in their flavour too – a little like fried sardines but with the chalky tang of smelt.

Part of the fun of eating at Aghios Stefanos lies in the display of the enormous searchlight just across the water in Albania. The country has been at war with Greece for forty years (during the '60s a Zervou man was imprisoned and his property confiscated for allegedly signalling to the Chinese troops massing across the Straits) but older ties remain. There is a large population of Greeks in southern Albania and every summer a few defect, drifting with the current on inner tubes to be washed up on the beach of some Corfiot resort. Albania takes these escapes seriously and is vigilant: the searchlight sweeps through the darkness of moonless nights and her gunboats prowl.

This is a cause of annoyance to the fishermen of Corfu. A legend has grown up, verified by the daring, that Albanian waters are teeming with every kind of fish. Undisturbed by tourists or shipping, they bask in the shallows of superb beaches untrodden for decades by anyone but soldiers. One need only lower a bucket . . . It is impossible to say who goes or how often, but people do row across before dawn to net what they can. If they are caught their boat and their equipment are confiscated and they are returned after a couple of days to a point on the mainland frontier, far from the sea. It used to be that those days were spent in jail, but there have been rumours on the island recently that trespassers have been fêted and shown the sights and virtues of the Communist system in the hope that they will proselytize on their return. Philip is intrigued by the idea. He has lived in sight of the bleak mountains above Sarranda all his life and he is a curious man. One day he intends to drift across and see for himself.

Most of the casual fishermen of Loutses, however, are content to work the waters they have always known, between Aghios Spiridon and Kassiopi. A lot of the men will go out once or twice a year in a borrowed boat, for sport as much as dinner, but a few still fish commercially. One such man is Ianni, who lives in Loutses but owns land behind Kalamaki beach, where he keeps his boat. He goes fishing often during the summer, using a single net three hundred metres long, which hangs vertically between floats and weights. This he lays in the evening, face on to the current, out where the sea is ten metres deep. Next morning at dawn, when the mountains of Albania are dark brown shadows and the still water reflects the grey and purple of the sky, he rows silently back, circling the net. He then begins to bang the side of the boat with a piece of wood. The knocking echoes from the hills above the bay and the fish hear it too and are driven by it, he hopes, into the net. As the sun finally rises, he is hauling them in.

These days, during the summer, even Ianni's experience cannot guarantee a decent catch. More often than not his net will hold little more than two or three kilos of *petropsaria*, rockfish, a name that embraces dozens of species too small to interest commercial fishermen, mostly varieties of wrasse and blenny. Too bony to fry, they are the basis, with carrots, onions and courgettes, of an impromptu stew that Ianni's wife Chrisoula has never bothered to name, though it remains an enduring memory for some of the tourists who visit Kalamaki, for three years ago Chrisoula and Ianni opened a restaurant on the beach.

Ianni's family have used their land behind Kalamaki as a vegetable garden for generations. Sheltered from the sea by thickets of tall bamboo and irrigated by a brackish stream, its produce, with the eggs from their chickens in Loutses, their own oil and wine, and the fish Ianni catches, make the restaurant virtually self-sufficient. Its menu is limited to chips, bread, Chrisoula's home-made *feta*, a salad of vegetables picked that morning in the garden, and one other dish – omelettes perhaps, or spaghetti with a sauce of tomato, onion and cinnamon, or the simple rockfish stew, all cooked on a single gas ring. The freshness of the food, right down to the pots of basil that line the pathway to the four tables, and the ramshackle charm of the surroundings have all contributed to the success of the enterprise; and Ianni has been able to do what few other Corfiots could: he has found a way to make a living from the tourist trade without abandoning his old work as a part-time fisherman and farmer.

In the winter, the sheltered waters of the straits are often whipped up into seas too high and powerful for boats as small as Ianni's, but there are days, particularly in January, when a spell of fine weather tempts him out. The fishing is better in winter, especially for the two fish that are found most often in shallow, sandy-bottomed water, the grey mullet and the sea-bass. These two species love bread and cheese and so a preliminary to the expedition is the baiting of a favourite spot at sea with a mixture of bread and the brine from a container of *feta*.

Grey mullet are delicious, with plenty of firm, white flesh. They can be cooked in a number of ways, particularly, on Corfu, as a *bianco*. With its Italian name and simple informality, *bianco* might be said to be typical of rural Corfiot cooking. In many families in Loutses it is among the first recipes children learn. Any fish can be used, or any mixture of fish, and the addition of the oddments of the catch – a single prawn, a stray squid – is welcomed. It is also very good with dried or salted fish, but the consensus is that a 'classic' *bianco* should be made with a couple of small grey mullet, each of about a half to three-quarters of a kilo.

To make a **Bianco** for five or six people you will need about 1½ kilos (3¼ lbs) of fish (ideally two grey mullet), 1 head of garlic, 150 ml (¼ pint, ⅔ cup) of oil, salt and white pepper, a pinch of *rigani*, 3 or 4 potatoes (of a waxy variety so that they do not break up during cooking), 750 ml (1¼ pints, 3¼ cups) of water, the juice of 1 large lemon, and as an optional extra, an onion.

Scale and clean the fish, leaving their heads intact but cutting off fins and tails, and then rinse them well in cold water and let them drain. Chop the garlic and onion and put them into a large shallow saucepan with the oil, salt and pepper, *rigani* and water. Let this simmer for half an hour. Peel the potatoes, cut them into large pieces and add them to the sauce. After fifteen minutes, move them to the sides of the pan and lie the fish side by side in the sauce. They should be at least half-covered by the liquid – if necessary add a little more water. Stew everything for a further twenty-five to thirty minutes until the gravy is thick. Squeeze lemon juice over everything just before serving. A very good accompaniment is fresh bread and a tomato salad, liberally dressed with oil and fresh basil.

Popular though a *bianco* is, the villagers are far more likely to grill any large fish caught during the summer-time. Grey or red mullet, sea-bass, saddled bream, and the pale pink Spanish bream are all superb when barbecued. The cook cleans and washes them, removing the fins and tail but not the head, leaves them to drain for a while in a colander, then finishes the preparation by cutting shallow vertical slits along the sides of the fish, a few centimetres apart, and rubbing salt into them. A dressing is made of oil and lemon juice and plenty of *rigani*. This is rubbed over the inside of the fish and once they have begun to cook on the grill, is also used to baste them, often with a paint brush kept for the purpose. An extraordinarily successful addition to this basic technique is to stuff the fish with a handful of whole, peeled garlic cloves. As if by magic, the fragrance of the garlic pervades the flesh without dominating the fish's own flavour, while the garlic itself ends up with a subtly nutty taste.

Another good fish for grilling is the *savrithia*, or Spanish mackerel, a firm, torpedo-shaped creature with dark oily flesh. When Kiki, who lives up on Zervou with her large family, grills them, she sets up the old barbecue on the patio, close to where the year's crop of walnuts are spread out on sacks to dry in the September sunshine. To feed seven she has four mackerel of three-quarters of a kilo each and because they are such solid fish she has scored and salted their flanks seven or eight times; lemon juice, oil and *rigani* stand already mixed in a shallow bowl beside the barbecue. This and the oil that seeps out of the fish themselves sometimes ignites on the charcoal so she has a plastic bottle of water to squeeze at the flames and prevent the food from actually burning. The charcoal smokes when this happens, adding to the flavour of the *savrithia*. The alluring scent of them spreads up and down the road, and passing neighbours pause to see what's cooking and to offer unnecessary advice. To stop the fish sticking to the grill, Kiki continuously moves and turns them. After thirty-five minutes they are ready, the skin charred and shrunken, the heads about to fall from the bodies. The last of the oil and lemon is used as a dressing. Kiki's daughters, Rania and Letta, help to make a cucumber and tomato salad and her husband returns from the morning's work in his carpenter's shop with two loaves of fresh bread. The table is laid in the shade of their enormous mulberry tree.

Savrithia are caught too far out to sea to be accessible to small boats like Ianni's. They are the prey of the fleets from Corfu Town and Kassiopi, and also of the fishermen from Orthoni, Mathraki and Erikoussa, the three small islands that lie on the north-western horizon of the view from Kiki's patio. The waters around them are deep and rich with fish, too far away to interest tourists and therefore, it is said, of use to the Italian Mafia, who use the islands occasionally in their smuggling activities, such as running contraband cigarettes from Albania to Italy, forty miles away. The Mafia have lean, unadorned ocean-going cruisers capable of sixty-five miles an hour for this work – a knot or two faster than any customs boat. In return for the islanders' discretion, the mafiosi sometimes help them out, bringing supplies in their cruisers or using them as ferries when the winter storms are too bad for local vessels to put out.

Few winds, however, deter the fishing fleets of Corfu – perhaps only a violent southerly wind called the *ostria*, and the *garbis*, a bitter north-westerly that sweeps down the Adriatic during December, January and February and forces even large cargo ships to anchor for a while in the roads off Akharavi. Otherwise the fishermen are out at all times, the lights of their boats strung out across the darkness of a moonless summer night. In the silence before dawn the noise of their engines, a mile out to sea, can even be heard in Loutses. At this time the boats are returning, and on a gas ring in the tiny cabin on deck someone may be making *kakavia*, a fish soup created long ago in the Aegean but beloved of all Greek fishermen, not least because it uses up the *petropsaria*, the bony rockfish too small to sell in the market.

 To make **Kakavia** for six people you will need about 1½ kilos (3¼ lbs) of any very small fish with white flesh (not, in other words, anchovies or sardines), ½ kilo (1 lb 1 oz) of onions, 200 g (7 oz) of carrots, 100 g (3½ oz) of celery, 150 ml (¼ pint, ⅔ cup) of oil, white pepper, a little salt perhaps, the juice of 1 or 2 lemons and water.

Pinch out the intestines and gills of the fish but leave their heads on and wash them in fresh or sea water. Chop the onions, carrots and celery and put all the ingredients except the lemon juice into a large pan with three litres of water. (Fishermen are said to use a glass or two of sea water to make up the amount.) Stew everything for two hours until the fish and vegetables have begun to dissolve and then sieve it. Add the lemon juice to taste, and some people give the soup more body by crumbling bread into it.

Kakavia is a magnificent soup. It can be made with half a kilo of tomatoes (added with the other vegetables) instead of the lemon juice, an addition which deepens its golden colour to a vivid orange and gives it a slightly more robust flavour, but its consistency should always be thin. It is also a superb court-bouillon in which to stew cutlets of a bigger fish or a kilo of large prawns, as well as being a mightily restorative breakfast for a boatload of cold, tired men.

The fleet from Corfu Town returns to the harbour at first light, and the majority of their catch is immediately taken off through the streets to the fish market. This is in fact a part of the vegetable market under the massive bastion of the New Fortress. The fishmongers' stalls are crowded together at one end, and competition between them is fierce. Summer visitors rarely see much of the action here: by nine in the morning most of the stalls have sold out and the men have gone home, while the few remaining open have only a crate or two of sardines to shout about. But in the winter, without the bottomless appetite of the hotels and restaurants to feed and with the coastal waters better stocked with fish, the variety is much greater. There are garfish, strange thin creatures with green bones – Philip often comes across them when snorkelling at night and takes them home to fry. There are amberjack and bonito, and swordfish two metres long, cut into steaks on the stall and sold at half their summer price; grilled with *rigani*, oil and lemon juice they are as succulent as salmon. There are mackerel in crates and gangs of the eccentrically finned John Dory, groupers to make into soup, and trays of octopus so fresh that they still pulsate from time to time, to the delight of vigilant children. In wicker baskets there are *petrokavouros*, small green crabs to be boiled, and on the slab above, a great *kavouromana*, a 'crab-mother' with half a kilo of roe under her tail, almost as good as caviare when eaten raw with a squeeze of lemon and a dribble of oil. There are also bogue and picarel, white-fleshed and about twenty-five centimetres long, and small black *cheruvla*, the fish that Loutsiotes choose when making *marinato*.

This is an old recipe and the details of its preparation vary from household to household, though its essentials are the same. It is one of those dishes that the villagers love because it can be eaten at any time of the day, as a snack or an hors-d'œuvre or as a meal in itself, always served cold and with bread. It was especially popular in the past, before refrigerators reached Loutses, for the salt, sugar and acids in the sauce combine to keep the fish fresh for at least a week. Perhaps the best English substitute for *cheruvla* would be smelt, though any larger white-fleshed fish will do, cut into finger-sized pieces.

 To make **Marinato** for six, you will need about 1½ kilos (3¼ lbs) of fish (see above), the juice of ½ lemon, 150 ml (¼ pint, ⅔ cup) of oil, 3 tablespoons of wine vinegar, 100 ml (3½ fl oz, a scant ½ cup) of dry white wine, 300 g (10½ oz) of tomatoes, a couple of sprigs of rosemary, 2 or 3 bay leaves, 1 teaspoon of dill weed or fennel leaves, 4 cloves of garlic, 2 teaspoons of white sugar, parsley, a handful of raisins, plain flour, salt and pepper.

Clean and wash the fish, then let them drain. Dip them in the lemon juice, sprinkle them with salt and pepper and roll them lightly in flour. Now peel and sieve the tomatoes, chop the garlic and set both aside. Put half the oil into a saucepan and fry two level tablespoons of flour, stirring until it begins to yellow, then stirring in the tomatoes, garlic and all the other ingredients except the fish and the remaining oil. Let the sauce simmer over a very low heat for ten minutes, stirring occasionally. Meanwhile, fry the floured fish in the remaining oil until they are golden. Lay them close together in a shallow bowl and cover them with the sauce.

The fishermen of Kassiopi do not supply the market in Corfu Town; their customers are the small winter population of Kassiopi and the people of the nearby villages. In vans fitted with loudspeakers and a set of old brass scales, they set off along the coast and into the hills to sell what they can; or else they supply wholesale to a middle-man. To qualify for a supplier's licence, a man must be receiving a pension as a veteran of the Second World War. His equipment is minimal: a wooden crate tied to the back of a motor-scooter, a set of scales, and a few sheets of paper to be twisted into conical containers.

Very occasionally, the Kassiopi fishermen will net a really big fish, a swordfish of twenty kilos for example, too big and too expensive for a single customer to buy. This they carry up from the harbour to the main square where they hang it up for all to see, proclaiming its excellence. A crowd gathers and the fishermen begin to sell tickets, raffling the fish. When its value has been reached, the winner's name is drawn from a bag to everyone's satisfaction. Greeks love to gamble and a lottery has the added virtue of being so aggressively democratic.

The problem remains for the winner of what to do with his prize. These days several families in Loutses have freezers, though the cost of electricity deters most, and perhaps the fish can be cut up and frozen. More likely, it will be distributed among family and friends. In the summer a couple of kilos of swordfish steaks would probably be grilled; in the winter, with the cooking done indoors in the oven of a wood stove, they might be baked as *psari plaki*.

 To make **Psari plaki** (baked fish) you will need a kilo (2 lbs 2 oz) of any white-fleshed, firm-textured fish, either steaks or enough other cuts to make up the weight, 1 large lemon, sea salt, black or white pepper, 3 onions, 180 ml (⅓ pint, ¾ cup) of oil, a whole head of garlic, 1 kilo (2 lbs 2 oz) of ripe tomatoes (or the equivalent weight of drained canned tomatoes), 120 ml (4 fl oz, ½ cup) of red wine, parsley and *rigani*. First make the sauce. Cut two of the onions into rings, and peel, chop and sieve three-quarters of the tomatoes. Fry the onions in half the oil until they yellow, then add the tomatoes, the chopped garlic, the pepper and the wine and let them simmer, stirring occasionally, for about forty-five minutes. Now take a large, deep baking pan and wet the inside with a tablespoon or two of oil. Lay the fish in the pan, squeeze the lemon juice over it, sprinkle on a little salt then pour on the sauce. Thinly slice the remaining tomatoes and cut the last onion into rings and scatter them on top of the sauce. Sprinkle on the chopped parsley, the *rigani* and a little sea salt. Bake it in a moderate oven for forty-five minutes. Five minutes before serving, take it out of the oven and pour the last of the oil over the top for flavour.
Psari plaki, like nearly all fish recipes, is traditionally eaten on its own or with a light salad and, of course, bread.

Westward, beyond the bay of Apraos, the mountains at last begin to recede from the sea and the coast road dips inland to cross a narrow plain. Between the road and the sea is a salt-water lake called Antinioti. The name means 'enemy of the young' and refers to the fact that it was a breeding ground for the malarial mosquitoes that once infested the low-lying villages in the summer. Surrounded by thickets of reed and bamboo, fringed on the coastal side by the scrubby dunes of Nissos and inland by orchards, olive groves and farmland, the lake has its own quiet beauty, particularly in winter when the beach at Aghios Spiridon is empty. Between October and April it is a place for hunters after duck or for courting couples seeking an hour of privacy – and also for the men who farm the waters for fish.

The lake was first stocked at the beginning of the century, a scheme devised by the twelve principal villages of north-eastern Corfu, one of which was Loutses, which shared a common administration led by an official with the title of Mayor of Kassiopi. The mayoralty has since disappeared, but the villages still share the ownership of the lake and they rent it out on a five year basis for an annual sum of 1,901,000 drachmas, about £9,000 or $15,000. The men who lease the water corral their stock of grey mullet, sea-bass and eel with a moveable maze of nets which hang picturesquely from poles and half-submerged bamboo screens. In the summer they sell all they can trap to hotels and restaurants and in the winter their fish is bought by individuals and to the fish market in Corfu Town. There is always a demand for the fish, but their most prized crop is the mullet roe, which these days is packaged elsewhere in genteel glass jars and sold as 'Greek caviare', but which until quite recently was pressed and salted locally as *tarama*.

Before it became Greece's most famous hors-d'œuvre, *taramasalata* was a Lenten delicacy, and it still retains those connotations in the villages. Tubs of *tarama*, no longer mullet but cod's roe, caught and salted in Iceland and packed in Greece, appear in the local shops in the early spring, to be sold by the spoonful in a twist of greaseproof paper.

Everyone in Loutses has a favourite recipe for *taramasalata*, even Kostantes, a master-builder in his sixties and a man with an almost superstitious aversion to all other cooking. His method is simple and requires a tablespoon of roe, half a lemon, and the family olive oil bottle from the cupboard under the sink in his kitchen. He puts the *tarama* into a basin, squeezes on the lemon, dribbles in a little oil and begins to mash it with a fork. He adds some more oil, then more again – the mashing has by now become a beating – and still more. After half an hour and a litre of oil he is left with a basinful of a pale pink emulsion that peaks to his fork, into which he can dip hunks of bread. It looks spectacular, but only the merest hint of the flavour of the *tarama* remains and the lemon is gone forever beneath the pervasive fragrance of oil – which is exactly how he likes it. On evenings when he is not in the mood for such industry, Kostantes foregoes the *tarama* and lemon altogether and just dips his bread into his own, thick, golden olive oil.

Philip's recipe for *taramasalata* is less idiosyncratic. It is a food that delights him and over the years he has found the perfect, crucial balances of the dish: between the *tarama* and the onion, and between the lemon juice and the oil. He prefers bread to boiled potatoes as a base since potatoes produce a texture he finds too heavy and glutinous and in some cases an unwanted additional flavour.

 To duplicate Philip's recipe for **Taramasalata**, which makes enough for at least eight people, you will need a large loaf of stale white bread, a dozen spring onions, 250 g (8¾ oz) of *tarama*, 250 ml (8¾ fl oz, 1 cup) of fresh lemon juice, and 350 ml (12 fl oz, 1½ cups) of the best olive oil.

Cut the crusts off the stale bread (a local loaf is perfect after four days in the bread bin), then cut it into four hunks and soak it in a bowl of water for half an hour. Grate the onions finely to produce four rounded tablespoons of pulp. Squeeze the water out of the bread very thoroughly indeed and crumble it carefully into a bowl. Now put the *tarama* and a quarter of the lemon juice into a separate, perferably wooden bowl and begin to blend. Philip uses an electric hand-blender on its lowest setting – the traditional pestle and mortar is too laborious. Add another quarter of the lemon juice. Still blending, tip in the onion and after two minutes more blending add a little oil and the rest of the lemon juice. By now it is a thick cream. Still blending, slowly begin to add the crumbled bread and more of the oil, alternating the two. It is most important to take your time and to persevere with the blender. After ten more minutes, he has used up all the ingredients and the *taramasalata* has acquired its characteristic texture – an aerated emulsion, heavy but at the same time wobbly, and peaking to a fork.

Other cooks will go on adding oil, as much as 800 fl oz for 250 g of roe, compensating with a little more lemon juice, but Philip's recipe preserves the rare flavour of the *tarama* in a tantalizing harmony

– a very different dish to the sticky, garlicky paste served by the tavernas on the coast.

The men who farm the lake at Aghios Spiridon take the mullet roe in the early summer, and this is also the time when they net their eels. The dangerous moray eels that lurk among the rocks around the island have always been welcomed by the cooks of Corfu (conger eels, unless very large, are considered too bony to be worthwhile) but those of the lake are *anguilla anguilla*, the common eel. Every January they migrate, writhing out to sea down the small river at the lake's mouth, travelling, it is said, in a single great rolling ball of eels as they head for the Atlantic to breed. They return in May to be caught and sold, many going to Italy in freezer lorries, others finding their way to the fish market in Corfu Town, and some to be bought on the spot by locals. These will be simply fried in salted flour and oil, or made into a *bourtheto*, or else baked in the oven to become *heli plaki*, a particular favourite of Alexandra, the wife of Kostantes the builder.

 To make Alexandra's **Heli plaki**, you will need a kilo (2 lbs 2 oz) of eels, 1 large onion, 2 ripe tomatoes, 100 ml (3½ fl oz, ½ cup) of oil, 3 cloves of garlic, 3 medium-sized potatoes, salt and pepper, water and a handful of fresh garden herbs – ideally parsley, dill weed or fennel leaves and if possible a little *selino*.
If the eels are freshly caught, Alexandra is always careful to make sure they are really dead by cutting off their heads below the gills. She throws the heads away and rubs the bodies with sand to clean the slime off the skin. Then she cuts the eels into pieces about ten centimetres long and puts them into an oiled baking pan. In another pan she makes a *sivrasi*, a separately cooked sauce, by frying the roughly chopped onions and garlic in the oil until they are yellow and then adding the chopped tomatoes and herbs and a glass of water. She lets this simmer for ten minutes while she peels and thickly slices the potatoes, laying them around the eels. Then she pours on the sauce and bakes the dish in the oven, at a moderate temperature, for an hour. The sauce should be thick, but more water may be needed; the result is marvellously rich, served at her table with a little more oil poured over each plateful and a loaf of fresh white bread.

Eel cooked into a *bourtheto* looks very similar to *heli plaki*, but the flavour is unique, a fact which has little to do with the eel and much to do with the deliberately large amount of red pepper in the recipe. *Bourtheto* is one of the few Corfiot specialities whose fame has spread throughout Greece. That it should be oily and hot and spicy, in contradiction to the general distinction between mainland cooking and the lighter Corfiot cuisine, is an anomaly that amuses Philip. He himself is not fond of *bourtheto*, explaining that red pepper, like all spices, is unhealthily full of vitamins. In fact there are two sorts of red pepper widely used on Corfu, and sold in the village shops as 'mild', which has the bitter tang of good paprika, and 'hot', which is our cayenne. Both are known in the rest of Greece but are far more popular here – a fact that may have something to do with the Venetians, who controlled the oriental spice monopoly for so long. A mixture of both are needed for *bourtheto*.

Precisely which fish to use in the recipe remains a matter of debate. Some Loutses families prefer a mixture of small fish, others a kilo of red mullet or of swordfish steaks, but the majority agree that the ideal choice is the scorpionfish, a rather grotesque creature that skulks among rocks in deep water and has long poisonous spines in its dorsal fin and gill covers which must be cut away before cooking. The fish is plump, its colour ranging from brown to orange and vermilion, its flesh soft and tasty. Scorpionfish come in all sizes from a hundred grammes to more than two kilos, but the variety most often found in the market are small, fat and brown. These are tiresomely bony to eat; two fish of half a kilo each would be perfect. Failing that, any white-fleshed fish with enough flavour to insinuate itself among the red pepper will do very well.

To make **Bourtheto** you need 1 kilo (2 lbs 2 oz) of fish (see above), 3 medium-sized onions, 180 ml (⅓ pint, ¾ cup) of oil, 2 large ripe tomatoes, 2 tablespoons of tomato paste, salt, 4 cloves of garlic, water and red pepper (to taste, but its heat and flavour should dominate the sauce – perhaps a tablespoon of mild paprika and a teaspoon of cayenne).

Clean and wash the fish but leave their heads on. If you have found scorpionfish be sure to cut off their dorsal fins and gill covers. If the fish are large (more than about 400 g) make four vertical cuts along their flanks and rub salt into them; if they are small add salt later to taste. Finely chop the onions and garlic and soften them in the oil. Stir in the tomato paste and the red pepper and let them

fry gently for two minutes. Stir in the chopped tomatoes and about
180 ml (⅓ pint, ¾ cup) of water and let the sauce simmer for five
minutes. By now it is essentially cooked and this is a good opportunity to taste it and correct the amount of red pepper, remembering
that its pungency will intensify slightly as cooking continues. Now
put the fish into the sauce and cover them with water. Bake the
bourtheto in the oven for about forty minutes until the sauce reaches
a good consistency: the oil should have separated, the fish should
be soft but still intact. Allow it to stand, covered, for five minutes
before serving.

 Bourtheto is eaten a lot in Mandouki, an area of Corfu Town near
the docks where many of the local fishermen live. Their recipe for
it is simpler: 2 tablespoons of mild paprika and a teaspoon of cayenne
are fried in 150 ml (¼ pint, ⅔ cup) of oil, and are then simmered
with salt and half a litre (1 pint, 2¼ cups) of water for twenty minutes
until they form a sauce which the red pepper has thickened as if
it were flour. The fish are laid side by side in this sauce and are
cooked for another twenty minutes.

Bourtheto is seen on the mainland as Corfu's great fish speciality,
but on the island itself other dishes are as highly prized. To Corfiots,
the bay of Apraos has always been associated with the best sardines
in Greece, fish as tasty and large as the more famous sardines from
the gulf of Kaloni in Lesvos. The only reason their reputation has
not spread across the country is that every single one is eaten by
the Corfiots themselves.

Until about twenty-five years ago, sardine fishing was something
of an industry in the area. All year round great shoals of sardines
would feed in the shallow waters of the bay of Apraos. With boats
scarce and trawl-nets unknown, the fishing was done by hand, by
laying nets off-shore and then laboriously pulling them in. The local
men and women did this together, standing waist-deep in the water
– uncomfortable work in a cold winter sea. But today the fish are
all but gone, caught further out in the Ionian by boats equipped
with the latest mechanical winches and radar. Strangely perhaps, they
are not missed: the income they brought seems negligible now, and
the new affluence and mobility of the villagers means that the old

reliance on preserved sardines as a winter food has gone. Only a few people still salt sardines, and they do it because they prefer the flavour of their own to that of the tinned equivalent sold in the shops and in the market in town.

Philip salts sardines once a year, so he makes a large amount – enough to fill a seven kilo *teneki* – packing them between layers of salt and a sprinkling of paprika, pouring on half a litre of oil and then weighing them down with a stone. After about two months, depending on the weather, they are ready to eat, either as an hors-d'œuvre, a *meze*, or as a light lunch by those working away from home. To serve, they must be peeled by holding each fish at the neck and gently scraping off the skin and fins with a piece of folded paper. They are then lightly rinsed and put on a plate with a dressing of oil and vinegar.

The decline of the coastal shoals of sardines is typical of the story of fishing on Corfu. Since the '60s, improved technology and a vastly increased demand has emptied the waters around the island. It is this and the sheer nuisance of the thousands of little boats with which tourists amuse themselves that is responsible, not pollution (a problem that plagues other parts of the Mediterranean) for except in the actual harbours of the town, the sea is as clean and clear as ever. The situation is being investigated by the government and a new law may one day emerge banning all fishing during the two months of the year when the fish are spawning. Until then, Greece meets the demands of her visitors by elaborate and little-publicized measures, the strangest of which is the bulk importation of fresh fish from Israel and frozen fish from the North Atlantic. Cunning restaurateurs bore holes in the frozen bodies and thaw them in sea water to restore a fresh flavour; only a faint grey spotting of their otherwise pure white bones gives the lie to the proud boasts of the menu.

There are, however, two other types of imported fish that have long been enjoyed in Corfu, as in the rest of Greece: the salted, smoked herrings from the Netherlands known as *renga*, and the dried, salted cod from the eastern seaboard of Canada, *bakalaros*, whose unique aroma dominates Stamati's dark emporium all year round. Despite the fact that it is imported it is cheap and an important part of the diet of those too old to make the trip out of Loutses very often. It can be cooked in many ways once it has been reconstituted by soaking: boiled and served with a dressing of oil and lemon juice, shallow fried, or as a *bianco*, or, its most popular incarnation, in a 'red sauce', when it is called *bakalaro yahni*.

To make **Bakalaro yahni** you will need 1 piece of dried, salted cod (which weighs about 700 g or 1½ lbs), 1 large onion, 150 ml (¼ pint, ⅔ cup) of oil, 1–2 tablespoons of tomato paste, 1 fresh ripe tomato, white pepper and water. Cut the dried fish into three or four pieces and soak it in warm water for twelve hours, changing the water several times. Chop the onion and soften it in the oil. Stir in the tomato paste and fry it gently for two minutes. Add the chopped tomato and perhaps half a teaspoon of pepper, place the fish pieces on top and cover them with water. Simmer them very slowly on top of the stove or bake them in a moderate oven for half an hour, until the liquid has reduced to a thick sauce. The fish should be firm and still in large pieces.

Everyone has additions to offer to this recipe, depending on the season and the family's tastes. Some add trimmed artichokes as the water boils, others add the sweet *horta* known as *seskolo*, or, most deliciously, a dozen bulbs of fresh garlic, trimmed as if they were spring onions. Anything can be claimed to be appropriate.

The Dutch herrings are not so versatile. Oily and shining gold, they appear in their crates in the shops in the early spring. They are eaten as they are, their very powerful flavour modified with oil and lemon juice (never vinegar), or else they are grilled, traditionally over a fire of newspaper. This is a favourite lunch for people working a long day in the olive groves, far from home. The herring is impaled on a stick, then the paper it was wrapped in is crumpled up and burned. With drops of oil oozing from it, the fish is held in the flames until its skin begins to char and break – in two minutes it is ready. The flesh is scraped off the bones and anointed with a little oil and the juice of a whole large lemon. Its flavour is fantastically strong and salty, but after the first mouthful one's tongue begins to understand what is happening. People can grow passionately fond of *renga*. When Philip was chief steward on a merchant ship, half way round the world from Corfu, he would often find a quiet corner of the deck and sear a Dutch herring in this way, seasoned a little with nostalgia.

For Philip's generation, the spectacular development of Greek shipping in the '60s provided a unique opportunity to see the world beyond the Ionian. It also offered culinary training to those with a knack for it. The chefs of both tavernas in Loutses learned to cook at sea, to menus and nutritional guidelines laid down by the shipping companies of Piraeus. That this might lead to a levelling of the differences in Greek regional cooking was not an issue that worried Philip; in fact he once had to fire a cook who came from near the Turkish border because the largely Corfiot crew could not eat the heavily-spiced, oily food he insisted on preparing. But the relationship between Loutses and the sea is much older and more deeply engrained. Through the millenium of poverty suffered by the working people of rural Corfu, it was fish rather than meat that provided a break from staple foods. Animals were the property of whoever owned the land where they were grazed; a fat mullet or a pail of sardines belonged to the man who caught them.

VINES AND FRUIT TREES

When Homer brought Odysseus to Corfu in Book Seven of the *Odyssey* he brought him to the end of the world – to the island in the west that has symbolized romance through centuries of European literature, a place of grace, beauty and magic. He gave to the island a miraculous climate and fecundity, listing the abundant gifts the gods had bestowed upon it, from the quantities of wheat to the quality of the water – that most important of elements to the Greeks. Then he peopled it with a race unparalleled in their art, their seamanship and their generosity, ruled by a king and queen, Alkinoos and Areti, in whom all the virtues of civilization had reached a peak.

To make it clear that this was indeed contemporary civilization, he added minutiae to the narrative: a synoptic history of the inhabitants, information about their personal habits, sleeping arrangements and laundry, their architecture, their diet, and sufficient nuances of personality to bring his characters vividly to life. In fact, by the time Odysseus leaves the island, the only part of it that has come to seem a little far-fetched is the description of the royal orchard, as seen through the hungry hero's eyes:

 To left and right, outside, he saw an orchard closed by a pale – four spacious acres planted with trees in bloom or weighted down for picking: pear trees, pomegranates, brilliant apples, luscious figs, and olives ripe and dark. Fruit never failed upon these trees: winter and summer time they bore, for through the year the breathing Westwind ripened all in turn – so one pear came to prime, and then another, and so with apples, figs, and the vine's fruit empurpled in the royal vineyard there. Currants were dried at one end, on a platform bare to the sun, beyond the vintage arbors and vats the vintners trod; while near at hand were new grapes barely formed as the green bloom fell, or half-ripe clusters, faintly colouring . . .

Pears, pomegranates, apples, figs, olives and grapes . . . the luxurious fruits of Bronze-Age Greece. There are no mysterious Hesperidean additions to the inventory. The exaggeration lies in the report of the weather with its ever-blowing west wind and in the fruits' own circumvention of any seasonal cycle. It might be thought that such botanical wonders would be presented as part of the welcome offered to Odysseus by the king, especially since his immediate needs were for food and drink, or that they would at least feature in the more formal feasting next day. Yet no mention is made of any fruit. There is plenty of wine to drink with the bread and meat, and the oil from the olives in the garden is ready as a rub after the bath, but the marvellous produce of the orchard never reappears in the poem.

That it is mentioned at all is interesting. Poetically, such pragmatic hyperbole suggests a delightful pastoral harmony between nature and a cultured race of people, but it also indicates that the island itself had already acquired a reputation as an earthly paradise. To a Greek from the Aegean – or even from barren Ithaca – the lush vegetation and gentle climate of Corfu must have been awe-inspiring.

Today some of the Loutsiotes believe that the climate of their island changes every twenty years or so. They remember that during the Second World War winters were particularly hard. Water barrels froze and split, icicles hung from the guttering and Pantokrator was white with snow. During the '60s and '70s the winter weather was milder – wet of course, but with only one or two days when the ground temperature dropped below zero. In the last two years December and January have once again grown colder. In 1985 and

1986 it snowed in Loutses, albeit for a single morning, and well into March there is still no warmth in the sun.

Loutses' position, so high on the exposed northern slopes of the great bulk of Pantokrator, inevitably means that the villagers will live with different weather conditions to the people of the town. Loutses is too dry, for example, for melons and water melons (it is left to the *karbouzi*-man to bring the latter up in his lorry), and too exposed for citrus trees to flourish as they do just down the mountain in Peritheia.

And yet there is a surprising variety of fruit trees in the village. On Nikolas Sarakinos's property, one of the larger, older farms in the valley, there are almond, quince, cherry, apple, pear and fig trees and an enormous old walnut tree, as well as olives. On his land in the mountains, in the valley around Ano Peritheia, he has a vineyard, more figs, and several wild pomegranates. Were it not for his continual efforts he would also have a blackberry thicket of several acres.

Scattered around Loutses in ones and twos are others: an apricot tree that leans over the main road at the turn-off for Zervou has been a source of plunder for children for generations, and across the road grows a jujube tree — its small tan-coloured berries taste faintly of caramel and were the original delight of the lotus-eaters. In other gardens a few of the enterprising do their best to coax forth the peaches and nectarines that are farmed so easily in the south of the island, and every June Kiki hangs fine nets from the lowest branches of the mulberry tree outside her house on Zervou to catch the sweet black berries as they fall. On the other side of the village, along a little-used track that winds down from the main road to end suddenly at the towering escarpment of the mountains, a pair of magnificent and ancient chestnut trees soar upwards, taller even than the fine old cypresses around them. The nuts fall on to the path where anyone can gather them; the trees themselves, in their hidden glade, are the most beautiful on the island.

There are others on the outskirts of the village: halfway down to Peritheia a prickly pear cactus casts its alien shadow on to the road. A little of its ripe fruit is a specific against diarrhoea; too much doubles the affliction. In Koulouri, in the feral gardens of the abandoned houses, greengages and damsons ripen in the dry heat of July and drop into the waist-high undergrowth; and in the wild places along the edges of the valley a type of arbutus known as the strawberry-tree or *koumaria* produces a summer crop of sweet scarlet berries – more treasure-trove for the local children.

In the springtime the fragrance and colour of the blossom of all these trees is breathtaking. Looking down on the village from the mountains the pinks and whites, mauves and purples leap out, iridescent, from the sober green of the olives. All year round, the procession of the different fruit seems endless as one crop ripens and is picked, only to be succeeded by another. Perhaps this was what Homer was referring to in his description of the old king's perpetually fecund garden.

The owners of such riches take what they want and share the rest with friends and relatives, sending their children to a neighbour's door with a bowl of persimmons or pears, or a heavily-laden bough from a cherry tree. A hungry man passing an orchard sees no harm in helping himself, picking an apple or gorging on plums. Fruit is essentially an informal food and this could be the reason why fruit plays no part in King Alkinoos's royal feasting – dangerous though it is to draw parallels between ancient and modern Greece. Only recently has fruit begun to appear on local tables at the end of a meal, an innovation due, perhaps, to the demands tourists make for a dessert.

When Philip was a boy he and his family would occasionally share a dish of melon or watermelon if they were still hungry after lunch or dinner, and in the winter chestnuts were roasted and eaten with a post-prandial brandy, but not because it was thought necessary to finish the meal with something sweet. Fruit was a snack, eaten when and where a person decided he was hungry, whether plucked from a convenient tree or on rare occasions purchased. One or two very scarce and special kinds of fruit were actively sought after, in particular the wild strawberries that still enthrall the gourmets of Corfu Town in May – they last only a few hours once they have been picked and their *fraise de bois* flavour is exceptional – but in general the local attitude to fruit was decidedly casual.

This nonchalance is one reason why fruit is so rarely used creatively in the Greek kitchen. Today only a handful of households bother to preserve fruits and, when they do, it is usually to make jam from their quinces – a fruit that can be eaten only after it is cooked. This has nothing to do with a changing social climate or any economic development – if anything, the availability and price of sugar today should encourage jam-making – for forty years ago the situation was exactly the same. It is unnecessary to bottle or preserve when there is such a wide variety of fresh fruit available all year round.

Quince trees have flourished in Loutses for as long as anyone can remember, growing in small plantations of three or four all over the valley. They resemble pear trees with long, pointed leaves and the quinces themselves look like knobbly, misshapen pears covered with a fine yellowish fur, an attribute that led Cyril Connolly to the conclusion that they were the original golden apples of the Hesperides. They are ready to eat in November, though in very hot, dry years they may ripen a month earlier, and with winter pears and the red and green local apples they are sometimes baked, whole and unadorned, in the oven – a popular recipe with children. Their flavour is unique – a little more tart than a pear, more musty than an apple – and it is this quality that the cook aims to capture when turning them into jam, though the tendency to smother the taste with too much sugar usually proves irresistible.

The best quince jam in Loutses is made by Nitsa. Charming, reserved and sophisticated, she and her husband moved to Athens many years ago but returned when he retired in order to restore their old family home in the village.

 To make quince jam, **Kithoni gliko**, like Nitsa's you will need 1 kilo (2 lbs 2 oz) of sugar and 300 ml (10½ fl oz, 1¼ cups) of water for every kilo of quinces, 2 large lemons and 3 or 4 sprigs of *arbaroriza*, a common herb that seems to be used for nothing else but quince jam with a flavour somewhere between vanilla and angelica – a few drops of vanilla essence could be used as a substitute.

Rub the fur off each quince, then peel and dice them (or grate them for a jam with a finer, more liquid consistency). Put the diced quinces into a bowl with the water. Cut a lemon in two, squeeze it into the bowl and then put it in as well. Let the fruit soak for half an hour, then remove the lemon halves. Put the liquid and the quinces into a large heavy pan and let it boil vigorously for half an hour. Stir in the sugar until it is completely dissolved and bring it quickly back to the boil for another fifteen minutes. Then add the juice of the second lemon and the washed sprigs of *arbaroriza* and let it boil for four or five minutes more. Remove the *arbaroriza*. Quinces are very rich in pectin and this much cooking should be enough for them : test for a set by spooning a few drops of the syrup on to a cold, dry plate and letting it cool in the fridge. If it wrinkles when you touch it with your little finger the jam will set. If not return it quickly to the boil and test again five minutes later. The village women let their jam cool before bottling it.

Quince jam is eaten as a conserve on bread and also as a sort of spoon sweet, the traditional Greek offering to guests, served in a tiny, ornate glass bowl, with a tall glass of water and a teaspoon. The guest eats a spoonful of the sweet, drinks the water and leaves the spoon in the glass, before turning to his coffee or liqueur. All this is a little pompous for Loutsiot tastes, but on very formal occasions, such as a visit to a household during the days leading up to a wedding, spoon sweets have been known to appear. True spoon sweets have a very different consistency to the rather runny local jams, since such fruit as cherries are left whole when made into spoon sweets, or cut into large pieces when pears or quinces are used. Quince spoon sweets are the favourite in Loutses, but in most of the rest of the island their popularity is easily outdistanced by the kumquat.

Kumquats, *citrus japonica*, had been cultivated in China and Japan for thousands of years before a certain Robert Fortune, collector for the London Horticultural Society, introduced them to Europe in 1846. Corfu was still part of the British empire at the time and the administration brought some of the shrubs to the island to see how they would fare in the climate, grafting them on to the hardier root of a wild variety known as *citrus trifoliata*. Today kumquats are a major crop on Corfu, and are sold both preserved in jars and as kumquat liqueur, a sickly-sweet orange syrup with the flavour of childrens' cough medicine. It is available in a seemingly limitless variety of miniature bottles, shaped like the Acropolis or an *evzone* soldier's kilt or the statue of Achilles in the garden of Corfu's casino, and it is a tremendous favourite of souvenir-hunting tourists. The fruit itself is like a very small, thick-skinned orange, with a rather bitter flavour, and like any other variety of orange will not grow in Loutses because of the altitude and the lack of shelter. Some, however, do well down in Peritheia, among the citrus groves in the moist valleys behind the village, and sweet-toothed Loutsiotes occasionally use them to make spoon sweets. Elsewhere in Greece tiny, unripe green oranges are used instead but the recipe is the same.

 To make two or three jars of **Kumquat gliko**, you will need perhaps 25 ripe kumquats, ½ teaspoon of bicarbonate of soda, 700 g (1½ lbs) of sugar, and the juice of 1 lemon.

Make a small hole in the fruit at the point where it was joined to the tree and with a needle remove the pips, taking care not to damage the appearance of the kumquats. Soak them in cold water for twenty-four hours, then boil them in fresh water with the bicarbonate of soda (to preserve their colour) until they are soft. Drain them and then soak them in fresh cold water for a further three or four hours. Drain them again and wrap them in a tea-towel to dry. Make a syrup by bringing to the boil the sugar and 250 ml (8¾ fl oz, 1 cup) of water, then add the fruit and simmer for ten minutes. Take the pan off the heat and leave it covered overnight. Remove the fruit and boil the syrup again, with the lemon juice, until it is thick – this should take about fifteen minutes. Put the kumquats back in and simmer on for another quarter of an hour. Test for a set by letting a drop of syrup fall on to a cold dry plate. If it remains like a bead and does not spread it is ready. Let the preserve cool and then seal it in jars.

The other great spoon sweet and jam made in Loutses uses the sour black morello cherries known in Greece as *vissino*, in a proportion of one kilo (2 lbs 2 oz) of sugar and 75 ml (2½ fl oz, ⅓ cup) of water for every kilo of fruit. The cherries are carefully pitted and then all the ingredients are boiled together for about fifty minutes, until the liquid has become a thick syrup. The juice of a lemon is added to prevent crystallization and the cook tests for a set, lets the jam cool a little, and then bottles it.

Vissino cherries are also the basis for a cherry brandy that Kleopatra makes to ward off bronchial problems. In June when they are ripe she picks a kilo of the fruit, takes out the stones and seals the cherries in a glass jar with half a kilo of sugar. This she sets outside in the hot summer sun until October. When the jar is finally opened she drops in half a cinnamon stick, two cloves and more than half a litre of brandy, then she leaves it to stand for another week before straining it into a large bottle. If the elixir is too sweet, more brandy can be added. The resulting drink is heavy and pink and the flavour of the fruit and spices is more than a match for the alcohol. Once the winter weather sets in, Kleopatra indulges in a tiny glassful of an evening, mixed sometimes with a little water, and this, with her other herbal remedies, keeps the worst of the damp from settling in her throat or chest.

A far more refreshing drink, and one that has become famous in the guidebooks as a quaint reminder of England, is ginger beer.

Tsitsibira, as the locals call it, was brought to Corfu by the British in the early nineteenth century, and like the game of cricket, England's greatest cultural legacy to the island, it remained in fashion long after they left. Lawrence Durrell describes the popping of corks from stone bottles as a principal sound of café society right up until the 1930s.

Cricket is still played on the old pitch in Corfu Town, but ginger beer, always a drink of the town rather than the villages, has virtually disappeared, displaced by Coca-cola and its kin. Nostalgiasts may mourn its passing but even in its heyday it was not quite the beverage it had been under the British. Once they had gone a change in the recipe began to evolve. Instead of ginger, expensive and difficult to obtain, the locals took to using bitter almonds as a flavouring, boiling them with sugar and water and then adding lemon juice and yeast when the decoction had cooled. Left in a covered wooden tub for three days and then strained, the resulting liquid could be drunk within a week of bottling – not quite ginger beer, but certainly *tsitsibira*.

In the villages a different drink with no foreign pretensions used also to be made from almonds, sugar and water, flavoured with *mastiha*, the powdered sap of the mastic tree. It was called *soumatha* and was produced in local bars to be drunk in the summer as a squash, but because of the hard work involved it was always considered something of a treat. The shelled almonds were blanched by dipping them into boiling water and then pinching off their thin brown skins. Then they were pounded to a pulp with an equal weight of sugar, the *mastiha* and a few tablespoons of water and forced through a sieve to produce a syrupy almond milk. It was the pounding that took the time – up to seven hours to produce five bottles of syrup, which was then mixed in the glass with an equal part of water.

There are many almond trees in Loutses. Nearly every household possesses three or four and a few families have hundreds, scattered about their various properties or growing in plantations that always seem neater and less haphazard than an olive grove. Philip's family used to own eighty almond trees. They collected the nuts towards the end of the summer, knocking them down with poles or pulling them off the trees with long-handled billhooks. The furry outer case was broken off and the nuts were put into sacks where they would remain until the winter or even until the following Easter. On long winter evenings the women would crack them, sitting on the floor, to sell them in the town. Their price was highest at Christmas and

Easter, when everyone buys sugared almonds, *koufeta*, from the confectioners' shops.

Almond farming is one of the old industries that has almost disappeared in Loutses. Only three families still bother to do it on a commercial scale, though everyone does their duty by their trees, collecting the almonds to eat during the winter with a glass of brandy or ouzo, either straight from the shell or else soaked in cold salt water and then briefly grilled. They are the principal adornment of many cakes and biscuits, and the heavy pruning that the trees need provides fuel for the stove. It burns faster and gives less heat than olive wood, but fills the house with a lovely fragrance.

The only savoury recipe for almonds known in the village is for a stuffing for the traditional Christmas turkey. In other parts of Greece such a stuffing might include a variety of minced meats or at least the diced liver of the turkey in question, but in Loutses they prefer the flavour of the nuts. The turkey is roasted just as it is in England or North America.

To make a **Nut stuffing** for a turkey you will need 150 g (5 oz) of shelled almonds, 150 g (5 oz) of shelled walnuts, 300 g (10½ oz) of chestnuts, 170 g (6 oz) of rice, 1 medium-sized onion, 3 cloves of garlic, 1 tablespoon each of fresh mint and parsley, salt and pepper and 100 ml (3½ fl oz, a scant ½ cup) of oil. (A handful of raisins can also be included, but most people find this makes the stuffing too sweet.)
Blanch the almonds and walnuts, removing their brown skins. Boil the chestnuts in salt water for fifteen minutes and peel off the shells and inner skins. Break the nuts into small pieces. Chop the onion and garlic finely and fry them in the oil until they are golden, then stir in all the other ingredients and a cup of water and let everything stew for twenty minutes, until the rice has absorbed the water. Stuff the turkey.

Sugared almonds are obligatory gifts at weddings and christenings, and in the past they also played an important role in traditional Orthodox memorial services, as part of a sweet called *koliva*. Made principally from whole-wheat kernels, dried and fresh fruit and almonds, *koliva* was cooked at home by the relatives of the deceased and then brought to Church to be distributed amongst those at the service.

Koliva is no longer prepared in the village, but a simpler, everyday version is still often made as a snack. It consists of three parts cracked whole wheat, boiled in water until it is soft, mixed with one part raisins and a great deal of sugar. The sugar and the liquid from the wheat combine to make a thick syrup. A bowl of the cold gruel is put down in the middle of the table and everybody helps themselves either with spoons or, rather messily, with their fingers.

Until quite recently the raisins used in this recipe would have been dried in the village. Just as Alkinoos's vintners did, the farmer used to choose the best bunches from the vine, pick off the grapes and set them out on a wooden tray to dry in the sun. These days the effort does not seem worthwhile as all manner of dried fruit can be bought cheaply in the supermarkets in Corfu Town.

Corfu wine had been renowned for two thousand years when the Angevin kings of Naples acquired the island in 1267. Like their Venetian successors, they immediately looked for a way to exploit the natural virtues of their territories, and they decided that the commodity most likely to bring them revenue was wine, particularly the fashionable sweet red wine known in England as Malmsey. The market for it in northern Europe was inexhaustible. So the Angevins set about turning the island into one enormous vineyard, using a variety of vine from the Peloponnese called *monemvasia*.

Today no trace remains of the hundreds of thousands of *monemvasia* vines, and nothing resembling Malmsey is made on Corfu. In the south of the island, around the town of Lefkimi, and in the village of Petalia in the northern mountains, some sweet, heavy wines are still made, but they are white not red – similar to the golden wine of Samos that Byron found so palatable.

Together with the produce of a few other private estates these wines turn up occasionally on the lists of good Athenian restaurants, but they are difficult to find on the island and are certainly unknown in establishments catering to the tourist trade, for it is a sad fact that these days the worst wine in Greece – perhaps in Europe – ends its short life in the tavernas of Corfu's resorts.

The cynicism of some restaurateurs reaches a new low when it comes to their wine lists. Recommended by the waiter as house red or house white, the stuff is mass-produced on the mainland and bottled behind labels composed of a confusion of Greek and French. The management relies on over-salted hors-d'œuvres and the near-

freezing temperature at which they serve the indigestible astringent
to hide its true nature. Only at the bottom of the list can the tourist
find anything worthwhile – usually a red Cava Boutari or a dry
white Calliga from Cephalonia – expensive by Greek standards but
a sound gastric investment.

Imported wines also form the main stock in trade of the vintners
of Corfu Town. These delightful wine shops are dark wet cellars
opening off the street, lined with enormous wooden barrels upon
which the merchant has chalked a basic description of the contents
– red or white, sweet or dry or resinated. The poorer people of the
town come daily with an empty plastic bottle to be filled – a purchase
as routine and necessary as that of a loaf of bread, and only a few
drachmas more expensive.

The wine is of a consistently high quality, particularly the *retsina*
from Attica. Resinated wines are not made on Corfu, largely because
there are no coniferous forests and no reason to adulterate a local
vintage unnecessarily, but they are drunk. When none is available
from the barrel there are always the small half-litre bottles on sale
in every shop and bar. It is a summer drink, light and refreshing,
a vital lubricant to much of the island's workforce, and in Loutses
at least, of value during August and September when last year's vintage of home-made wine has all been drunk.

Wine-making has a unique place in the psyche of the villagers.
The Loutsiotes are not a people with a deep awareness of history,
but part of the enjoyment they derive from the process stems from
the fact that they are doing what their forbears have done for thousands of years. Moreover, wine-making is an activity that is suffused
with family pride. Every family does it, using techniques and equipment that are passed on from father to son, and there is a profound
loyalty to the resulting vintage. Men will compare it favourably or
unfavourably with their own wine of other years, but not, except
among close friends, with the wine of others. It is almost as if there
were an unconscious agreement amongst the villagers to avoid doing
so – as if any public criticism would be tantamount to a criticism
of the traditions of the family itself.

This is not to say that wine-making is a mystical event in the
villages. It is both too merry an occasion and too down-to-earth
to be anything of the kind, but as the grapes are trodden there is
definitely a feeling in the air that the work is important, that it contri-
butes in some way to the sense of identity of a family, though only
the men are actively involved with the pressing. This may have some-

thing to do with the fact that the treader must work in his underwear; it is also part of a very ancient division of labour between the sexes: the same instinctive proprieties that send only the men out to hunt.

Village wine-making begins, of course, with the grapes. Twenty years ago, when Loutses was obliged to be more self-sufficient, every household grew enough to meet all its needs. Today such enterprise is rare, though a handful of farmers who own land up in the valley around Ano Peritheia still cultivate fair-sized vineyards. The extraordinary root systems of the vines find water throughout the long summer, burrowing as deep as thirty metres down into the rocky soil. Above the ground the farmers train them up fruit trees (never olive trees) to support and protect them from the wind, but they are as vulnerable as any other plant to the bushfires that sweep the hills in the late summer, when the surrounding undergrowth is tinder dry. After a fire it is only necessary to trim the vine back to within a centimetre or two of the ground; the roots will do the rest. Within two years the vine will be producing grapes again.

In the village itself one or two small vineyards remain, and keen gardeners like Maria Vlahou grow vines along fences and trellises among the honeysuckle. Otherwise the vines are restricted to the *klimaterias*, the scaffolds of wood or metal that extend from a wall of the house, providing a shady place to sit and easy access to the grapes.

Petros Parginos has a steel and bamboo *klimateria* above the yard outside his kitchen – an area of about fifteen square metres. In the early spring he cuts fifty poles from the bamboo thickets behind Kalamaki beach and takes them back to Loutses tied to the side of his old Vespa scooter. His vines have been left untouched since the previous October when he harvested the grapes from them. The leaves had turned the colour of copper before the wind stripped them away, and the months of rain have split the old bamboo and rusted the wire until it crumbled. Now in March the first hint of new growth is visible on the twisted vines and it is time for Petros to repair the winter damage.

His first job is to prune the vines themselves. Vines grow fantastically quickly; left to their own devices as some up on the ruined houses in Koulouri have been, they will double their size in a season, covering everything in a luxurious profusion of leaves but producing only a few tiny bunches of grapes. Even with regular annual pruning the development is prodigious, but the growth of the previous season does not have the strength to fruit and each yearling shoot must be removed. Petros does this with a sharp pair of secateurs, cutting them back to the third 'knuckle' along from the main stock. Next he unties last year's twists of wire and pulls down the useless bamboo canes. The wind has caused the wire to rub off some of the paint from the steel frame of the *klimateria* and he touches it up before mounting the new bamboo and fastening the vines to it. In a month he will spray the new leaves with a blue solution of copper sulphate to protect them from disease, and if there is heavy rain before the summer he will spray again. In June the young bunches of grapes will need the same treatment to prevent the incursions of greedy wasps, and he will also have to pick off most of the growth of leaves, so that the energies of the plant are all directed into the grapes.

June is also the best time for picking tender young vine leaves to make *dolmadakia yirlandzi*, stuffed vine leaves. This is another dish that has earned a reputation beyond the Mediterranean as a quintessential part of Greek cuisine. On Corfu it is acknowledged to be an eastern recipe, from the old Greek territory around Smyrna, but the centuries have changed the ingredients to suit more delicate local tastes. Convention dictates that they should be cooked in and served from an open clay pot.

To make **Dolmadakia yirlandzi** (stuffed vine leaves) you will need about 20 leaves (from any vine, but they must be young and tender and without blemish), 200 g (7 fl oz, a generous ¾ cup) of oil, 170 g (6 oz) of rice, 200 ml (7 fl oz, a generous ¾ cup) of water, ½ kilo (1 lb 1 oz) of onions, plenty of fresh fennel leaves and fresh mint, salt, pepper and a lemon.

Put the vine leaves carefully into a pan of boiling water for five minutes, then drain and wash them in plenty of cold water. Cut out a little of the stalk from each leaf if it seems tough. Chop the onions very finely and fry them in half the oil until they are yellow, then add the rice, salt, pepper, and the finely chopped fennel leaves and mint and let them fry for a couple of minutes more. Add the water and let the mixture simmer for five minutes before letting it cool. Now lay two teaspoons of the rice mixture on to each leaf and roll them up, folding in the sides first. Lay them tightly in the clay pot in two layers, with the fold in the leaf underneath. Pour on half a litre of water, the rest of the oil and the juice of the lemon. Weigh the leaves down with a small plate and put the pot into a very low oven for an hour. Let the vine leaves cool before serving them and dress them with a little plain yoghurt on each plate.

In Loutses wine is made during the last week of September and the first week of October, when the grapes are swollen with sweet juice and before the first storms of autumn, but preparations for the vintage begin many days before as equipment is checked and cleaned and if necessary repaired. The principal piece of apparatus whose appearance announces the coming labour is the *skafoni*, an enormous wooden tub whose straight sides widen upwards from the base, for it is in this that the grapes will be pressed.

Philip's *skafoni* is a century old and more than a metre and a half tall, the wood smooth to the touch and stained black by the years. Its diameter has dwindled as slats, warped by a cold damp winter and the summer's heat, have been removed and the metal hoops retightened, but it still holds 400 kilos of fruit. Its great age is a tribute to the dedication to wine of Philip's family, for it is only through annual use that a *skafoni* will survive: miss a vintage or two and the wood swiftly begins to rot. All year it has stood in a corner of the family *apothiki*, but now it is brought out into the sun to be scrubbed and sluiced and meticulously inspected. Then it is turned upside down and water is poured on to its lipped base. Topped up occasionally over the next few days this will swell the old wood and seal the tub.

Philip has four varieties of vine trained up the expansive *klimaterias* outside the bar. There is *moskato*, with tight bunches of small black grapes; *kerino*, also called *politiko*, a white grape with large pips; *phithia*, a word meaning snake, so-called because its grapes hang in long thin black bunches; and finally *fraoula* meaning, literally, strawberry. *Fraoula* grapes are useless for both wine-making and the table. The small black fruit has a taste uncannily like a strawberry, but it leaves a lingering flavour of vinegar in the back of the mouth. The vine was planted decades ago giving excellent shade because of its thick cover. It is strong and virtually immune to disease and needs no spraying or tending of any kind. Philip has never bothered to cut it down.

Down the road, Petros grows two different varieties of vine over his small, well-swept yard with its fringes of geraniums and roses. One is the black *petrokoritho*, locally reputed to be the best type of vine in Greece for making wine; the other is *kakotria*, producing large green grapes that grow in loose bunches and derive their name, which means 'hard to cut', from the toughness of their stems.

Petros's *skafoni* stands ready in the yard, but his harvest is too small for the family's appetite for wine, so he must wait, like most of the villagers, for the grape lorries that arrive every year from the mainland or from the other Ionian islands of Zakinthos and Lefkada, where the varieties of grape grown are the same as those of Corfu. Eventually they come, labouring up the mountain in the hot sun, packed with oozing plastic crates of fruit, in a haze of wasps and fruit-flies. This year Petros buys six crates to add to his own produce and early the following morning while it is still cool he tumbles them all together into his *skafoni*, strips to his vest and paisley-patterned underpants and climbs in. The contrast between his tanned, leathery arms and face and his thin yellow legs is startling.

So is his energy. Well into his seventies, he has no one to help him tread the grapes this year, for his son is a successful accountant in Cephalonia and his brother Kostantes, a builder, has work in town, but Petros is equal to the task. For long periods of the morning he keeps up a steady rhythm, periodically climbing out of the barrel to see to his other equipment. This is partly improvised, partly trusted and ancient. The *skafoni* stands on three supports – a log and two rocks. At its base is a small hole into which Petros has wedged a conduit made from a nine-inch length of bamboo. Inside the *skafoni* a curved roof-tile holds back the pulp from the mouth of the hole, but the bamboo is frequently blocked and Petros uses a thin stick to poke it clean.

The must runs into a sturdy, V-shaped, wooden trough called a *skafi* – a rare object in the village these days. Years ago, before the Greeks began their love affair with plastic and when people baked their own bread, every household owned a *skafi*. It was used for mixing dough and perhaps some awareness of the crucial role of yeast in both baking and wine-making suggested it might be appropriate for receiving must. Alternatively, perhaps, it was just a convenient size and shape.

Petros treads and the must oozes from the pulp. It is sickly-sweet and has the colour and opacity of blood from a piece of liver, somewhere between brick-red and maroon. A passing neighbour comments on this '*oreia chroma*', beautiful colour, and without breaking his rhythm Petros glances up, chuckling in agreement. When the *skafi* is full, he climbs out and with a plastic jug pours the must into a rectangular aluminium barrel. This will hold his hundred litres for a month while the sediment settles and the natural sugar turns to alcohol; then he will funnel it into bottles that he has collected during the year. Some, still stuck with labels of brandy and ouzo, were bought for a few drachmas from the bar; some other two-litre plastic flagons that once held Coca-cola or 7-up, came from the shop.

By eleven o'clock in the morning he has finished. The yard is sluiced down, though the smell of must still hangs in the motionless air. In two days time he will borrow a hand-press from a neighbour and squeeze the last juice from the *tsipura*, the mash of pulp and pips he has crushed into the bottom of the *skafoni*. Within a month, bottles of the new vintage will be on his table for the midday and evening meals. Thick, a little opaque and violet in colour, with a pungency both sweet and acrid, he will mix it with a third of water in the glass. It is his wine, made to his own taste, and his delight in the whole process recurs every time he proudly opens a bottle.

Philip's approach to wine is more sophisticated. Every day of the year, with their afternoon and evening meals, he and his father drink an average of two litres of their own manufacture, and in common with most of the village, he prefers a lighter wine to Petros's – something with the character of a rosé. He has therefore bought 450 kilos of grapes from the lorries, some black, some white, to add to his own 400 kilos of fruit. From them he will make 600 litres of wine – just enough to last him and Leonidas to the end of the following summer. The grapes fill two enormous *skafonia* which have been mounted on bricks on the flagstone floor of the old family home up on Zervou.

Coming in out of the bright sunshine the single downstairs room appears at first to be in total darkness, filled with the sweet smell of grapes already beginning to ferment and the continuous splashing of must into the modern plastic *skafi*. Light from the arched double doors is muted by a low overhanging roof outside and the only window, tiny and square, is filmed with cobwebs and dust. Since Philip built a new house behind the bar, this one has been used as an *apothiki* – though on very hot summer nights Leonidas returns to sleep in his old bedroom upstairs, with its view of the distant sea and its constant, faint breeze. Today the ancient woodstove and the iron bedsteads that normally dominate the downstairs room have been moved to one side to make room for the *skafonia*, and in one of them Philip is hard at work in his underwear, crushing the grapes with the methodical double rhythm of a long-distance cyclist.

Leonidas is busy at the *skafi*, straining the must into a large jug and then into two barrels that Philip bought this year from a whisky distillery near Athens. Ideally, he would like to leave his wine in them for a year, for even after six months there is room for improvement as regards clarity and depth of flavour, but he has never managed to do this. In a month he will take out the working wine, clean the barrels of sediment and pour the wine back in; by Christmas it will be bottled in a row of wicker-covered demijohns which he keeps in his new *apothiki* down in the village. A little will remain here on Zervou, joining the rows of bottles up on the dusty shelves, for every summer, when the wine is as good as it will ever be, Philip corks and waxes four or five bottles of the previous year's vintage, as his father and grandfather did before him. He opens them very rarely : the pleasure is in having them there, and knowing that some of the oldest wine was bottled before he was born.

To ensure that this year's vintage will be up to his usual standard, Philip has a moustometer – more commonly known as a *grado* on Corfu, where the Italian influence is detectable in such matters – which measures the specific gravity of wine and the relative percentages of alcohol and sugar. It is a slender glass rod, bulbous at the base and about a foot long, containing what looks like the sensitive innards of a barometer and a three-sided scale. It was Philip's grandfather's and is still accurate to a single per cent. Philip handles it with respect, dipping it into the liquid that wells up from the mash of grapes at his feet.

Testing the amount of sugar in the must has always been important as it determines the potency of the resulting wine and, in extreme cases, whether wine will be made at all. In the days before the *grado* a more rudimentary but equally foolproof method was used: a fresh egg was put into the must in the *skafi*. If it sank, it was necessary to add sugar; if it rose so that enough of its surface stuck out as to be visible beneath a two drachma piece all was well. The same experiment was used to test the brine in which *feta* cheese was to be kept. If the egg was not eclipsed by the coin then the brine was more than 13 per cent salt – an important reading in the days before refrigeration. At any lower level of salinity the cheese would spoil. The *grado* vindicates the egg: if the must contains less than 11 per cent sugar no shell protrudes beneath the two drachma piece.

The issue proves academic where this year's vintage is concerned, for the must is of a high quality. However, Philip will add 1 per cent of sugar to the *tsipura* once the first pressing is over, leaving it for three days and then using a hand-press to squeeze out what he can. This wine will be no sweeter than the other, but the sugar will speed up the metamorphosis into alcohol and give him something to drink during the three months in which the better wine is in the barrel.

Philip and Leonidas work into the afternoon, both becoming a little light-headed in the close but effervescent atmosphere of the old house. At last, as the sun sinks low enough to bring some light into the room, the treading is over. A drop of must hangs on the tube above the *skafi*. Philip says his legs feel as if he has run a marathon. A final step remains: to pour a bottle of brandy into one of the oak barrels, an addition made for the sake of flavour, though the difference is so subtle as to evade most palates. This year a far more intrusive bouquet will be given by the barrels themselves – a distinct aroma of whisky in the dry rosé wine. Jugs and *skafi* are washed, the *grado* is returned to its cloth wraps and the must awaits the hand-press. Philip goes home for a bath, though his feet and shins will be stained for days.

Meanwhile, down in Koulouri at the other end of Zervou, more wine is being made in the yard outside Spiros Vlahos's big house with its fine view over the sea and the Albanian coast. Since he retired from his business in Athens Spiros has been restoring his old family home in Loutses. He has planted new vines and trained them towards his high, welded steel *klimateria* but they are far too young to be of interest for this year's harvest. As a gesture Spiros throws the few bunches into his magnificent *skafoni*, already full of a thousand kilos of *petrokoritho* grapes bought from a merchant in Corfu Town.

This year no one will tread Spiros's grapes. He has borrowed a rudimentary *égrappoir* from a relative – an electrically driven Archimedes screw that breaks the bunches without pulverizing them. It is hoisted up on top of the *skafoni* on long stanchions and the grapes are fed into its broad funnel to fall into the barrel below. Spiros leaves the brimming *skafoni* for five days, unconsciously imitating commercial carbonic maturation. The top is not covered, though the whole apparatus is set beneath his new concrete balcony. The weight of the grapes themselves extracts the juice, and the waiting permits fermentation to begin before the must is transferred to the scrubbed barrels inside the *apothiki*. When this finally takes place, a brass tap is driven into the bung hole at the base of the *skafoni* and the must, creamy yellow and foaming, pours out into the waiting trough.

Once the *skafoni* has been drained and the must is safe in the barrels, Spiros's son Kosta sets to work with a handpress. First he scoops off the brown, rotting mash from the top of the *skafoni* where the *tsipura* has been in contact with the air, ignoring the million fruit-flies beneath the balcony and a pair of two-inch hornets spiralling, drunken, above the surface of the fermenting fruit. Then he sets up the equipment.

The handpress is an old machine, something like a French *maie*, and consists of a vertical screw that protrudes from a loose-slatted barrel. Since it holds very little it will take him hours to press the contents of the giant *skafoni*. Each horizontal pull on a five-foot lever lowers a weighted plate down the screw, crushing the *tsipura*. The must seeps out between the slats, draining into the *skafi*, from where it is poured into a waiting barrel.

As Kosta toils away his assistants are women, friends of the family and neighbours, informally recruited. Their children are with them, running about and playing and there is a holiday atmosphere in contrast to the more self-important pleasure of an all-male treading.

Six weeks later the new wine, dry and tasting something like sherry, is ready to be drunk. Spiros draws off the clear honey-coloured liquid into a variety of bottles and delivers them to Kosta's helpers and other friends. As a rule, however, he does not bottle, emptying the barrels only as he needs to and saving the others, unbroached, for the coming year.

It is easy to pontificate against wines of the kind made in Loutses, and anyone used to drinking those of France or Italy is startled by the apparent crudity of what connoisseurs refer to as 'peasant beverages'. But the Loutsiotes are not fools and the results of their labours are deliberate. To them, many wines with better pedigrees taste thin and sour, and most of the available Greek alternatives, encountered by the tourist in coastal tavernas, are inferior in every way. One crucial criterion is the way the head and stomach feel the morning after : the village wine, free from both chemicals and added water, rarely produces a hangover. But the real proof is in the drinking. An evening spent with a magnum of family wine, in the company of those who made it, and at a table loaded with the food it was made to enhance, will convince anyone that comparisons are odious and that in its own place nothing else will do.

The pressing of the year's new wine is one of the few activities that has retained all its old importance in the life of the village. Unlike the harvesting of the olives it is not an event with any great economic significance and despite the opinions of a few it is not a matter of life and death as the preserving of vegetables used to be. Also, because it takes place within the relatively small scale of the family it has avoided technological evolution. Wine is made as it has always been made, not for commercial enterprise but as a necessary personal self-indulgence.

For these reasons, perhaps, the peripheral activities of wine-making have also survived intact where other similar occupations have not. The end of the summer is a productive time in the village and many less important crops share the seasonal cycle of the grapes. Over the years aspects of the long process of wine-making have merged with the tasks these other harvests demand. One of the most traditional of these concerns the preserving of figs for the winter.

Loutses is full of fig trees. Somewhere close to every old house a fig tree stands, gnarled and twisted and ancient, as cherished as any generous old provider. They ripen in the late summer and platefuls of bulging green fruit, washed and shining beneath a paper napkin, are a frequent gift between friends. Figs for preserving, however, must be left on the tree a little longer, until they have started to shrivel. Because the last pressing from the *tsipura* will be needed in the recipe, the figs are generally picked the day before the grapes are trodden and are then laid out on mats in the sun. While the *tsipura* sits waiting for the hand press, the figs dry into flat, leathery knobs.

Figs are the sweetest of all fruits, but when preserving them it is necessary to add sugar to the sticky must as it comes to the boil in a heavy pan. The figs are lowered carefully into this syrup, left in it for ten minutes, and then removed one by one to be threaded on to a length of strong twine. This will be hung up in a well-ventilated spot so that the figs can dry out again. They last all winter, to be eaten with a glass of wine or brandy on particularly cold nights.

A rather more elegant way of preserving figs is to turn them into *sikopsoma*, fig bread. This is not a bread at all, but a flattened round cake of solid fruit that is sold wrapped in vine leaves and tied up with rafia. In Athens it is thought of as a Corfiot delicacy; on Corfu it is often referred to as *kalamata*, since most of the *sikopsoma* on sale in the town comes from Kalamata, the famous olive-producing area in the far south of the Peloponnese.

Some *sikopsoma* is still made in the villages, however. The green figs are again left on the tree until they have begun to shrivel, but are cut into four being set out to dry in the sun. Then they are put through a mincer, a little ouzo and a lot of white pepper are added, with enough of the must from the *tsipura* to make a sticky dough. This is shaped into balls about the size of a grapefruit which are then flattened to produce the characteristic shape of the patties. They are set out to dry again before being wrapped tightly in vine leaves and bound. *Sikopsoma* is eaten in small slices as a *meze* or as an accompaniment to brandy after a meal. It is sweet, heavy and aromatic, especially if fresh bay leaves have been used with the vine leaves as a wrapping.

Many of the Loutsiotes use the last must squeezed from the *tsipura* to make vinegar. It is a simple process in which the must is bottled with a couple of tablespoons of last year's vinegar. The enzyme goes to work, fermentation ceases, and within days the family has a supply of fine wine vinegar, twice as pungent as anything available commercially, and of an exquisitely beautiful coral colour. Vinegar is an essential ingredient to the Corfiot palate and a large household makes as much as twenty litres a year, storing it in bottles in the *apothiki* as far away from the wine as possible, since any contact could ruin the vintage overnight.

One of the first uses to which the new vinegar will be put is to replenish the *skorthostoupi* bottle. Most of the more old-fashioned cooks in the village keep a supply of *skorthostoupi* in their kitchens at all times, to use as part of a salad dressing, as a sauce for certain fish, and also as a vitally important flavour when preparing tripe. It consists of a head of garlic, peeled and broken into large pieces, and then dropped into a small bottle of vinegar, where it should remain for at least a month before it is used. It is, inevitably, strong stuff. Only a little is needed and then only the highly aromatic liquid – the garlic itself is inedible.

Vinegar is also an indispensible part of two of the best recipes in all Greek cooking: *stifatho* and *sofrito*, a speciality of Corfu. *Sofrito* is basically slices of steak braised in a particular sauce, but when cooked well the meat and the sauce combine to create something altogether unique. Various cuts of beef can be used, but it is essential that the meat should be meltingly tender: fillet steak is certainly preferable.

 To make **Sofrito** for four or five people you will need a kilo (2 lbs 2 oz) of good steak, flour, salt and black pepper, 5 cloves of garlic, 150 ml ($\frac{1}{4}$ pint, $\frac{2}{3}$ cup) of oil, 1 tablespoon of finely chopped parsley, a generous pinch of finely chopped fresh mint, 2 tablespoons of strong wine vinegar, 4 tablespoons of brandy, and some water.

(Corfu brandy is slightly flavoured with aniseed, and it is difficult to find off the island, so an alternative would be a Greek brandy such as Metaxa with the addition of a teaspoon of ouzo.)

Trim any fat off the steak and cut it into slices no thicker than a pencil, then hammer it well. Dust each slice with flour and fry them all together in the oil in a heavy frying pan until they are golden-brown on both sides. Pour in the vinegar, brandy and about 300 ml (10½ fl oz, 1¼ cups) of water and stir them a little, then add the crushed garlic, the herbs and the seasoning. Let everything stew on a low heat until the sauce is thick. Serve it at once with either chips or mashed potatoes.

Contrary to the apparent belief of some Greek restaurants in England, *stifatho* is not simply a translation of 'stew'; it is a specific way of cooking meat and its personality is created by two particular ingredients: wine vinegar and a large quantity of the sweet, tiny onions that are used in England for pickling. Unlike the rest of Greece where a variety of meats are acceptable, only game, particularly duck, rabbit, and hare, and also ox-tongue are considered appropriate for a Corfiot *stifatho*. Since the hunting season opens just as the baby onions arrive in the market and just when the new vinegar is being made, *stifatho* was always an autumnal speciality, though since game on Corfu is becoming increasingly scarce, it is usually a hutch-bred rabbit that finishes up in the pot these days.

Everyone in Loutses has their own preferred recipe for *stifatho*. Spiros Vlahos marinates his jointed rabbit in vinegar with a sprig of bay leaves for twenty-four hours and begins by browning the meat in oil. Philip disagrees: the marinade makes the meat taste too much of vinegar, hiding its delicate flavour, so he will boil it to make it more tender; but first it must be divided into portions. With an old knife, as thin and sharp as a stiletto, he cuts off the ears and feet of the skinned rabbit that lies on the marble counter in his kitchen, then separates it into nine pieces: the head, two forelegs, the breast split in two, and each hind leg, divided both at the spine and where each leaves the body. He discards the stomach, lungs and intestines, but keeps the liver, heart, kidneys and the rest of the offal to include in the sauce. There will be enough meat for five people, so he will need at least a kilo and a half of baby onions to achieve the correct proportions for a *stifatho*. While the rabbit boils in a deep pan of water and oil he sets about the tiresome task of peeling them.

To make a rabbit **Stifatho** you will need a large rabbit, 1½ kilos (3¼ lbs) of pickling onions, 250 ml (8¾ fl oz, 1 cup) of olive oil, water, 100 ml (3½ fl oz, a generous ⅓ cup) of good wine vinegar, 3 cloves of garlic, 2 bay leaves, 2 ripe tomatoes, salt and white pepper. Cut the rabbit into portions and put it into a heavy saucepan with half the oil. Cover it with cold water and let it simmer, covered, for an hour. Peel the onions and fry them whole in the remaining oil, in an ovenproof casserole, for one minute, with the peeled, chopped garlic. Roll the pan a little to turn the onions – using a spatula or spoon may break them. Lift the meat from its juice and add it to the onions, with the chopped tomatoes, bay leaves and pepper. Pour on the juice and add a little more water if it is needed to cover the rabbit. Put the open pan into a moderate oven for a little less than an hour, until the water has nearly evaporated. A *stifatho* should not be swimming in gravy: at this stage there should be only enough liquid left to prevent it sticking to the pan, and the meat should be falling from the bones. Take the pan out of the oven, sprinkle a little salt over it and pour on the vinegar. Cover the pan and shake it gently from side to side so that the vinegar covers everything. Let it stand for ten minutes, covered, before serving.

This is the purest form of the recipe Philip uses to make a rabbit *stifatho*, but his libertarian principles demand that he add this or that as the fancy takes him, substituting halved large onions for the tiny onions when they are not in season, throwing in a handful of chopped parsley or leaving out the tomatoes altogether. Sticking rigorously to a recipe bores him; his mood invariably finds its way into the pot. In spite of this he can be intolerant of the preferences of others. Down in Peritheia, in the mini-market on a Saturday morning, the air is rich with the fragrance of a rabbit *stifatho* that Marietta is cooking for the family in her tiny kitchen behind the bar. Amongst the meat and onions in the pan is a quantity of *orzo*, tiny grains of pasta. She added it half an hour before, when there was still plenty of gravy in the pan, and it has cooked in the liquid, absorbing some of its pungent flavour. The rabbit was marinated, and the dish is ready to serve now, without the addition of any more vinegar.

Philip greets a report of Marietta's recipe with a grimace and a joke. He might cook potatoes, rice or pasta as an accompaniment to his *stifatho*, but never in the same pan. Both methods are traditional; it is a matter of taste which is chosen. To complete the meal a separate salad is needed: *horta* perhaps, boiled briefly and anointed with oil, or a finely shredded cabbage salad. And of course there will be bread on the table, to wipe up the last of the gravy from the plate.

A *stifatho* is the main meal of the day, eaten usually for lunch, but also in the evening if the family has been out working during the afternoon. The key to its success lies in the proportions of ingredients used – so many onions, enough oil – and also in the cruelly tantalizing ten minutes in which the dish cools after cooking, when the nuances of flavour are released.

This year the summer that has lingered deep into October breaks suddenly with a fall of rain, the first since May. It begins an hour or so before sunset – heavy drops spattering into the dust at the roadside, staining the warm stone of the buildings and washing the summer's detritus from the roof-tiles. As yet it makes no impression on the near-empty cisterns, but it brings some relief to the parched ground.

The rain keeps up for a week, drizzling steadily out of a flat grey sky. At night violent squalls blow out of the north-east, gusting against the shuttered houses and driving the rain almost horizontally down the street. Then it is gone, as suddenly as it came, and the day breaks to cold sunshine and a new silence in the clear, still air. Spiders and large mantises hop about the flattened yellow undergrowth in the olive groves, but the swallows have left, as have the crickets and cicadas.

The temperature has fallen twenty degrees in a week and it seems as though nothing could remain of the summer, but there are still some English tourists down in Kassiopi. They wander about the streets in their shorts and T-shirts and some even pay tribute to the autumnal sun by stubbornly parading in bathing suits. Their skin is blue with cold. The Greeks, comfortable in jeans and sweaters and jackets, look at them with sympathetic curiosity.

The season has changed in Corfu Town as well. Within days of the first rain the market is once more full of *horta* and the year's first oranges – yellow and pithy and swollen with juice that is still a little sour. There are chestnut vendors on the street and down in the old Jewish quarter the tinsmiths are busy hammering out stove-pipes. In the cafés along the Spianada, where the teenaged schoolchildren meet for coffee before lunch, the girls have assumed their winter uniforms of denim skirts and short white boots. Gypsy women move among them in long full dresses of red, black and orange; and their children follow, grubby and barefooted, pausing at tables to beg.

Out in the countryside, October is the busiest time of the year for olive farmers. After the first rains of the autumn, they must assess any damage caused to the trees by the long summer drought. In very dry years one olive in every five may be shrivelled and useless, a dark brown skin withered around the pit.

This is the season, too, for clearing the land beneath the trees, cutting back the damp dead undergrowth of the summer with scythes and raking it into piles to burn. Blotches of smoke linger above the hillsides on crisp cool mornings. Frequently these days the bar and shops are shut, for everyone has their nets to lay. The two tavernas have already closed until the following May.

Life, in fact, has changed in Loutses. As the landscape tautens with the change in the weather, so the village draws in upon itself. Tourism becomes a remote idea and older, simpler occupations reassert themselves. Buildings must be repaired and *sternas* emptied of their sour residue of water before the torrential rains of November set in; winter forage must be gathered for the animals and wood collected for the stoves. Daily now, old Tomas makes his way down to his olive groves to look for logs and kindling. Nut trees are pruned and any that are expendable or diseased are now felled: the valley echoes with the sound chain-saws.

🍇 THE SHOPS

In the first half of this century, before tourism turned the coastline of the island into the sole focus of attention, Loutses was not the isolated community it now appears to be. The scattered distribution of land and the strong family links between Ano Peritheia, Loutses and Peritheia gave the people the feeling that they belonged to a general area rather than to a specific village, and Loutses, halfway between the two Peritheias, lay at its centre.

This geographical convenience brought advantages. For one thing, all the local elections were held in Loutses, and since the Mayor of Kassiopi, who headed the administration of the twelve villages of Oros, was for many years a Parginos from Zervou, it was inevitable that the village should become the centre of political life in the area. Five hundred adults lived here then, almost double the present population, and the school had seventy pupils, instead of the twenty of today. Once a month their classroom served as the regional courthouse.

More relevant to daily life was the Loutses general store, which acted as a trading post for all the mountain farmers and shepherds as well as for the villagers themselves. It was run by Philip's grandfather and his brother, in a large house they rented on the corner of Zervou and the main road, and it supplied the whole area with anything and everything that was needed. It was also the export outlet for local produce – wood, cockerels and lambs as well as oil – all of which were taken by donkey down to the beach at Aghios Spiridon to be shipped along the coast to Corfu Town. The business was big and there was money to be made, but Philip's grandfather took to spending it on drink and women. He died just after the end of the war, at the climax of a week-long wedding party, leaving the family with enormous debts.

Today there are two shops in Loutses – Stamati's and Andrei's – though neither is anything like as active as the old general store that Philip's forebears ran.

Andrei's is the senior establishment, occupying the ground floor of his house and run to the rather idiosyncratic rules that he and his wife live by. Often on hot summer afternoons prospective customers climb the stone steps to the open door and enter the large, airy room to find nobody there, except for the two finches who live in a cage that hangs from the ceiling. Along the wall to the right are stacked rows and rows of tin drums for keeping *feta* cheese and olives; coils of wire and rope hang from nails, and a forest of broomsticks stands in the corner, bound with a piece of string. Across the creaking wooden floor, under an open window, is an enormous nineteenth-century iron and brass set of scales, a souvenir of days when village trading was busier, and on the other side of the room is a television, mounted high on a shelf above a single table and two chairs. Andrei has a licence to sell drinks, but he discourages any but a few very old friends from taking advantage of the opportunity.

Where food is concerned, Andrei's can offer only a limited choice of certain imperishable basics and one or two luxuries like tomato ketchup, but his stock of hardware is legendary. If a local workman suddenly needs some particular, rare item he need only go to Andrei; if it isn't in the hundred cardboard boxes under the counter it is certainly in the pitch-dark and mysterious backroom where the barrels of turpentine and paraffin are stored. This sepulchral chamber is also where Andrei keeps his most coveted commodity: the eggs from his chickens, which he sells when he has a mind to, to a favoured clientele.

Stamati Parginos, who owns and runs the other shop in the village, spent most of his life as a shoemaker. Then, twenty years ago, having sold a piece of olive-covered land to raise the capital, he bought the building three doors down from Philip's bar, installed his family in the upstairs rooms and opened the ground floor as a general store. The small cement courtyard in front of the premises is separated from the road by a low wall and shaded by a tangle of gourd and grape vines. Here in the summer the regular customers can sit at four or five ricketty, tin-topped tables and drink coffee, ouzo or orange squash as they play cards together and generally watch for interesting things happening up and down the street. The postman stops here four mornings a week, just as he does at Philip's, and once a month he brings the pension money for the elderly of the village, sitting at one of the tables with a coffee while the beneficiaries stare intently at his computations.

Stamati's establishment is as much of a social rendezvous as Philip's bar, an impromptu gathering-place both for passers-by and for a coterie of regulars who enjoy its familiar environment. Somewhere to do the shopping or to do business, to electioneer, to play cards or just to sit and talk, it is a true and traditional village *kafepantopoleion*, a word without an English equivalent that can be translated as a combination grocer's, bar and coffee-house. It opens every day of the year. In the summer, when Stamati's wife Maria gets up at dawn to look after her sheep, the doors are unlocked at about seven o'clock in the morning – a convenience for some of the village men who can stop by for a brandy before going off to work. They close in the middle of the day and the family has lunch and then sleeps until half past three, to be open again for the arrival of the four o'clock bus from Corfu Town. By six the place is full and it remains that way until eleven o'clock, when Stamati and Maria finally go to bed. During the winter the shop is open from about eight in the morning until the last customer goes home for the night. Stamati bought a television set six years ago and keeps it on a shelf above the cigarette and sweet displays. On winter evenings the small room is crowded with a dozen elderly regulars, sitting behind glasses of ouzo, talking through the soap operas but gazing up in silence at the weather report.

Inside, the shop is cool even in the summer, and dark, for Stamati is careful with electricity. A set of scales hangs from the ceiling above the gas ring where coffee is made, and an ornately mounted photograph of his son Babis in national service uniform faces the door.

The only significant change in the size of Stamati's clientele takes place during election time, and then the shop is always packed. Perhaps because they are less concerned with the past than in continually assessing the relationship between the present and the future, or perhaps because they are so much more interested in people than in anything else, the Greeks have a passion for politics. That they were denied a political voice for two thousand years may also have something to do with their fervour and may explain why they are equally delighted to debate the smallest local question or the most whimsical abstraction of political philosophy. In Loutses it would be difficult to find a man under sixty who does not believe that his grasp of current affairs is as great or greater than that of the Prime Minister; and every Corfiot knows that his island has provided more than its share of the nation's leaders.

The voters of the village are roughly divided between the socialist Pasok and the conservative New Democrats, with a fringe of individuals on the far left and far right, but in recent years Pasok has had the advantage. Usually this division is neither very important nor very apparent, but in times of national or local elections it re-emerges and everyone is obliged to declare their interest. One way of showing loyalty is by a careful choice of where one goes for coffee, a drink or conversation. Followers of Pasok favour the unofficial campaign headquarters in Philip's bar; diehard New Democrats head for Stamati's shop. Only the village priest must remain neutral: after the morning service on Sunday he has a glass of coffee at Philip's, then he strolls down to the shop where Maria cooks him lunch.

The priest has a standing invitation, but from time to time during the year Maria and Stamati find themselves asked to feed strangers. In the past, and especially on the mainland, a hungry traveller might have expected to be able to get something to eat in a village *kafepanto-poleion* – some bread and cheese perhaps, or a fried egg – but Stamati has never followed the tradition. Now he is filled with alarm when on some parched August afternoon a family of tourists push open the gate into the shady courtyard, sit down at one of the tables and ask to look at a menu. They may have smelt something delicious cooking in Maria's kitchen, or glimpsed the family eating inside the shop; they may just have assumed that the presence of tables and chairs means the place is a restaurant, but many of these people show considerable resentment when they discover their mistake. To avoid such tantrums, Stamati's English daughter-in-law Michelle sometimes makes them a cold lunch if she is not too busy with her two young daughters. At the end of the meal she offers Nescafé and the bill and the tourists leave, happy and none the wiser.

In Greece all instant coffee is called Nescafé, or just 'Nes', no matter what company makes it, though villagers of Stamati's generation refer to it as *mavrozoumi*, an uncomplimentary word that means black juice. It is still very expensive and Maria treats it warily when a passing tourist calls upon her to make it. If the customer asks she will open a tin of evaporated milk, but the idea of putting it into coffee seems somewhat revolting to the more old-fashioned villagers. To them, coffee means Greek coffee, one of the principal supports of village life, as dearly beloved as wine and the crucial adjunct to any serious conversation.

The ability to make a good cup of coffee is of great importance to the Greeks. They prepare it in a *briki*, a long-handled, wasp-waisted metal pot that comes in a variety of sizes to make one, two, four or even six tiny cups, though it is best to make Greek coffee individually. For *kafe metrio*, medium sweet coffee, a teaspoon of the especially finely ground beans and half a teaspoon of sugar is put into the *briki* with a coffee-cup of water. Greek stoves have a small burner at the front just for making coffee and the *briki* is put on to it over a hot flame. The coffee is stirred regularly until it begins to boil and rise, then it is taken off the heat, stirred again, set back to boil once more and poured quickly into a cup or glass. The grounds sink to the bottom and the sweet, hot liquid is sipped noisily from the top. A glass of water is always offered with the coffee to clear the palate.

Today most of the ground coffee sold in the tiny, dark, aromatic coffee-shops in Corfu Town is African, but when Philip was a boy the beans that reached Loutses came from Brazil. The villagers bought them green so that they would keep longer, and roasted them themselves in a long cylindrical metal drum called a *broustouli*. This was suspended on two uprights over a charcoal grill and turned very slowly, filling the air with a marvellous smell; then the roasted beans were ground in the family coffee mill. Very poor households made their own *broustouli* from tin cans, and their own mill from a stone with a hole in it and a metal pestle. Sometimes, to eke the coffee out, they roasted and ground grains of wheat with the beans.

Stamati makes what little profit he does by providing coffee and drinks for his customers, for the turnover of the place as a grocery shop is minimal. Babis has to buy everything in Corfu Town and then bring it up to the village in his small van, and where food is concerned government price controls regulate the mark-ups Stamati can impose. As a result, his stock of fresh food is limited to a couple of sacks of onions and potatoes. His range of dried goods is a little larger, however. There is a good selection of tinned fish and meats, different pastas and rice, tinned and longlife milk, dried fish, Nescafé, mustard, sugar, flour and often four or five old but palatable salamis, hanging on strings from the low ceiling. There are bottles of wine and brandy, kumquat and cherry liqueur for villagers to give as presents, and a great many cigarettes, sweets and biscuits. In wintertime it is possible to buy a little of Maria's deliciously creamy home-made *feta*, and during Lent there are always blocks of *halva*s and tubs of *tarama* on the counter. In the summer they double their stock of Nescafé, milk, kitchen paper and ketchup for the handful of tourists who might be staying in the village.

Stamati's local customers are mostly those who for one reason or another cannot do their shopping in Corfu Town, where things are cheaper. To encourage their patronage, Stamati used to offer credit but he was recently obliged to stop the practice after certain of his debtors left bills unsettled for months. The worst offender was a local policeman who decided that paying for the things he took undermined his authority in the village.

The usefulness of the Loutses *kafepantopoleion* as a local grocery shop, like the regional prestige of Loutses itself, has dwindled over the years, but it will no doubt continue to survive for as long as the Loutsiotes need somewhere to talk. In other parts of the island, however, the shops are changing, both because of tourism and also, one suspects, because of a process of modernization that is moving slowly over the whole of Greece. Ten years ago, tourists staying in a rented villa on the coast would have had to go to Corfu Town to do most of their shopping, now even the smallest seaside community has a mini-market stocked with curious imports in cans and bottles and packets. The impact of this new variety on local cooking has been negligible, partly because the prices for such delicacies are high, and partly for the simple reason that Greeks prefer fresh food, but in Corfu Town there have been many casualties among the specialized, family-run businesses that once made shopping there so delightful.

For example, three years ago there used to be several small dairies close to the busiest thoroughfares of the town – tiny, dimly-lit rooms that opened off the street and were furnished with one or two old tables, some chairs and a cold cupboard that also served as a counter. The temperature in these places was always lower than in other shops and the air smelt strongly of curds. The dingy walls were decorated with a fusebox, a calendar and a dog-eared representation of a saint. The only visible merchandise was in the cold cupboard, where arrayed on shelves of metal wire sat dozens and dozens of small plastic pots of yoghurt. There was yoghurt made from cow's milk, and from the fatter milk of goats or ewes, yoghurt with a natural crust of yellow cream and yoghurt sprinkled with a teaspoon of sugar that had dissolved and percolated down to transform it into the simplest but most delicious confection. The business of these dairies was equally divided between those who came in off the street to eat a bowlful at one of the tables, and those who bought one or two to take home. The pots had no lids and the dairyman would spend a long time wrapping a purchase, laying a piece of cardboard between each pot, folding it round with paper and binding everything into as stiff a construction as possible with yards of string. The yoghurt itself was superb, whichever type one chose – as rich and sweet as Devonshire cream.

The shops have gone now. Perhaps the rent rose too high in that part of town where every second door leads into a boutique or souvenir emporium, but they do not seem to have reappeared in any other quarter. In their place are two modern dairies, tiled and gleaming bantlings of the EEC, selling longlife milk from France, Danish *kephalotyri*, Kerrygold *kasseri*, and the yoghurt of the new age – low-fat, liquid and lifeless in foil-sealed tubs.

Greeks eat bread with every meal – ubiquitous soft, white loaves which are bought, never made at home. Bread is an important part of their diet and a necessary balance to the oil and heavy sauces that dominate their cooking. It is also immensely popular: people love bread and choose to eat it whenever they can. And yet there has never been a bakery in Loutses. Even in its heyday it would not have been commercially viable.

Many years ago, before cars and vans reached this part of the island, villagers made their own loaves from their own flour. Wheat was cultivated wherever it would grow, especially down on the plain between Peritheia and the sea, but also in the more sheltered valleys higher in the mountains. Ears of domestic wheat still ripen among the wild grasses of the hills.

On one hilltop above Loutses there is a flat stone circle, about twenty paces in diameter, with a small hole in the centre and a narrow trough running round its circumference. This was the place where the wheat was winnowed, in the most primitive fashion imaginable, by throwing it up into the air and letting the wind blow away the bran. The central hole was the mounting for a post and beam which acted as a loose axel for a millstone; a horse provided the power, walking round and round the stone circle, pulling the quern over the grain. A small pear tree grows on the otherwise open hilltop, planted deliberately as a shady place for the miller to doze. The techniques and apparatus would have been familiar to Greeks of Homer's day; in remote settlements like Loutses they were still in operation a hundred years ago. The grain grown and used in the villages of north-east Corfu was of a standard that is considered today to be unfit for human consumption, and the coarse, grey *babota* bread it produced, despite being sweetened with a third part of cornflour, contained nothing of nutritional value.

Better flour was available, however, to the population of Corfu Town, and after the war various laws and restrictions were passed all over Greece to ensure that bread of the same quality was accessible to everyone. The laws themselves have come to seem extraordinarily illogical, especially since they are applied to the village bakeries as strictly as to the urban businesses they were designed to control. In Spiro's bakery in Kassiopi, for example, the law insists that an ordinary loaf should cost 63 drachmas, while a round loaf, made from the same amount of the same dough and differing only in its shape must be sold, in the afternoon, for 153 drachmas. An 'ordinary' loaf of bread is one that has been baked in his new electric oven and then glazed with water; bread baked in his old stove oven and unglazed with water is known by law as 'village bread' and should cost 86 drachmas. By arguing that all bread baked in a village is village bread, Spiro has been able to circumvent the absurdity.

The business is very much a family concern. Spiro's father was one of the two bakers in Kassiopi and it was always understood that Spiro would inherit the firm. For this reason he spent many years in France and Belgium, perfecting his knowledge of the trade as apprentice to a baker-*pâtissier*. Today his younger brother assists with the baking and deliveries to Peritheia and his mother is in charge of preparing the cakes and pastries; his wife helps out in the front of the shop.

The presence of another bakery in Kassiopi and the naturally frugal attitudes of the local people limit Spiro as a baker. He would love to produce bread and especially croissants in the ways he learned in France and Belgium, but to do so would raise prices and his custom would vanish overnight, however marvellous his product.

The great feature of Spiro's bakery is undoubtedly the old oven set into the rear wall of the building. Through its arched opening one can look into the low domed chamber with its lining of grey Cephalonia stone. Spiro fires it every morning at five o'clock and the flames lick upwards through the round hole in its floor, fuelled from below by wood and the peaty *liosta* from an olive press. The loaves are slipped in one at a time using a very long wooden pole with a flattened end like an oar, some in tins but most in nothing at all, sitting on the bare stone. Once they are inside, the opening of the oven is sealed until the bread is ready, at which point Spiro and his brother leap into action with the pole, pulling the loaves out as fast as they can to make sure they are all cooked for the same length of time. In the winter Spiro makes 350 every day; in the summer, catering to the tourist trade, his workload doubles. The bread is soft and very white with a thick, chewy crust. It contains little salt and therefore draws very little moisture from the air, with the result that it is noticeably stale within a day and as hard as stone after a week, but never shows a sign of mould. Since Greeks buy their bread daily such considerations are academic, except when stale bread is needed for such dishes as *taramasalata*.

Spiro buys three types of flour from two different sources: a basic strong flour for bread, a finer, softer flour for special breads and pastries, and a third kind for cakes, known as American flour. Because the strength of flour varies with the weather and he sometimes needs a blend to reach his own high standards, he also has an arrangement with suppliers in the Thessaloniki area where the best wheat in Greece is grown.

Only the farmers' cooperatives around Thessaloniki still produce genuinely pure, additive-free flour, grinding and bolting it to their own specifications and for the exclusive use of their own bakeries. The brown flour available on Corfu is of a very poor quality and Spiro, remembering the wholemeal flour he worked with in France, will have none of it.

On the other side of the room from the oven is the enormous steel mixer where the dough is made. It is old and slow and this, coupled with the fact that he cuts the dough by hand means that Spiro needs less yeast for his bread than he would if the bakery were fully automated. The yeast comes from Athens and last year a pro-tracted lorry-drivers' strike left him without any. But he remembered the way his father had made bread and imitated it, using a dough made from just flour and water and leaving the unbaked loaves to sit for twelve hours, relying on the wild yeasts in the air to leaven them.

One small but important product of every Greek bakery is *frigonia*, the dry toast that is sold in cellophane packets. It is very light and crisp, keeps for months and is particularly popular with old people, whose teeth may not be a match for the thick crust of an ordinary loaf. They crumble their *frigonia* into milk or tea for breakfast. Spiro makes it with his basic dough to which he adds a small amount of butter. The loaves are baked in tins with the other bread, allowed to cool and are then sliced and set aside for twenty-four hours. The next morning they are put back into the oven for ten minutes to dry them thoroughly before they are wrapped.

There is one loaf that Spiro makes every week with special care: the *Prosphoron*, the offertory bread for the church in Loutses. For this he uses his best flour, mixing and kneading it by hand before shaping it into two different-sized balls. The smaller of the two is pressed down on top of the larger and then it is left to rise in its own tin, covered by a cloth kept specifically for the purpose. Just before it goes into the oven, Spiro presses a circular carved wooden seal down on to the top and pierces the pattern twelve times with a nail to prevent the bread breaking as it rises. The resulting loaf with its elaborately etched crust is very beautiful; the priest will break it into pieces to distribute during Holy Communion and also at the end of the service.

While Spiro and his brother are busy making bread every morning, his mother is hard at work in a small kitchen in the back of the shop preparing the pastries that make up the other side of the business. These can be divided into two distinct groups: sweet *pâtisseries* and cakes, and *pittes*, sweet or savoury individual pies.

Pittes are one of the great traditions of Greek cooking. The ancient Greeks made pastry and there is some reason to suppose that they used it, in their wisdom, for *pittes* even then. Today *pittes* can be found throughout the country, sold in every bakery and on every street corner of the larger towns, to be eaten as a snack by passers-by or taken home for a simple meal. In Kassiopi most of them are devoured by the school children who make a beeline for the shop as soon as they are released for their morning break.

Mainland Greeks make their *pittes* with paper-thin *fyllo* but Spiro's mother prefers to use a rough puff pastry. She mixes it in a purpose-built machine, using a blend of butter and margarine as a fat, and has another device the size of a table-top which rolls the pastry out almost as thinly as *fyllo*. All her *pittes* and cakes are baked in a modern electric oven.

Without such professional equipment it is difficult to achieve the exact texture of the pastry Spiro's mother makes. *Fyllo* has the necessary delicacy, but it is really too crisp; puff pastry is closer to what is needed but it has to be light and not too flaky.

However, the fillings of the three kinds of *pitte* the bakery sells are easily imitated. *Tyropittes* are basically cheese puffs about four inches square, packed with two or three tablespoons of crumbled *feta*. The *feta* is made locally, creamier in texture but a little stronger than some that is made for export, and Spiro's mother moistens it with a teaspoon of the brine from the tin, some of which she also uses in the pastry mix. Since commercially made *feta* may travel in a variety of liquids and preservatives, the practice is not advised elsewhere.

Loukanopittes are sausage rolls made with slim, lightly spiced frankfurters that Spiro buys in town, and *milopittes* are apple pies. Spiro's mother prepares the fruit for the filling by stewing it twice with sugar and a pinch of cinnamon until it turns into a smooth jam, and she dredges the pies with icing sugar and cinnamon after they are baked.

All these *pittes* are popular throughout Greece, but the bakery also makes another, more unusual snack called *varkas*. The name means 'small boats' and describes gondola-shaped pastries with a filling of minced meat, vegetables and cheese – as Spiro's mother says herself, they contain all the constituents of a complete and balanced meal.

The temptation when making them at home is to turn them into a kind of pizza, but in Spiro's mother's recipe the emphasis is on the meat, which should be so smooth in texture as to seem almost like a paste. *Varkas* need a shortcrust rather than a puff pastry base. They are at their best when they are still warm from the oven and not too heavily laden with meat and cheese. Such a *varka*, eaten late in the morning, should prompt an almost irresistible urge for another.

 To make about a dozen **Varkas** you will need, for the pastry, 250 g (8¾ oz) of plain flour, ½ level teaspoon of salt, and 110 g (4 oz) of a mixture of butter and margarine. For the filling you need 250 g (8¾ oz) of finely minced lean beef or veal (doubly minced if possible), 1 small onion, a tablespoon of tomato paste, a small pinch of powdered cinnamon, a pinch of finely chopped fresh mint, 3 or 4 tablespoons of olive oil, salt and pepper, and 150 g (about 5½ oz) of any waxy cheese like *kasseri* – a mild Gruyère will do very well.

Sift the flour and salt together in a bowl and rub in the margarine, making sure it is at room temperature before you start. When they are well mixed stir three tablespoons of water into the bowl and then tip the pastry out on to a clean surface to knead it briefly into a soft dough. Form the dough into a ball and seal it in a polythene bag while you make the filling.

Brown the meat very slowly in a dry saucepan, stirring and breaking it up into grains, then set it aside. Grate the onion and soften it in the oil on a low heat, then stir in the tomato paste, two or three tablespoons of water, the cinnamon, mint, and the seasoning. Add the meat and mix it well, stirring frequently over the next thirty minutes and adding a little water from time to time if it threatens to become too dry. The mixture should be smooth and of the viscosity of porridge. Allow it to cool before using it as filling.

Now take the pastry and roll it out fairly thickly, to about the depth of a pencil. With a sharp knife cut out the shape of the boats which should be about fifteen centimetres long and eight centimetres wide at their broadest point in the middle; they should taper to a blunt prow at either end. Turn up the ends and the sides to form a hollow in the middle of the boat. Smooth two tablespoons of the meat filling into the boat and lay a thin strip of cheese on top. Moisten the cheese with a wet finger and lay the *varkas* on a baking tray moistened with a few drops of water. Put them into a moderate oven until the pastry is golden – for perhaps thirty minutes – and serve them while they are still warm.

Walking into the bright, airy front shop of Spiro's bakery, the first things to meet the eye are the three refrigerated cabinets where the cakes and pastries are displayed. In the largest are the metal trays of *baklavas* and *kataifi*, golden and glossy with syrup, that Spiro's mother makes.

Alongside them are other trays piled with marvellous, rich confections of flavoured creams and chocolate, gâteaux and tarts smothered in white and silver dragées, angelica and pastel-coloured icing, éclairs and doughnuts and *koks* that seem at first glance to be chocolate-covered hamburgers. The variety is startling, but in fact none of them are made in the bakery – the shop's resources could not possibly meet such a challenge. They come from a *zacharoplasteion*, a confectioner's shop in the town, and identical delights can be found all over Greece and in Greek delicatessens from Toronto to Sydney.

These shops and their *pâtisseries* are very much a part of urban life in Greece. In the mornings they supply the populations of the cities with a sweet snack, at night those who have eaten out stroll along the street to take their coffee and a dessert there, and their offerings are always in demand for family occasions or national holidays. Their contribution to the national appetite is neatly defined, for Greeks prefer a clear separation between sweet and savoury; they do not consider coffee an appropriate accompaniment to a meal, or a dessert a necessary finale.

The traditions of the *zacharoplasteion*, however, have never extended to the countryside. If someone from Loutses wanted a box of elaborate cream cakes for some special event such as his child's nameday he would have to go to town to buy them, or at least to the bakeries in Kassiopi where all manner of treats are available during the tourist season. In fact very few of the villagers ever do this, partly because those grand confections taste far less interesting than they look, and partly because the Loutsiotes are proud of their own baking and consider a home-made cake or pastry best for a family celebration.

The villagers' repertoire of cakes and biscuits contains nothing that is not cooked elsewhere in Greece, in rural or urban homes. Furthermore, everything they make could be found in a good bakery or *pâtisserie* anywhere in the country, prepared in virtually the same way and with virtually the same ingredients, though the tender loving care a housewife lavishes on her *kourabiethes* may be missing from the recipe.

The devotion to tradition noticeable in all Greek cooking is at its most obvious when it comes to sweet things. Recipes for pastry or bread or sponge cake always lean towards the finite, but the Greeks are further limited by the fact that most of these creations are associated with a particular day or festival when it is desirable to reproduce some seasonal favourite.

The recipes for pastries and cakes are therefore among the oldest in the Greek chef's canon. Cynics suggest that their nation-wide uniformity proves them to be a legacy of the Turks; patriots claim that they were first devised in the Hellenistic period, when Alexander the Great was alive and eating. Judging from the writings of Apicius, the second provenance is the most plausible. The Romans, whose cuisine was the creation of Greeks, ate many different sweets with a basis of dough covered in honey and chopped nuts, the fundamental adornments of many traditional Greek pastries to this day. Wherever the recipes may have come from, their immutability is seen today as a virtue. Even the simplest festive biscuit is beloved by the Greeks and greeted rather as a Christmas pudding is by the English – with an innocent pleasure in something familiar and good and deliberately old-fashioned.

There are some baked goods, however, which transcend the calendar and are always appropriate, and the first among them is *baklavas*.

Because of its ubiquity in Greece and abroad, *baklavas* has become the quintessential Greek pastry, though like so many of the mainland specialities its origins are disputed between Greeks and Turks, and even, in this case, Russians. Its principal ingredient is the pastry called *fyllo*, which Corfiots invariably buy frozen from supermarkets. Some advice on using frozen *fyllo* appears on p. 35.

When making *baklavas* it is important to use the correct baking tray: one that is rectangular, without curved corners and with perpendicular sides of smaller dimensions than a rectangular leaf of *fyllo*. The trays used on Corfu are twenty-five by thirty-five centimetres, and about nine centimetres deep.

To make **Baklavas** you will need 500 g (1 lb 1 oz) of *fyllo* pastry, 500 g (1 lb 1 oz) of shelled walnuts, 130 g (4½ oz) of blanched almonds, 170 g (6 oz) of butter, 130 g (4½ oz) of sugar, 2 teaspoons of powdered cinnamon and ¼ teaspoon of powdered cloves. For the syrup you will need 400 g (14 oz) of sugar, 350 ml (12 fl oz, 1½ cups) of water, a cinnamon stick, a large piece of lemon peel, 4 cloves, and half a cup of runny honey.

Take the frozen packet of *fyllo* out of the freezer and let it thaw, unopened, for three hours. Chop the nuts finely and mix them with the sugar, cinnamon and powdered cloves. Melt the butter in a small pan without allowing it to brown. When the *fyllo* is properly thawed, open the packet and gently unfold the wad of leaves. Grease the bottom of the baking tin with a little melted butter and lay the first *fyllo* leaf into it. Brush it with melted butter and carefully fold in its edges until it fits snugly in the pan. Do not try to trim the edges of the leaf. Repeat the procedure with four more leaves, then add a fifth without brushing its top with butter. Sprinkle some of the nut mixture evenly over the leaf in a thin layer. Lay another leaf over the nuts, brush it with butter and lay a second leaf on top, unbuttered. Make another thin layer of the nut mixture. Repeat the procedure until all the nut mixture has been used. Lay a final four leaves of *fyllo* over the top, brushing each with butter, and buttering the top leaf particularly well. Now take a very sharp knife and carefully score the *baklavas* into strips, then squares, then triangles, taking care to cut no deeper than the top layer of nuts. Sprinkle the top of the *baklavas* with about ten drops of water to prevent it curling up in the oven, then put it into an oven preheated to 325°F (170°C, Gas mark 3) for about an hour and a half until the pastry is golden brown.

Meanwhile make the syrup by heating the water and dissolving the sugar in it before bringing it to a fast boil. Then add the cinnamon, cloves and peel and let it simmer for twenty minutes. While it is still hot, stir in the honey.

When the *baklavas* is out of the oven, pour half the syrup carefully over it, wait half an hour, and then pour on the rest. Let the *baklavas* rest undisturbed for at least twelve hours before finally cutting it through, following the lines cut before the baking. To refresh the palate, Greeks always serve a glass of water with a pastry, and usually a tiny cup of hot sweet Greek coffee as well.

Corfiot cooks have traditionally looked for alternatives to *fyllo*, but there is another pastry that, like *baklavas*, demands it, whether prepared professionally or at home. *Galaktoboureko* is a pie with a top and bottom crust of *fyllo*. Recipes for the filling vary with every household, especially in the proportions of milk and eggs to semolina and cornflour, with the result that in some kitchens it is thought of as a custard pie, in others as a semolina pie. The following recipe is the version favoured by Philip's aunt Paradisi. It is sweet and firm and decidedly more like semolina than custard, and she does not insist on soaking the finished product with syrup as some cooks do, or on following the alternative of a generous dusting of icing sugar and powdered cinnamon. One potentially delicious amendment, however, might be to include some grated nutmeg in the filling. Paradisi cooks her *galaktoboureko* throughout the year, serving it as a sweet snack in the morning or afternoon or an hour or so after dinner, but in common with most traditional households on the island, she makes a particularly large one for the last Sunday of the Carnival week – the day before the beginning of Lent.

 To make Paradisi's **Galaktoboureko** you will need 1¼ litres (2¼ pints, 5 cups) of evaporated milk, 300 ml (10½ fl oz, 1¼ cups) of water,

8 drops of vanilla essence, 1 cup of semolina, 1 cup of cornflour, 4 eggs, 1 cup of sugar, ½ lemon, 11 sheets (about 350 g) of *fyllo*, and at least 100 g (3½ oz) of butter. *Galaktoboureko* should be baked in the same size and shape of tin as *baklavas*.

Scoop out the flesh and pith from the lemon and put the whole piece of peel into a large saucepan with the milk, water and vanilla. Bring it to the boil then remove it from the heat. Combine the semolina, cornflour and sugar, and add them slowly to the milk, stirring well to discourage lumps. Bring it to the boil again, stirring continuously, then turn off the heat and let it cool, stirring from time to time, until it is lukewarm. Remove the lemon peel. Beat the eggs and fold them into the mixture. Melt the butter gently so that it does not brown, and let it cool for five minutes, then use a little to grease the bottom and sides of the baking tin. Following the instructions for using *fyllo* as described on p. 35, lay one leaf over the bottom of the tin. Brush it with melted butter and lay another leaf of *fyllo* on top. Repeat until there are six leaves of *fyllo* in the tin, but do not butter the top one. Pour the semolina filling on to the pastry and smooth it gently into an even layer. Lay a leaf of *fyllo* on to the filling, brush it with butter and repeat the procedure with the remaining four leaves. Fold in the edges of the leaves, buttering them too, and sprinkle a dozen drops of water over the top. With a sharp knife, score the top leaves of *fyllo* with five parallel lines about three inches apart. Bake it for forty-five minutes in an oven preheated to 400°F (200°C, Gas mark 6) until the pie is golden brown. Let it stand for five minutes then cut it into three-inch squares. At this point the pie could be soused with the same syrup as was made for the *baklavas*, but many people find it is sweet and moist enough already.

Semolina is still a widely used cereal in Greece. The inefficiency of the old horse-driven millstone or the small hand-mills that village women operated in their yards or kitchens is part of the reason and explains the number of local recipes for using up cracked wheat or semolina. The most basic amongst them is for a kind of porridge or gruel called *poulenta*. No doubt the Venetians prepared and ate *polenta*, the northern Italian staple made from ground maize, when they were on Corfu, but the same food was known to the ancient Romans as *pulmentum* and was probably introduced to the island in ancient times. Until the 1930s *poulenta* was the mainstay of the very poor. Roughly ground wheat, semolina or cornflour was added to boiling ewe's milk or water with a little salt and then simmered until it was very thick. A slightly more extravagant dish called *kofto* was made from cracked wheat in the same way but with the addition of some honey or even sugar. Some old people, living alone and with little money, still cook it.

Poulenta, like the rough peasant bread *babota*, carries bad associations for those villagers who had to eat it as children, but *revani*, another old recipe that uses semolina, is remembered with delight. It is basically a sponge-cake, delicately flavoured with orange and lifted by the eggs in the recipe, soused with a thin, fragrant syrup. It is eaten all over Greece and is enjoyed all year round.

 To make **Revani** you will need 6 eggs, 6 tablespoons of semolina or cream of wheat, 3 tablespoons of flour, 100 g (3½ oz) of butter or margarine, 6 tablespoons of sugar, 1 teaspoon of baking powder, a teaspoon of finely grated orange peel, 2 tablespoons of fresh orange juice, 2 tablespoons of Greek brandy, ⅓ teaspoon of bicarbonate of soda, and 3 drops of vanilla essence. For the syrup you will need 250 g (a scant 9 oz) of sugar, 400 ml (14 fl oz, 1⅔ cups) of water, ½ a cinnamon stick, 2 cloves and a tablespoon of Greek brandy. First make the syrup by dissolving the sugar in the hot water, adding the cinnamon and cloves, and then bringing it to the boil. Let it simmer for about twenty minutes until it is a pale brown colour, then add the brandy and simmer it for two or three minutes more. Remove the cloves and cinnamon and let the syrup stand while you bake the cake. Sift the flour, semolina and baking powder into a bowl. Melt the butter carefully in a pan without allowing it to brown. Separate the eggs and mix the yolks with the sugar, then stir in the peel, brandy and vanilla, and the melted butter. In a large bowl, beat the egg whites until they peak and then fold in the dry ingredients, spoonful by spoonful. Dissolve the bicarbonate of soda in the orange juice and stir that in too. Fold in the yolk mixture. Take a large deep baking tin, grease it and pour in the mixture. Bake the *revani* for half an hour in an oven that has been preheated to 350°F (180°C, Gas mark 4). When it is ready, pierce the cake all over with a knitting needle, let it stand for no more than five minutes and then slowly pour on the syrup until it is absorbed by the cake. Some people find so much syrup rather sickly, but without it a *revani* can be too dry. Allow the cake to cool before serving. Although not authentic, an excellent variation of the syrup can be made by melting 6 tablespoons of icing sugar in about 300 ml (10½ fl oz, 1¼ cups) of fresh orange and lemon juice, simmering it for five minutes and then pouring it hot over the punctured cake, saving the last few spoonfuls to smooth over the top as a glaze.

In the past, the women of Loutses were too busy for anything like a regular baking day to become commonplace, and though most of the ingredients such as flour or semolina, eggs, nuts, oranges and brandy were readily to hand, others were often expensive or scarce. Sugar in particular has always been a troublesome commodity to get hold of. Village shops invariably buy it in bulk and measure it into kilo bags on the premises and its price and availability still fluctuate wildly. Brown sugar is restricted to the cosmopolitan supermarkets of the town.

The old alternative to sugar is of course honey, and several villagers keep hives for their own use as they have always done. Up in Ano Peritheia, in a small garden surrounded by ruined walls and shaded by fig, cherry and white mulberry trees, one local apiarist has a dozen square, wooden *kypselia*. The hum of the bees can be heard a long way off along the deserted lanes, giving a voice to the heat of summer. They feed on clover and herbs and the hundreds of varieties of wild flowers that every year reclaim a little more of the old town. Their honey is superb, thick and creamy and a pale yellow colour, in contrast to the runny brown, refined honey on sale in the shops. The owner makes more than he can use and sells his surplus to friends at a competitive price.

It is said that the best honey in the world comes from the bees of Mount Hymetos near Athens, but modern Greek cooking has only one or two formal recipes that use honey, except as an ingredient of a syrup to pour over pastries, and even then sugar generally takes its place. In Loutses it is still sometimes used by the elderly to sweeten warm milk and it remains a favourite specific against sore throats, either taken by the spoonful or dissolved in a small cup of clear tea. There are, however, a few recipes for which honey is considered absolutely necessary and one of them is for *loukoumathes*, the yeast-risen fritters that are certainly the most popular sweet dish in Loutses.

At Easter and Christmas time, and particularly just after midnight on New Year's Eve, nearly every family in the village will be frying their *loukoumathes*. Even Philip has been known to make them – the only cake or pastry he ever cooks. The dough will last for a day in the fridge, but the *loukoumathes* themselves must be eaten within minutes of being made, still hot and as light and delicate as bubbles. Because Greek families gather in the kitchen (always the most welcoming and most central room in the house) the cook will not find herself alone at the stove at the height of the festivities – indeed there can sometimes be too many experts crowding round the pan with advice on how to drop the dough. Professionals do it in one swift gesture, squeezing an actual bubble of batter up from their fist and twitching it into the oil, but as long as the oil is hot enough the results can be perfectly satisfactory using two teaspoons – one to dig a rounded teaspoon of batter from the bowl, the other to scrape it quickly off into the pan. In certain parts of Greece milk or yoghurt is included in the recipe, but Loutsiotes rely on creating a soft enough dough without either.

 To make about 30 **Loukoumathes** you will need a packet (8 g) of dried yeast, 1 level teaspoon of sugar, 550 ml (19 fl oz, 2¼ cups) of warm water, 250 g (10 oz) of plain flour, a pinch of salt, and plenty of oil for deep frying. Their syrup is made from two parts honey and one part water, flavoured with half a cinnamon stick and, if you like it slightly less sweet, a teaspoon of lemon juice. A little icing sugar and powdered cinnamon can be sprinkled over the *loukoumathes* after they are fried.

Prepare the dough well in advance as it will need three or four hours to rise properly. Stir the dried yeast into a cup of hand-hot water in which the sugar has been dissolved, and let it stand undisturbed for ten minutes until it is frothy. Sift the flour and salt into a bowl, add the yeast and the remaining warm water and whisk them into a sticky batter. Cover the bowl with a damp cloth and set it aside in a warm place until it has risen and bubbles are forming on the surface. Heat the oil until it begins to smoke. Check the oil is hot enough by dropping a morsel of dough into it – the dough should move around and fizz. Now drop teaspoonfuls of the dough into the oil and let them fry for five or six minutes, turning them continuously with a slatted spoon. They will swell to five times their size. Remove them and lay them on paper towels to drain. Bring the honey, water and cinnamon to the boil and let the syrup thicken for a few minutes, then dip each of the cool *loukoumathes* quickly into it and set them out on a plate. Sprinkle them very lightly with cinnamon or icing sugar or both and serve them immediately.

Kourabiethes, Greek shortbread, is also baked for the Christmas holiday and the New Year, the one time of the year apart from Easter when everyone seems to be busy at their ovens. Philip's aunt Paradisi, whose version of the recipe this is, makes the biscuits in vast quantities just before Christmas and offers them to all the visitors to her house until New Year's Day. Smothered in fine white icing sugar, the pale biscuits look marvellous piled on top of a doily on a silver tray. The recipe has supposedly come down to us from the early Middle Ages, but the addition of the alcohol is Paradisi's own idea, much approved of by her family.

Kourabiethes are made in a variety of shapes, but the crescents Paradisi favours are unpopular in certain parts of Greece. A legend persists that it was the Turks who ordered all *kourabiethes* to be cut that way as a mark of respect for Islam; after the liberation of the country patriotic cooks dispensed with the design. A charming mainland tradition is to form the biscuits into the shape of pears and to stick a clove into each one for a stalk, but perhaps the best idea is to vary the shapes as much as possible.

According to Paradisi, the key to perfect *kourabiethes* is the beating of the butter, both on its own and then with the other ingredients. It takes a very long time, even with an electric blender and calls for more patience than most cooks can muster, especially just before Christmas. However, since her *kourabiethes* are indeed perfect, rich and with the texture of the very best shortbread, it might be as well to follow her advice.

 To make a good quantity of **Kourabiethes,** you will need 500 g (1 lb 1 oz) of the best butter, 100 ml (3½ fl oz, a generous ⅓ cup) of olive oil, 4 tablespoons of pure alcohol and 2 of brandy, half a teaspoon of vanilla powder or 5 drops of vanilla essence, 500 g (1 lb 1 oz) of blanched almonds, the yolks of 2 eggs, 500 g (1 lb 1 oz) of flour, just over 4 tablespoons of sugar, and 500 g (1 lb 1 oz) of icing sugar.

Beat the butter in the bowl of an electric mixer on its lowest speed for half an hour. Meanwhile chop the almonds very finely and fry them briefly in a little oil, until they are golden. Put them on to a paper towel to absorb any oil. With the mixer still beating, slowly add the sugar, oil, egg yolks, brandy, vanilla and the almonds. Let the mixer continue its work for a few minutes before gradually adding half the flour. Slowly pour in the alcohol and then the rest of the flour. All this should take another half an hour. While the oven reaches a temperature of 200 °C (400 °F, Gas mark 6), roll the dough out to a thickness of one centimetre. Paradisi uses a small glass to cut out crescents and other shapes which she then lies, spaced well apart, on a baking tray, greased with melted butter. Bake them in the oven for twenty minutes. When they are cooked, lie them close together on a sheet of greaseproof paper and dredge them with sifted icing sugar.

Koulouria Paschalina are a very different kind of biscuit, made and eaten at home during the week after Easter. A plate of them is left on the table in the parlour for visitors, with another in the hall to tempt people coming in and out, and they are a favourite gift between friends.

Koulouria is almost a generic term for the many dry, bready biscuits that are found everywhere in Greece. Crisp, round, very thin *koulouria*, often covered with sesame seeds, are sold on the street in Athens, especially by boys who wait at sets of traffic lights during the early morning rush hour. When the cars stop they dash into the road, passing a warm biscuit with a piece of cheese through the window to any driver who has the right amount of money in his hand – the boys have no time to fumble for change. This modern tradition stems from the old city practice of selling *koulouria* from door to door. Today few bakeries offer such service but it is still possible to buy them from less frenetic salesmen who wait with their trays at strategic corners, or move along the boulevards.

In Loutses if anyone wanted fresh *koulouria* for breakfast they would have to make them themselves, but nobody does, except at Easter.

The recipe calls for a little carbonate of ammonia. This is used fairly widely in Greek baking as a raising agent, but its powerful smell may discourage cooks who have not encountered it before. The smell, like the powder itself, vanishes during the baking. In shaping the biscuits remember that they will double in thickness in the oven, so tight knots may not be successful. Because it is Easter, many Greeks like to twist the dough into alphas and omegas, the first and last letters of the alphabet and therefore symbolic of God's omnipresence and infinite dominion, the beginning and the end – but part of the fun of making *koulouria* is to be creative with the design.

 To make **Koulouria Paschalina** (Easter biscuits) you will need 4 eggs, 230 g (8 oz) of butter, 230 g (8 oz) of sugar, a teaspoon of carbonate of ammonia, 120 ml (4 fl oz, ½ cup) of milk (ideally ewe's milk, since it gives a better flavour), 1 kilo (2 lbs 2 oz) of flour, 1 heaped tablespoon of grated orange peel, 1 tablespoon of brandy, 3 drops of vanilla essence, and a small pinch of baking powder.

Beat the butter well until it is a smooth cream. In a separate bowl, beat three of the eggs with the sugar and the vanilla until they too are smooth and creamy and fold them into the butter. Warm the milk and dissolve the carbonate of ammonia in it, then add it to the butter mixture, stirring well. Mix in the brandy and peel. Sift the flour and the baking powder and fold it into the mixture to make a soft dough. Pull a little off and roll it between your hands until it is as thick as a pencil. Twist it into a pleasing shape and lie it down on a greased baking tray. Continue to do this, making sure that there is plenty of room between the biscuits, and when the tray is full beat the remaining egg and brush it over each biscuit. Put them into an oven preheated to 200 °C (400 °F, Gas mark 6) for about twenty minutes.

Fogatsa, which is also known as *tsoureki* or *Christopsomo*, is a sweet bread that like *koulouria paschalina* is baked at Easter time as part of the reward for a long Lenten abstinence. It is eaten informally, by anyone who happens to be passing the kitchen, and also as a traditional breakfast on Easter Sunday, like hot cross buns in England.

Mahlepi, one of the flavourings for *fogatsa*, is the name for a powder dried from the bitter fruit of a variety of cherry tree called *mahlepi* in Greek, or St Lucie's Cherry in English. It is sold in Greek shops primarily for this recipe, but if it is unavailable, substitutes will do, particularly sweet aniseed boiled for twenty minutes in a very little water, or a similar infusion of cinnamon, cloves and bay leaves. One tablespoon of the liquid would replace half a teaspoon of powdered *mahlepi*.

 To make **Fogatsa** you will need 500 g (1 lb 1 oz) plus 140 g (5 oz) of flour, 1 tablespoon of dried yeast, ½ a cup of butter, ¾ cup of sugar, 4 eggs, the grated peel of half an orange, half a teaspoon of powdered *mahlepi* or a tablespoon of an infusion of *glikanison* (sweet aniseed), 100 ml (3½ fl oz, a scant ½ cup) of milk, ½ teaspoon of salt, and a small handful of blanched, silvered almonds for decoration.

Warm the milk and dissolve the yeast into it, leaving it for ten minutes until it begins to froth. Then stir in about ¼ of a cup of flour and cover the bowl with a cloth. Sift the rest of the flour and the salt into a mixing bowl. Melt the butter without allowing it to brown and pour it into the flour; add the *mahlepi* or the essence of *glikanison*. Add the whole eggs, sugar, peel and yeast paste and mix them all together into a soft dough. Cover the bowl with greaseproof paper and a damp cloth and leave it in a warm place for an hour, until it doubles its size. When this has happened, knead the dough again briefly and divide it into three large pieces. Roll each piece out until it is as thick as a length of rope, tapering at either end, and braid the three pieces together, or roll them up like a hose. Put them on to a tray that has been greased with butter, cover them with a cloth and leave them to rise again for half an hour. Now beat the last egg, brush it over the top of the bread and sprinkle on the almonds, either in a pattern or at random. Bake it in a moderate oven for thirty minutes.

Almost as popular as *loukoumathes* with the people of Loutses are soft and sticky *melomakarona*, halfway between a biscuit and a cake, and fragrant with the flavours of orange and honey. They are also called *finikia*, a word which is translated as either Venetian or Phoenician, depending upon whom one asks, though since most people agree that the recipe dates from the fourteenth century, the first provenance seems the most likely. Either way, they may well have originated in Corfu. If they really are an extraordinary legacy of the Phoenicians then they should by rights have entered Greek cuisine through the good efforts of King Alkinoos's chefs; if they are actually Venetian then they were surely brought from Venice to Corfu, or else created here for the delight of the island's Italian masters.

One final derivation of the name might be from the Greek word *finix*, which means both a date-palm tree and the mythical phoenix. *Finikia* are certainly as sweet and sticky as dates, and they are also Phoenix-like in a way, emerging transformed and magnificent from the oven's fire.

To make **Melomakarona** you will need 500 g (1 lb 1 oz) of plain flour, 200 ml (7 fl oz, a generous ¾ cup) of olive oil, 125 g (4½ oz) of sugar, ½ teaspoon of baking powder, ¼ teaspoon of bicarbonate of soda, 2 tablespoons of Greek brandy, 4 tablespoons of fresh orange juice, 1 level tablespoon of grated orange peel, 1 level tablespoon of grated lemon peel, a pinch of powdered cinnamon, and

60 g (2 oz) of finely chopped walnuts. The syrup is made from 3 parts sugar, 2 parts honey and 2½ parts water.

Beat the sugar and the oil in a slow blender for a very long time (local cooks keep beating for an hour) until they form a smooth cream. Dissolve the bicarbonate of soda in the orange juice, add the brandy and peel, and mix them well into the oil and sugar. Sift the flour and baking powder into a bowl and fold in the oil and sugar mixture, mixing everything into a soft dough. Mould the paste between your hands into finger-sized cakes. Lie them, spaced well apart, on a greased baking tray, then press the top of each one gently with the flat tines of a fork – these indentations will hold the syrup once the *melomakarona* are cooked. Put the cakes into an oven, preheated to 200 °C (400 °F, Gas mark 6), for half an hour. Remove them and let them stand, for the cakes must be cold and the syrup hot when they finally meet. Make the syrup by bringing the sugar, honey and water to the boil and letting them simmer together for five minutes, then dip each of the *melomakarona* into the syrup and lie them side by side on a plate. Dust them lightly with the cinnamon and sprinkle them with chopped walnuts.

Any attempt to find true desserts in Loutses will end in failure. The villagers often eat some sweet or other if they are hungry, at any time of the day or night, but not as part of a meal. The nearest thing to a dessert is *rizogalo*, rice pudding. Sweet and rich, more of a custard than a real pudding, it is as popular with children here as it is anywhere else, either warm or ice-cold from the refrigerator. Because Corfiots prefer tinned evaporated milk to fresh milk, the recipe below, which Koula Parginou often prepares for her daughter, is even sweeter than it might otherwise be.

 To make Koula's **Rizogalo** (rice pudding) you will need 100 g (3½ oz) of long-grain rice, 500 ml (17½ fl oz, 2 cups) of water, 500 ml (17½ fl oz, 2 cups) of evaporated milk, a pinch of salt, 150 g (5 oz) of sugar, 1½ tablespoons of cornflour, 2 eggs, 1 teaspoon of vanilla essence, and a pinch of powdered cinnamon. Bring the water to the boil, add the salt and rice, and let it simmer for five minutes. Pour in all but two tablespoons of the milk and when it returns to the boil, let it simmer for half an hour longer. Meanwhile, beat the cornflour and the vanilla into a paste with the last of the milk and, in a separate bowl, thoroughly beat the eggs. When the rice is very soft, slowly stir in the sugar until it has all dissolved. Add the cornflour liquid and let it simmer for a further five minutes, stirring continuously, then remove it from the heat. After a quarter of an hour, take three or four tablespoons of the rice mixture and stir it vigorously with the eggs, then pour it back into the pan. Return the pudding to the heat and keep stirring but do not let it boil again. Tip the *rizogalo* into a bowl, sprinkle the cinnamon on top and put it into the refrigerator until it is cold.

Neither cakes nor breads nor indeed food in general were ever an important stock-in-trade of the shops of Loutses, even in the days when Philip's grandfather kept his general store. The *kafeantopoleia* were always more use as suppliers of the hardware of the kitchen. Isolated in the mountains, the villagers might have been obliged to pay heavily for such goods, but in fact there was always an alternative source from whom they could buy – the travelling salesmen of the countryside. Tinkers, ironmongers and haberdashers, gypsies for the most part, they still come up into the mountains every winter, driving gaily-painted vans with tiers of plastic bowls and buckets tied precariously on the roof. Through a loudspeaker they play alluring bouzouki music at shattering volume and wherever they stop the women come out of their houses to see what is for sale, crowding around the piles of woollen blankets and giggling at jokes as they hold up underwear against each other, doing their best to bewilder and embarrass the salesman into a bargain.

The women's social life moves indoors during the winter. After a long day's work in the olive groves they must prepare the family meal and do the housework, but there is also time for visiting friends. Alone together, they relax and their conversation becomes more animated, often bawdy, revolving around illnesses and gossip, for as in any small community information about neighbours is extraordinarily detailed and frequently scurrilous.

The traditions of embroidery, crochet-work and knitting continue to flourish as an evening pastime. Silks, brocade, and patterns are bought from the vans or from the shops in Corfu Town, as is an enormous variety of wools, though many of the older women still card the fleeces from their own sheep. In the past a girl's early teens were spent making her trousseau, but the custom has faded away; today the women stitch their doilies and antimacassars to adorn their home or to give away to friends. Two women still weave carpets at home on traditional wooden looms.

A seasonal change has also taken place up at the bar. Throughout the summer business is quiet for Philip and Leonidas. The men go down to the coast for their late-night recreation, or to the tavernas, and only a few of the older men sit outside under the vines after dark, playing cards and assessing the issues of the day. In the winter, the scene is very different. From six until eleven the place is packed. In the true tradition of the *kafeneion*, the Greek coffee-house, it becomes an arena for debate, negotiation, drinking and card-playing. Philip, from his position behind the long bar is both arbiter and participant as well as the master of ceremonies, dispensing beer and large amounts of whisky to the younger men, ouzo to the old, and good advice to anyone who asks for it. Because of his discretion and ability to keep a secret he is known to his friends as 'The Grove', a soubriquet he is proud of. The card-players shout their orders above the din and he keeps tabs for them on long strips of cardboard with one hand, using the other to dial a number for anyone unfamiliar with the bizarre idiosyncracies of the village telephone. The air is opaque with cigarette smoke, and as hot from political argument as from the wood stove that stands in the middle of the room. Philip is in his element.

Gambling is and always has been a vital necessity to the men of Loutses. By a cruel irony the most charming casino in Europe is to be found on Corfu but only Corfiots of a certain income are permitted to play there – the government wants tourist currency not an island of bankrupts – so the men must exercise their skills at Philip's tables. The games are lethal to the outsider and can be to the *aficionado*: when the fit is upon them, large proportions of the men's income are won and lost – to the dismay of their wives who must scrimp for the smallest luxury. Big games are watched by whole support teams and in the event of a cash-flow crisis, Philip will supply credit. As at any poker table, banter is brisk and centres around jokes about who has to get home when and whose wife has threatened to lock him out if he is late for dinner again. On New Year's Eve, however, the game goes on from dusk until dawn and on this special occasion women play as well, a most rare occurrence. The ruthless cunning of some of the village grandmothers is awe-inspiring.

To mark New Year a special sponge cake is baked, called *vasilopitta*, after Saint Basil, patron of New Year. Most families bake their own and will go home after midnight to eat it, but Philip always has one in the bar, made by his cousin Vivi in Kassiopi. At one minute to midnight he turns off the lights (leaving the television on for the countdown from Athens) and as the chimes ring out the cake is cut.

 To make **Vasilopitta**, you will need 250 g (8¾ oz) of butter, 340 g (12 oz) of sugar, 6 eggs, 4 or 5 tablespoons of Greek brandy, 2 tablespoons of a sweet orange-flavoured liqueur (on Corfu this is naturally kumquat), 2 teaspoons of baking powder, 500 g (1 lb 1 oz) of hard flour, 200 ml (7 fl oz, a generous ¾ cup) of evaporated milk, 1 teaspoon of vanilla powder or 6 drops of vanilla essence, the grated peel of 2 oranges, and enough slivered, blanched almonds to decorate the top of the cake. Mix the butter and sugar very well, then stir in the egg yolks, the vanilla, the orange peel, the brandy and the liqueur, until they form a thick paste. Combine the flour and the baking powder; beat the egg whites until they are stiff. Then, alternating the flour, the egg whites and the milk, fold them into the paste a little at a time. Pour the mixture on to a baking tray greased with butter, and put it into a moderate oven for forty-five minutes, until it is golden brown.

When the cake is cool decorate it with the almonds by arranging them into words: the two most common messages are either EFTI-HISMENO TO NEO ETOS (followed by the number of the year) or KALE HRONIA (also followed by the year), both of which mean Happy New Year.

Hidden in every *vasilopitta* is a coin wrapped in foil. Whoever finds it in his or her slice will enjoy good luck during the coming year. The fortunes of everyone else can be predicted from how well or how badly they are doing at the card table on the stroke of midnight.

For those who stay at home there is an even older tradition to ensure good luck – first-footing by a child of six or seven. The child knocks on the door just after midnight and is admitted. He or she must head straight for the fireplace. Earlier on, members of the household have hidden eggs among the cold ashes, saying as they do '*Ta avga poulia*', literally, 'The eggs birds', an incantation designed to guarantee fertile eggs from the family chickens. Once inside, the child must sit down and begin to play with the eggs. If all goes according to plan, the household will prosper in the new year. The child is given money and the small cakes called *loukoumathes* as a reward.

Vasilopitta is the only food Philip serves in his bar, though during the summer he sells packets of biscuits, chocolate and ice creams, especially to the children when they come out of the village school in the mornings. As a *meze* for the men he offers only peanuts, and those only in the winter time.

At eleven o'clock, when the last card-players have settled their tab and left, he sweeps up the shells and puts them into the wood stove. Then Leonidas switches off most of the lights in the bar, turns up the sound on the television and lets in his cat and Philip's dog, Proudon. Philip sets off into the darkness, heading for the kitchen of their house behind the bar and returning a few minutes later with their dinner. He uncorks a bottle of their wine, sets it down on the table nearest the wood stove, and together they sit and eat and watch the news reports from Athens.

Outside the wind grows stronger, bringing rain down out of the mountains, buffeting the houses and tossing the trees in the blackness. The dim light in the windows of the bar is the only sign of life in the sleeping village. Soon it, too, is extinguished.

🍇 ANIMALS

Winter, it is said in Loutses, really begins on 14 November, St Philip's day. For a month or so the weather has been violently changeable. There have been days when the wind howls across from Albania so hard and cold that children are kept indoors and woollen cloths are wrapped about the necks of the goats in their byres to protect them from the chill; and there have been days when the wind drops to nothing at all and the sun, in a few short hours, warms the island into an illusion of springtime. Nights begin calm and still, with the moon riding low in the east, gleaming on the cold sea. Then at two in the morning clouds come streaming over the mountains behind the village, the vanguard of vast, towering thunderheads that blot out the stars. Their extraordinary detonations shake the houses and make the windows buzz, driving hail knocks rooftiles to the ground and strips the last leaves from the vines. The storm lasts twenty minutes before it passes on, a monstrous anvil of darkness over Albania, continually illuminated by flashes of forked lightning.

The summer recreations of the village have also disappeared. People who have some reason to be outside hurry up the street, moving faster than they have for months, the women hunched against the cold with scarves tied tightly, the men striding up to the bar with jackets thrown over heavy sweaters. It seems as though the only people who are out and about voluntarily are the hunters.

There are certain autumnal mornings in Loutses, just after dawn, with a cold mist hovering among the trees and spirals of woodsmoke drifting into the air from the houses of early risers, when every man in the valley seems to have gone out hunting. Grim-faced with masculine concentration, they prowl like ghosts through the olive groves, clutching their shotguns and staring keenly about for something to shoot. A law forbids them from firing within 200 metres of the last house in the village, but many see this as an unpardonable infringement of personal liberty and those who are unable to muster the energy for a real expedition sometimes take up position on their balconies, their expensive automatic shotguns aimed at the sky, ready for something feathered to come within range. It is rare that anything does.

However, down at Antinioti, the small lake where the fish are farmed, there are still a few wild duck to be had. They are cooked in a casserole and served in their rich thick gravy with either rice, chips or mashed potatoes. To get rid of the fishy flavour in their flesh, the inside of the bird is scorched with a lump of charcoal, or else half an apple and a celery root are secreted inside the carcass, to be removed halfway through the cooking.

 To make **Agriopapia salmi** (salmis of wild duck) you will need a duck, 150 ml (¼ pint, ⅔ cup) of oil, a large onion, a whole head of garlic, salt and pepper, 3 or 4 sprigs of parsley, 200 ml (7 fl oz, a generous ¾ cup) of white wine, 150 ml (¼ pint, ⅔ cup) of chicken stock and the juice of a large orange.
Pluck the duck, discarding all the offal and the head. Sear the inside with a charcoal ember or put half an apple and a celery root into the duck. Fry the whole duck in the oil in a large casserole on a low heat, turning it frequently until it is browned. Add the stock and the salt and pepper and simmer the duck on a low heat for half an hour, until nearly all the water has evaporated. Remove the duck, cut it into pieces and throw away the apple and celery. Chop the onion and garlic and fry them briefly in the fats in the casserole. Put the duck back in the pot and add the wine, orange juice and the chopped parsley. Leave it on a low heat to stew for between thirty and forty minutes until the liquids have reduced to a thick sauce.

The hunters of Loutses shoot for the pot. That this requirement encompasses species not eaten in England horrifies some visitors, but the criterion is culinary rather than aesthetic, and is undeniably logical. The mauve flesh of a grilled songthrush has a delicately perfumed flavour and the bird itself, it is pointed out, has no special right to an amnesty just because it sings. Corfiots are fond of the company of robins when working out of doors, but they used to eat them too. In the past rich farmers would send their hands out to trap the birds fifty at a time to make a *rouvellopitta*, a robin pie.

Birds that taste bad flourish around Loutses. Crows and magpies and sparrows are unmolested, hoopoes and all species of owl are protected, and the many varieties of swallow and swift are positively encouraged because they eat mosquitoes. There is one bird, however, that is rarely mentioned by hunters. Nobody has ever seen it and it is called simply '*striglo pouli*', the screaming bird. If anyone hears its call close to their house it means that a family member will die, but if the bird were to be shot and killed the curse would be lifted. Obviously no one has ever managed to do this or they would know what it looked like.

For most of the local hunters the favourite game is woodcock. They are well-flavoured but small and one needs several to make it worthwhile cooking them in a stew or a *rizatha*. The birds are served on slices of bread that have been fried in butter – an idea foreign to Corfiot cuisine. The notion may have been brought to the island in the Middle Ages, when the European habit was to use bread trenchers as plates.

 To make **Bikatsis krassatas**, (woodcock stewed in wine) you will need 4 woodcock, salt and mild paprika, 100 ml (3½ fl oz, a generous ⅓ cup) of oil, 1 large onion, 1 tablespoon of flour, 120 ml (4 fl oz, ½ cup) of red wine, and 3 large ripe tomatoes.
Pluck the woodcock and discard their heads. Remove the offal but keep the livers and hearts and chop them up very finely. Wash the birds, pat them dry and then rub a little salt and paprika into the inside cavities. Brown the woodcock slowly in the oil, then dust them with flour and fry them for two or three minutes more with the chopped offal. Pour on the wine and braise the birds until about half the liquid has evaporated. Grate the onion, peel and chop the tomatoes finely, and add them to the casserole with 150 ml (¼ pint, ⅔ cup) of water and some more salt and paprika. Let everything stew on a low heat or in a moderate oven until the woodcock are tender and the sauce thick. Serve them either on fried bread or with rice or macaroni. Fried wild mushrooms are considered the perfect garnish.

Just as the fishermen gaze greedily towards Albanian waters, so the hunters stare at the mountains of the mainland with undisguised longing. The reputation of Epirus and what is now southern Albania as a home for vast quantities of game is centuries old. Today a few of the most dedicated shots in Loutses make an annual trip to hunt in the hills of Epirus, but there is one man, though not a resident of the village, who ventures over into Albania in order to do a little shooting. He carries dozens of packets of coffee to bribe border guards and to offer as gifts to his friends across the frontier. He stays for a couple of days, and then hikes back to Igoumenitsa and the ferry for Corfu.

Some years ago a wild boar also managed to cross the iron curtain, and by a far more direct route. It had been cornered by huntsmen in Albania and driven down to the sea, but instead of standing at bay it jumped into the water and swam straight across to Corfu, coming ashore near Aghios Stefanos. Judging from the succession of local reports, it then made its way up into the mountains. Excitement among the guns was intense, but the animal was never seen again.

Twenty years ago the northern mountains of Corfu had abundant game. There were plenty of rabbits and hares in and around Loutses, and the trees were full of pigeon and woodcock. In those days, though, there were less than twenty guns in the village; now there are more than a hundred and the amount of wildlife in the area reflects the fact. The hares have disappeared, no one has seen a wild rabbit in Loutses for almost a decade, and as a result the animals that preyed upon them, foxes, eagles and jackals, have also dwindled in number – the last two are probably gone for good. Were it not for the fact that the bird population is largely migratory they would certainly have vanished too. The government attempts conservation measures from time to time, printing them on the back of hunting licences, and there are volunteer rangers in some areas of the countryside to make sure that these rules are enforced, but until some restriction on the sheer number of hunters is agreed upon things will not improve.

By mid-November the weather has settled down. The rain is steady, washing the summer's detritus down from the mountains to the sea, filling the villagers' cisterns in a few short weeks, and seeping up as damp into the walls of every building. Sunshine will be rare until the clear, cold days of January. The women, bundled up against the season, their fingers numb and aching, are out each day from the early morning until dusk, laying nets in the dripping olive groves. Diversions are few, and even those involving hard work are welcomed. Though by no means a holiday, except for Philip and his namesakes, 14 November represents one such break – at least for those families with a pig – for this is the traditional day of its slaughter.

In the past, when Loutses was a more self-sufficient community, winter brought a dramatic change of diet to the villagers. *Horta* was scarce and the variety of fresh vegetables dwindled. Hunting brought in game for those with guns but the fishing boats were taken out of the water until the following spring; most of the chickens that had kept the family supplied with eggs all year stopped laying and became eligible for the pot.

In those days every household of any size kept a pig, bought as a piglet in the spring and fattened over the summer on leftovers from the family table, the whey from *feta*-making, corn meal and *horta*. The animal was slaughtered by a professional butcher and its meat was packed into barrels or tins between layers of sea salt to be soaked and cooked when it was needed over the coming year.

Because of its harsh climate, its poor soil and the poverty of its population, meat has always been scarce in Greece. It is surprising therefore that the villagers made so little use of their pigs. Traditionally, the head would be boiled and made into brawn, and the liver, heart and kidneys were fried and eaten on the day of the slaughter, sprinkled with salt and pepper and vinegar, but the rest of the offal was thrown away. The villagers did not make their own salami or sausages or blood pudding as did their counterparts in Italy or even England. It was not a matter of squeamishness or laziness – the Loutsiotes use up every tiny scrap of offal from a lamb and relish the dishes they create from it – so much as a diffidence of taste. Old Tomas Vlahos's attitude that you don't miss what you never had may partly explain it, but the fact is Corfiots are not greedy for meat. In a country where sheep and goats are ubiquitous, and a roasted milk lamb is the hero of the feast, goat meat and mutton are actively disliked.

In the last few decades the animal population of the villages has declined in an exact ratio to a general increase in meat-eating. The reasons for this apparent anomaly are of course economic. Thirty years ago the family flocks of sheep and goats existed to provide milk and wool and to sacrifice an animal for the table was to jeopardize the meagre income of the household; these days the villagers can afford to patronize the butchers in Kassiopi or Corfu Town. However, the ways in which the Loutsiotes cook their meat have not kept up with the change in their fortunes. Recipes that evolved to stretch the extravagance of half a kilo of veal into a meal for the whole family, or to disguise some ancient hen whose laying days were over, are as popular now as they ever were.

The most beloved of them all is *pastitsatha*. The islanders consider it the best and most typical of all their specialities and the Loutsiotes never tire of it. When guests or relatives are entertained at home some version of it will often be at the centre of the meal both because of its delicious flavour and because, with a little imagination, what is really one dish can be made to seem like two.

At the heart of a *pastitsatha* is its sauce. The recipe begins as a pot roast, whether of a chicken or of a piece of beef or the yearling beef the Greeks call veal. The meat is cooked in a rich gravy and then removed and its place is taken by partly boiled pasta, which finishes its own cooking by absorbing the flavours of the gravy. At this point the pasta can be offered as a course in itself with the meat held back as an entrée, or the two can be combined on the same plate; or else, as is usually the case, platefuls of pasta can be set before the guests while the pieces of meat are put on to a plate in the centre of the table, next to the salads and the *feta*, to be shared when the pasta has been eaten.

Traditionally, and owing perhaps to the local habit of using only one cooking pot for a meal whenever possible, the gravy and the pasta are divided into portions before they are combined. If four people are dining, the cook leaves a quarter of the gravy in the pan and adds a quarter of the pasta, cooks it, serves it, and then returns to the stove to prepare the next plateful. This somewhat staggered arrangement is no more disconcerting to a Loutsiot than is the luke-warm temperature of the early portions when the conversation finally pauses for the eating to begin.

 To make **Pastitsatha** you will need either 1 large free-range chicken, or 1 kilo (2 lbs 2 oz) of veal or beef of any cut, though well-flavoured rump steak is perhaps the best, 200 ml (7 fl oz, a generous ¾ cup) of oil, 2 large onions, 2 or 3 cloves of garlic, salt and mild paprika, 3 cloves, a pinch of cinnamon, 1 kilo (2 lbs 2 oz) of ripe tomatoes, 120 ml (4 fl oz, ½ cup) of red wine, 1 tablespoon of wine vinegar, 2 bay leaves, plenty of grated *kephalotyri* or Parmesan, and 500 g (1 lb 1 oz) of pasta – either the thickest spaghetti, sold as number

6 in Greece, or the thinnest tubular macaroni, number 5. Divide the chicken into portions or cut the meat into a dozen large pieces and brown it in the oil. Grate the onions and add them to the meat. Wait a minute or two then add the finely chopped garlic. Peel and chop the tomatoes and when the onions are soft and the garlic is just beginning to brown, add them to the pan with 400 ml (14 fl oz, 1⅔ cups) of water and all the other ingredients, except the macaroni and the cheese. Let it simmer until the meat is well-cooked and tender, then remove it from the heat. Take the meat out of the sauce and set it to one side. Boil the pasta for five minutes less than is recommended by the advice on the packet and drain it thoroughly, then add it to the sauce and simmer it very slowly for five minutes, stirring continuously. Serve it with the grated cheese on top. The meat can be offered as a separate course or at the side of the same plate.

Pastitsatha is not, in the opinion of the villagers, a suitable fate for a hen bought from the freezer of one of the new supermarkets in Corfu Town. Tender and white though these chickens are, they are seldom found in a Loutsiot kitchen for the flavour of poultry is far more important to the villagers than its texture. The majority of households in Loutses still keep chickens. Vasiliki Sarakinou, whose husband Nikolas is a busy and prosperous farmer, has between twenty and fifty during the summer. She buys them from the lorries that come up to the village in the springtime, bearing crates of cheeping yellow chicks.

For the first few weeks, these new arrivals will be kept indoors, but when they have learned to come to her call in the evening to be fed and when they are big enough to defend themselves, at least against a cat, Vasiliki releases them to forage among the olive groves around the farm.

Surprisingly, perhaps, the villagers have considerable respect for chickens. They are by no means as confused a species as they appear to the passing motorist. Philip has twice seen a chicken attack and kill a snake, fluttering up as the snake strikes and then pecking down on its head. In an area where several people a year still die from the bite of the Mediterranean viper, chickens, like cats, are especially valued as a deterrent against snakes.

Vasiliki confesses to a certain fondness of her flock, particularly for those hens that produce plenty of eggs. She encourages them to lay in the wire coop in the farmyard where they spend the night, but inevitably many of them prefer to build their own nests under the trees. From twenty hens Vasiliki can expect between ten and twelve eggs a day during the summer and from time to time during the year she will let some of them hatch. Her daughter Maria is married to Spiro, the baker in Kassiopi, and Vasiliki gives the bakery those eggs she does not need herself. Her grandson has an egg for breakfast every day as most young children do, soft boiled and mashed into a glass with some crumbled bread, but it is always an egg from the day before, since it is considered unhealthy to eat one on the day it is laid.

Vasiliki kills a chicken when one is needed for the table, cutting its throat (not without some qualms) and plucking and cleaning it herself. She spares her best layers as long as she can, but a free-range chicken is very old if it should live to be much more than two, and even at a year they are too tough for roasting. Vasiliki is very fond of *pastitsatha* and most of her birds end up this way. Otherwise she will boil them simply and serve them with an *avgolemono* sauce, but once or twice a year she makes a *kotopitta*, a chicken pie.

Encased in *fyllo* pastry, filled with the chopped meat in a rich, firm sauce, *kotopitta* is eaten all over Greece, though some Loutsiotes think of it as a speciality from the largest of the Ionian islands, Cephalonia.

 To make **Kotopitta** you will need a well-flavoured chicken of about a kilo (2 lbs 2 oz), 3 onions, a generous litre (1¾ pints, 4 cups) of water, salt and plenty of white pepper, 2 tablespoons of fresh chopped parsley, 6 eggs, 50 g (1¾ oz) of semolina, 50 g (1¾ oz) of butter, 120 g (4¼ oz) of grated *kephalotyri* cheese (or Parmesan), 75 ml (½ fl oz, a scant ⅓ cup) of evaporated milk, and 14 leaves of *fyllo* pastry.

Boil the chicken in the water for a good hour. Remove it from the pan and take all the meat off the bones. Cut the meat into small pieces and set it aside. Into the stock (there should be about 300 ml (10½ fl oz, 1¼ cups) of liquid left in the pot), put the grated onions and the semolina. Stirring, bring the stock back to the boil and let it simmer for five minutes, then set it aside for half an hour to cool. Melt the butter in a saucepan and use a little to grease the bottom of a rectangular baking tin with sides at least ten centimetres deep. Following the directions for using *fyllo* described on p. 35 lie a leaf of *fyllo* in the bottom of the tin. Brush it with melted butter and lie another leaf on top. Repeat until there are eight leaves of *fyllo* in the tin. Separate the eggs and beat the whites until they are fluffy. Fold them into the cool stock with the yolks, the milk, parsley, salt and pepper, and most of the cheese. Stir in the chicken, then tip the mixture into the baking tin. Sprinkle the rest of the cheese on top and lie a leaf of *fyllo* over everything. Brush it with butter and lie on five more *fyllo* leaves, each one brushed with melted butter. Score the top three layers of *fyllo* with parallel lines to serve as a guide when cutting the pie later, sprinkle the top with a few drops of water to prevent the pastry shrinking too much and put the pie into a moderate oven for forty-five minutes, until the *fyllo* is golden. Let is stand for fifteen minutes before serving.

Kotopitta is a marvellous way of dealing with a chicken that might be rather tough, but younger birds can of course be roasted. In the winter when her hens stop laying, Maria Parginou, whose husband Stamati owns the *kafepantopoleion*, often prepares roast chicken, baking it in the oven of the woodstove in the kitchen next to the shop. It is a good stove and the oven is properly sealed so no woodsmoke ever taints what is cooking, but out in the courtyard the fragance of smouldering olive or almond logs mingles delectably with the aroma of chicken and garlic on a cold morning.

 The recipe for **Roast chicken** is simple. Maria cleans the bird and then splits it in two down the breastbone. She cuts a lemon in half and rubs the skin with it, then squeezes the juice over the meat. Then she makes three or four incisions in the skin and rubs into them a mixture of salt, black pepper and *rigani*. The joints are put into a baking tin in a quarter of an inch (1 cm) of oil and sprinkled again with the salt, pepper and *rigani*. Around them are scattered eight or nine peeled and split cloves of garlic and half a dozen potatoes, peeled and cut into large pieces.

The heat in the oven of a woodstove is very low. Maria will put a chicken prepared in this manner into her stove at nine and eat it at one, basting it occasionally during the morning, and turning the potatoes once or twice. It is served with plenty of the oil from the pan as a gravy, while the giblets are often fried or braised in a sauce as an impromptu *meze*.

Like Vasiliki, Maria buys her chicks from the lorry that comes up to the village once or twice a year. The tradesmen are for the most part gypsies – not the colourful families whose enormous brown canvas tents can be seen at the side of the road during the summer and whose women walk from house to house begging for money or oil with their babies in carpetbag slings, but the gypsies who actually live, in relative permanence, on the island.

Animal husbandry has always been their main occupation. In the thirteenth century they were encouraged to settle on Corfu by the Angevins who valued them as horsebreeders. They were given land to the north of the town as a small but comparatively autonomous fief, and they continued to use it and to live there, unmolested, for the next seven hundred years. Then, in the 1960s, the Colonels passed a law forbidding gypsies to stay for more than two days at a time on Corfu, since their presence, it was feared, might discourage tourism. Only when the Colonels fell from grace was the law revoked. Today the gypsies still deal in livestock – a few horses, donkeys which are brought to local centres like Peritheia in a lorry and auctioned, chickens and particularly turkeys. The turkey chicks also travel in crates on the back of a truck and many Loutsiotes buy five or six at a time to raise for the table. Less intelligent than chickens they are often restricted to an enclosure, but occasionally in the summer a cock escapes into the olive groves to terrorize passing children with his rainbow face and unearthly thrumming call.

The villagers eat turkey on special occasions throughout the year, roasting it or making it into a *pastitsatha*, and an increasing number now cook a turkey for Christmas, either boiled with *avgolemono* sauce if the bird is no longer young, or stuffed and roasted. The idea is not a new one but there are some families in Loutses who preserve the prejudice of their grandparents and dismiss it as an urban fad, preferring lamb on Christmas Day.

At the heart of the island of Corfu, protected on all sides by hills and mountains, is the plain of Ropa. The grass is deep and green, watered by the Ropa river and its tributaries, and the farmers who live there describe it, with some justification, as the best grazing land in Greece. At a time when beef was a rare import in the rest of the country, the Ropa valley supported herds of fat cattle, the cherished source of the sweet butter for which Corfu was famous. Then, during the 1970s, cattle farming and dairying on the island went into a dramatic decline. In 1972, when Philip was working for a dairy in Corfu Town, local herds produced 25,000 litres of milk; today, the figure has dropped to 8,000 litres a day.

Tourism has been entirely responsible for this decline, offering more lucrative employment, investment and land-use to the farmers – part of the Ropa valley is now a golf course – but since Greece's entry into the Common Market and the resultant availability of subsidies, some men are going back to cattle farming, even in the northern hills. In a valley beyond Akharavi a local farmer is breeding calves and selling them as yearlings for meat.

It is this yearling beef that is described by restaurateurs and anglo-phone butchers as veal, despite its mature flavour, texture and colour. It is a problem of translation rather than an attempt to deceive, for the pale pink, milk-fed veal of western cuisines is unknown on the island. There are other differences, too, between the traditional Corfiot butcher's shop and one in England or North America. The map of a cow on the wall shows divisions that correspond fairly accurately to French cuts – the names for *noix, filet,* and *contre-filet* are even transliterations – but in practice such distinctions become academic. The Corfiot butcher does not present prepared joints to his customers. Instead the housewife tells him exactly what she wants, often by pointing at the carcass hanging behind the counter, and watches with an eagle-eye while the meat is cut. To satisfy his regular clientele, a butcher is often obliged to extract some particularly lean half-kilo from the middle of the chuck or flank and if it is needed for a recipe requiring minced meat to put it through his machine several times until the texture is satisfactory.

Like *moussaka,* most of the minced meat recipes prepared on Corfu originated in eastern Greece, where they were devised to stretch a small amount of meat and to disguise the strong flavour of the mutton from a slaughtered ram or a ewe too old for breeding. On Corfu, however, cooks are far more likely to use minced beef or veal in such dishes, since it is cheaper and, to their minds, more palatable than mutton. Other than that, most of the recipes have remained unchanged since immigrants brought them from the mainland. An exception to this is the recipe for *keftedakia.* In other parts of the country *keftedakia* are sizeable patties of minced lamb, flavoured with *rigani* and thyme, but on Corfu they are no bigger than golfballs and the thyme has been replaced with fennel.

Up in her house on Zervou, Koula Parginou makes wonderful *keftedakia.* Her secret is to knead the ingredients into the mixture very throughly, one at a time. If she makes them late in the year when there is no fresh fennel, she uses the dried yellow flowers of the herb and adds a tablespoon of ouzo to fortify the flavour – a most successful improvisation.

To make enough **Keftedakia** (fried meatballs) to feed six, Koula uses a kilo (2 lbs 2 oz) of lean minced beef, 1 medium-sized onion, 4 cloves of garlic, 8 slices of *frigania* (dry toast), 2 thick slices of stale bread, 1 egg, 1 teaspoon of salt, 1 level tablespoon of fennel leaves or flowers, a pinch of mint, 2 generous tablespoons of *rigani*, black pepper, a tablespoon of ouzo, flour and (olive) oil for shallow frying.
Crush the *frigania* on to a plate until they are a heap of dry crumbs. Grate the onion into a large bowl and add the finely chopped garlic and the mince, then knead them together thoroughly. Add the crumbled *frigania*, the crumbled bread and the beaten egg and knead the mixture again. Add the fennel, mint, *rigani*, pepper, ouzo and salt one at a time, kneading vigorously for a minute or so after each addition to distribute them evenly through the mixture and to make sure it is sufficiently dough-like in texture. Now form the mixture into spheres the size of golf balls. Roll each one carefully in the flour and put them into a pan of hot oil to fry – when the pan is full the oil should cover two-thirds of each ball. Turn them often until they are brown. The surface of the *keftedakia* should be crisp and dark, the inside soft. Serve them hot with a little more salt and some lemon juice squeezed over the top. Koula also dribbles a little fresh oil over them.

Youvarlakia are very different from *keftedakia* – soft, lightly spiced rissoles made with minced beef or lamb and rice, that are braised in stock and served in a delicate *avgolemono* sauce. A more festive minced-meat creation, and one which conjures memories of Scotch Eggs in the hearts of English ex-patriates is *rolo apo kima*, mince roll. Something like a meat loaf, this *rolo* is rendered particularly rich by the sauce, which is baked into it.

To make a **Rolo apo kima** you will need 750 g (1 lb 10 oz) of minced beef, 1 egg, 1 large onion, 200 g (7 oz) of soft breadcrumbs, salt and black pepper, 1 tablespoon of finely chopped parsley, 200 ml (7 fl oz, a generous ¾ cup) of oil, 120 ml (4 fl oz, ½ cup) of red wine,

350 g (¾ lb) of tomatoes, 3 cloves of garlic, and 3 peeled and hard-boiled eggs.

Grate the onion, beat the egg and knead them very thoroughly with the mince, breadcrumbs, wine, salt, pepper and parsley and half the oil. Add a little more oil if the mixture is too dry to mould. Lie a large piece of greaseproof paper on the table, wet it slightly, and tip the mixture on to one half of the paper. Fold the other half over and press the mixture into a rectangular shape about three centimetres deep and broad enough to be wrapped around the eggs. Peel back the fold of paper and lay the hard-boiled eggs end to end along the middle of the meat. Roll up the paper so as to fold the meat mixture over the eggs and press the ends of the roll of meat together to seal them. Oil the paper and lie the whole thing on a greased baking tray. Put it into a hot oven for thirty minutes. Take the tray out of the oven and carefully peel off the paper. Pour half the remaining oil over the roll and put it back into the oven for twenty minutes more, or until it is brown, turning it once.

Make a sauce by stewing the peeled, crushed tomatoes, the crushed garlic, the remaining oil, 100 ml (3½ fl oz, a generous ⅓ cup) of water, salt and pepper together in a pan for ten minutes. Pour the sauce over the roll and return it to the oven for a further half an hour. Cut it into slices to serve, accompanied by rice, pasta or chips, and vegetables.

It is often claimed that Greeks eat more pasta than anyone else in the world – more even than the Italians. Certainly, if Loutses were to be chosen as representative for such an important survey, the question would be quickly answered, for *makaronia*, the word Greeks use for all varieties of pasta, is superceded only by oil, bread and wine in the diets of the villagers.

The Venetians brought pasta to Corfu, and it seems likely that the introduction took place at the lower levels of society, perhaps between the Italian garrison and that part of the population with whom they mixed, for the role of pasta in Greek cooking is central but also humble, and it is plausible to suppose that it was always so. The islanders took to it immediately and their enthusiasm soon spread to the rest of Greece. Somewhere along the way, though, the creative genius Italians bring to their pasta dishes was lost. Only certain recipes petrified into tried and trusted favourites.

Today Greeks treat pasta very much as the English once did, baking macaroni in the oven with a cheesy béchamel sauce, putting vermicelli into soups, and eating spaghetti either with a basic tomato sauce or unadorned except for salt and pepper, butter and cheese. In many households the only time butter is ever eaten is when it is allowed to melt among a bowlful of plain boiled pasta. At the head of this simple band, however, is a triumvirate of more exceptional recipes: *pastitsatha, yiouvetsi* and *pastitso*.

Pastitso is basically a pie of tubular macaroni, minced meat, cheese and béchamel sauce, baked in one of the deep, rectangular baking tins so indispensible to Greek cooks. Texture is everything with a *pastitso*. It is served in square or rectangular slices which should be able to stand unaided on the plate without collapsing into their constituent parts, but which should still be as light as possible. Venal or lazy restaurants use the alarming amounts of flour in their béchamel sauce as a kind of glue, but in this recipe of Philip's, the eggs, a sufficiently moist meat sauce, and a thorough packing of the various layers of the dish achieve a much better consistency and flavour.

 To make **Pastitso** for six people you will need 500 g (1 lb 1 oz) of minced beef or veal, 250 g (about 9 oz) of medium tubular macaroni, 100 g (3½ oz) of grated *kephalotyri* or Parmesan, 1 large onion, 120 ml (4 fl oz, ½ cup) of olive oil, salt, white pepper, 1 tablespoon of chopped fresh parsley, a pinch of *rigani*, 2 bay leaves, 1 carrot, 2 tablespoons of tomato paste, a large ripe tomato, and 2 eggs; and for the béchamel sauce, 2 eggs, 3 tablespoons of butter, 3 tablespoons of flour, 500 ml (17½ fl oz, 2 cups) of milk, a pinch of grated nutmeg, salt and white pepper, and 6 tablespoons of grated *kephalotyri* or Parmesan. Brown the mince in a dry, heavy pan, then add the oil, chopped onion, grated carrot, parsley, *rigani*, bay leaves, pepper, a little salt and 200 ml (7 fl oz, a generous ¾ cup) of water. Let it stew very slowly for about twenty minutes. Add the chopped tomato and the tomato paste and continue stewing for ten minutes more. Meanwhile boil and drain the macaroni. Take a deep-sided baking tray and moisten it with two tablespoons of oil, then tip the macaroni into the tray. Beat the eggs and pour them over the macaroni, sprinkle on the grated cheese, and then pour in half the mince mixture. Mix it thoroughly with the macaroni, then press them down into an even layer over the bottom of the tray. Pour on the rest of the mince and smooth it into a second layer. Make the béchamel sauce by stirring the flour into the melted butter, beating the egg into the milk and stirring it slowly into the butter until the sauce is smooth and creamy. Add the seasoning and the cheese and pour it over the top, sprinkling a few drops of water on to the sauce to prevent it browning too quickly. Put the *pastitso* into a moderate oven and bake it for forty minutes. Let it cool before serving.

There is a well-known restaurant in Corfu Town that offers yet another kind of meatball – or so it appears from the column of the menu that has been translated into English. Tourists ordering 'meatball' at this establishment will indeed be faced with something spherical, but it is smooth, dark brown, glossy and the size of a grapefruit – the whole braised spleen of a calf.

Dishes using calves' offal are popular throughout Greece, though they do not approach the inventiveness that is brought to bear upon the delicate lights of a lamb. Since classical times tripe in particular has been renowned all over the country as a settler of stomachs and as the best possible remedy against a hangover. It is cooked primarily in the winter in a soup called *patsa* that has a unique and rather viscous texture, similar to the English tripe and onions, but with its flavour cut by the addition of lemon juice or of *skorthostoupi*, garlic-vinegar.

Tripe must be thoroughly cleaned before it is cooked – both to rid it of any lingering taste of bile and also to achieve the snowy whiteness local gourmets insist upon. In Greece this is done at home rather than in the butcher's shop. Washing it thoroughly in the sink is the best way, but there are people who resort to a sprinkling of lime or even bleach to speed up the process, followed by a good rinsing – a method that is not recommended.

 To cook **Patsa** (tripe soup) for five or six people, you will need 1 kilo (2 lbs 2 oz) of tripe, 2 medium-sized onions, salt and white pepper, and either 2 lemons or *skorthostoupi* to add to the soup when it is served. On the mainland, 4 or 5 cloves of garlic are included in the recipe as well. Thoroughly clean the tripe and then cut it into finger-sized pieces. Immerse the tripe, the peeled whole onions and a generous amount of pepper in a large saucepan of water and simmer it slowly for five or six hours, adding more water as it is needed. By the end of the cooking there should be between 1 litre (1¾ pints, 4 cups) and a 1½ litres (2½ pints, 6¼ cups) of liquid in the pot. Add salt to taste for the last ten minutes of cooking and anoint each bowlful with lemon juice of *skorthostoupi* as it is served.

Ox or calves' tongue is a great deal more popular on Corfu than in the rest of Greece – another legacy, perhaps, of the superior grazing found on the island. Corfiots cook it in many ways – as a *stifatho*, a *yiouvetsi*, and in a number of sauces. In all cases the tongue must first be soaked for twenty-four hours in cold water, boiled in fresh water for at least two hours, trimmed and skinned before the recipe can proceed. Philip often prepares tongue, and the most interesting of his recipes for it is for *glossa latholemono*, tongue in oil and lemon sauce.

To make **Glossa latholemono** you will need an ox-tongue, 3 litres (5¼ pints, 12½ cups) of water, 2 onions, 250 g (about 9 oz) of celery, 250 g (about 9 oz) of potatoes, 250 g (about 9 oz) of carrots, salt and white pepper, 1 large juicy lemon, 250 ml (8¾ fl oz, 1 cup) of oil, and a good pinch of *rigani*.

Treat the tongue as suggested above, skimming any scum from the water as it comes to the boil. Put the boiled, skinned tongue into the three litres of fresh water with the halved onions, celery, carrots, salt and pepper and boil them for a further hour. Peel the potatoes, cut them into large pieces and add them to the stew; boil it for a further twenty minutes until the potatoes are soft. Remove the tongue and cut it into slices. Garnish the individual plates with the vegetables and pour the little juice remaining in the pan over them. Beat the oil, lemon juice and *rigani* together until they thicken, then pour this sauce over each portion.

Long before olives became the central industry of the region, long before Loutses even existed, the people of the hills bred lambs to sell. As recently as thirty years ago there were five thousand sheep in the area, and the lambs of the region were famous for their tender, well-flavoured meat; now there are perhaps a thousand. One or two shepherds still tend flocks of a hundred or so up in the mountains, but the rest belong to individual farms and households, kept in groups of between two and twenty. Maria Parginou, whose husband Stamati runs the *kafepantopoleion*, owns a typical number: seven ewes and a ram.

Every day Maria rises early, at dawn in the summer, an hour after first light in the winter, and walks up the road from the shop to the land where she keeps them. The pasture is rented and in return for its use, Maria clears it and looks after the trees and fences and the fold where her sheep sleep in the winter. They are restless after the long night, especially those ewes that have milk but no lambs, and Maria's first job is to milk them, sitting on a low stool in the cold morning air. The ewes come to her and she is finished with each one in less than five minutes, then she leads them off through the trees to pasture. In the evening she returns for them and brings them back to the fold to be watered and milked again.

The lambs are born between December and January and the ewes give birth without her help, unless she happens to be with them at the time. Occasionally the newborn have strange deformities such as missing ears, but a more serious problem arises when a ewe gives birth to two or even three young. A ewe will have only enough milk for one lamb and so Maria has to bring the twin home to the shop where she keeps it in the *apothiki* in a cardboard box stuffed with straw and rags, and she feeds it from a bottle. Maria invariably becomes fond of these nurselings and they grow deeply attached to her, sniffing her jumper and crying when she leaves the room; when they rejoin the flock a little of the bond remains.

The women who keep sheep in Loutses do so for the milk, for the wool and for the commercial value of the lambs themselves, rather than for meat. A healthy ewe produces between half a kilo and a kilo of milk daily and will do so from lambing time in December until April. The villagers do not drink the milk – they prefer the taste of goat's milk – but they turn it into *feta* cheese, both for their own table and to sell.

The process of cheese making can be an almost continual one during the winter and spring. Every afternoon Maria strains two kilos of milk into a large metal saucepan and brings it very slowly to the boil, before transferring it into a plastic container to cool. She takes a Greek coffee-cup of cold water and stirs in a quarter of a teaspoon of *pitia*, the powdered rennet she sells in the shop. Then she adds this to the milk and leaves it for two hours while the curds sink to the bottom of the container and the whey rises to the top. Pouring off the whey, she then cuts the curds with a spoon and puts them into a muslin cloth she calls a 'chandilly', which she hangs from the ceiling over a pan. By the next morning, the last of the whey has drained through the cloth and the curds are ready to be formed into a brick of cheese. Maria does this by hand, patting the curds into a cuboid, sprinkling each side with a tablespoon of coarse salt, and patting it again.

The cheese is then put into a special wooden box, made for the purpose by a carpenter in the village. Two feet long, six inches wide and deep, the box is divided inside by two wooden partitions, each of which has a notch cut into its bottom. The new cheese goes into one of the end compartments which has a small hole for liquid to drain out, for the salt will draw moisture from the *feta* in the days to come. On the second day, Maria takes the cheese out, rolls it in salt, and puts it into the second compartment while a new brick of *feta* goes into the first. On the third day, both are moved up a compartment and a third cheese fills the box. The salty whey, called *armi*, that drains out of the box is kept to put into the large tin, the *teneki*, with the blocks of *feta* and brine. A stone on a block of wood supplies constant pressure during the weeks it takes to fill the tin.

Feta will keep in its brine for a year. The younger the cheese the milder its taste, and opinions differ about when it is at its best – Philip says after two months. Very new *feta*, washed under the tap to reduce its saltiness, can be marvellously creamy, while a cheese that has been maturing in a tin for twelve months has a strength and vigour to match that of a stilton. There is even a *feta* made elsewhere in Greece called *feta fotias* (fire-*feta*) with a flavour so powerful it seems to burn the tongue. The taste of the cheese also varies according to the diet of the sheep. If the ewes have been grazing in the olive groves and have eaten too many fallen olives, their milk and therefore the *feta* can taste unpleasantly bitter, so when she can Maria prefers to pasture her small flock beneath almond trees. In her opinion cheese made earlier in the year is superior because the ewes' milk is naturally richer.

The very first milk of the season from the ewes is not used for *feta* at all but for a special *tyropitta*, a cheese pie that in flavour and texture is more like the most delectable custard, since it has no crust or pastry at all and is made with fresh unsalted curds.

 To make **Tyropitta**, Maria strains about three litres (5¼ pints, 12½ cups) of the milk through muslin to remove any impurities, then she gently heats it in a heavy saucepan until it is hand-hot. Just as if she were making cheese, she pours the milk into the plastic container and stirs in a quarter of a teaspoon of rennet, then leaves it for three hours to separate. She drains off the whey then transfers the curds to a different bowl and sets about breaking them up with her fingers. Then she sifts in about 250 g (8¾ oz) of self-raising flour, and because she likes her *tyropitta* sweet, about 100 g (3½ oz) of sugar.

In yet another bowl, she separates two eggs (Maria Vlahos uses four in her recipe), beating the whites until they are fluffy and then folding them into the beaten yolks. These she folds into the curds, sometimes adding a pinch of powdered cinnamon or a tablespoon of finely chopped orange peel for flavour.

The pie will be baked in a *rihia*, the large, round, flat-bottomed pan with sides seven or eight centimetres deep, that must first be warmed in the oven and then moistened with olive oil. Maria pours the mixture into it and lets it stand for a few hours so that it can further solidify, then she bakes it in a low oven for about an hour, until the top of the custard is golden. If she has included no cinnamon in the mixture, she now sprinkles a little on top, then she lets it cool. The *tyropitta* is surprisingly solid, especially if it has stood for an hour or so after baking, and its taste lies somewhere in the Elysian hinterland between home-made egg custard and clotted cream.

Feta is the only cheese made in the village, though sometimes the recipe is varied by the addition of a little goat's milk. Less fat than the milk of ewes, its inclusion results in a firmer cheese.

Goats themselves are not as popular on Corfu as they are in southern Greece, where the hot, dry climate is so well-suited to the animals. Even the pale, sweet, turkey-flavoured flesh of a milk-kid roasted whole upon a spit will draw no crowds. In Loutses goats are kept for their milk and the one or two kids each nanny bears every spring are slaughtered. Their hides are sold on the coast to be turned into handbags and tourist souvenirs, while their carcasses end up in the butcher's shop – though if local demand for the meat is too low even for that they will be sold on the mainland. Philip is not particularly fond of kid, but there is a restaurant near Athens that he sometimes visits where it is prepared so well as to be irresistible.

The place is out in the country and so high in the mountains that the air is cold even in summer, and customers hoping to get there must use a Land Rover or a van to negotiate the steep tracks. The owner, Ianni, keeps large numbers of goats and sheep in the fields around his establishment and his speciality is *arni* or *katsikaki sti stamina*, lamb or kid cooked in an amphora-like clay pot. Raw meat, potatoes and herbs are stuffed into the pot which is then sealed with wet clay and put into the embers, completely covered by glowing charcoal. Five hours later the pot is broken and the contents tipped out on to a plate. The meat is fantastically tender, deeply permeated by the fragance of thyme, *rigani* and rosemary, and well worth the trip into the mountains.

Arni sti stamina is not cooked on Corfu, and neither is *kleftiko*, 'thieves' meat', the traditional meal of bandits and resistance fighters in which the meat of a lamb was rolled in garlic and herbs, wrapped in the hide of the animal and buried underground in a pit of glowing charcoal so that no smoke or smell gave away the location of a hideout. Corfiots do, however, cook *yiouvetsi*, a delicious combination of meat and the smallest of all the varieties of pasta stocked by the shops on the island: the tiny seeds that look like slightly flattened grains of rice and that on Corfu are called *orzo* or *sporo* or *manestra*, or sometimes *kritharaki*.

Like *pastitsatha*, the point of a *yiouvetsi* is to insinuate the delicious juices and gravy of a piece of meat into the accompanying pasta, but in this case the initial cooking is done in the oven. The meat remains in the baking pan after the *orzo* has been added, unless everything is to be transferred into several individual *yiouvetsi* pots, the small earthenware bowls which give the recipe its name.

Since the meat carries most of the responsibility for the flavour of the dish, it might be a good idea to marinate it beforehand, perhaps in a mixture of oil, lemon juice, crushed garlic, *rigani* and pepper; this marinade could then be used as the liquid in which to bake the meat.

Lamb is the traditional meat cooked in a *yiouvetsi*, but it is excellent with kid or beef. Neither of these is as fat as lamb, however, so a little more oil will be needed in the baking pan. On Corfu *yiouvetsi* is also made with ox or calves' tongue, though the meat can be too bland for some tastes.

 To make **Yiouvetsi** for six people you will need about 1 kilo (2 lbs 2 oz) of lamb (either the leg or the shoulder), 75 ml (2½ fl oz, ⅓ cup) of olive oil, the juice of 1 large lemon, 3 cloves of garlic, 1 tablespoon of *rigani* or a mixture of *rigani* and fresh mint, salt and black pepper, 1 onion, 1 kilo (2 lbs 2 oz) of ripe tomatoes, 400 g (14 oz) of *orzo* pasta (see above), 100 g (3½ oz) of grated *kephalotyri* or Parmesan or 6 thin slices of *feta* cheese.

Cut the lamb into small cubes and marinate it in the oil, lemon juice, garlic, herbs and pepper for about six hours, then transfer the whole thing to a baking pan. Peel all the tomatoes except one and put them into the pan, sprinkling everything with salt. Bake the lamb in an oven set at 220°C (425°F, Gas mark 7) for forty-five minutes, occasionally turning the meat, then stir in 1½ litres (2½ pints, 6¼ cups) of water, breaking up the tomatoes as you do so, and bake it for a further fifteen minutes. Take the pan out of the oven and stir in the pasta. If you have proper *yiouvetsi* pots, divide the *yiouvetsi* between them (if not, use the pan) and put it back into the oven for forty minutes, stirring once, until the liquid has been absorbed by the pasta. The finished *yiouvetsi* should be moist and slippery but without any actual liquid remaining. Garnish it with a sprinkling of grated cheese or a slice of *feta* and a slice of tomato.

A simple and old-fashioned, everyday way of cooking any cut of beef, or indeed any kind of poultry or meat except kid, is to boil it and then serve it with rice and an *avgolemono* sauce. Such a dish is deliberately bland and those who are not such devotees of the simple flavour of the sauce often begin by sautéing the meat in a little oil and then add other vegetables to the stewing meat – carrots or spinach, or endives or artichokes if the meat used is lamb, and nearly always onions.

The archetype of all such recipes, both for its delicate flavour and pale appearance is a fricassee (in the original, general meaning of the name) of baby lamb and leafy cos lettuces, often prepared at Eastertime, and known on Corfu simply as *frikase*.

To make **Frikase** you will need 1 kilo (2 lbs 2 oz) of the boned meat from an unweaned lamb (shoulder or leg are the best cuts), about 24 spring onions, 120 ml (4 fl oz, ½ cup) of oil, 1 tablespoon of cornflour, 1 kilo (2 lbs 2 oz) of cos lettuces (types of lettuce with firm white leaves will not do), salt, white pepper, plenty of fresh chopped parsley and dill weed, and for the *avgolemono* sauce 2 eggs and 1 or 2 lemons, depending on the degree of astringency preferred. Cut the meat into four or five large pieces and let it begin to fry in the oil in a large, shallow pan. After three or four minutes, before the meat begins to brown, add the trimmed spring onions and fry them until they are soft but again not brown. Stir the flour into the oil and let it fry for a minute, then stir in a generous litre of water. Add the herbs and seasoning and let everything stew, covered, for half an hour. If using a shoulder of lamb, there may be too much fat on top of the liquid in the pan for the *avgolemono*

sauce to be as good as it should be, so spoon out a little. Cut out the hearts of the lettuces and eat them as a salad. If the leaves are large cut them in half and put them into the pan with the lamb, moving the meat to one side so that the lettuce has the benefit of the liquid. Cover the pan again and let it stew over a very low heat for at least an hour more, until the meat is very tender and the liquid almost gone. Remove the pan from the heat and let it stand for five minutes then make the *avgolemono* sauce. Strain off six tablespoons of the liquid into a bowl. Separate the eggs and beat the whites for a minute, then fold them into the beaten yolks. Beat in first the lemon juice then the liquid from the pot, one tablespoon at a time. Pour this sauce back over the meat and set the pan on a very low flame for two minutes, shaking the pan continuously. Let the sauce thicken but on no account allow it to return to the boil. Remove the pan from the heat, leave it covered for five minutes and then serve up the *frikase*.

The milk, cheese and wool from a sheep have always been of more value to the villagers than the meat, especially of a ewe with a record of producing good lambs which could be sold in the market in Corfu Town. To slaughter a lamb was to destroy a proportion of the family's income, and it was therefore only for some momentous occasion such as a wedding or christening, or for Easter, the most important event of all in the Greek calendar, that such an indulgence could be permitted.

It can be difficult for foreigners to appreciate how much Eastertime matters to the Greeks. In some ways the feelings it engenders can be compared with the shared emotions of an old-fashioned, pre-commercial Christmas in the west, but the analogy is not really good enough. The Passion, after all, is a very different series of events to the Nativity, and the Greeks continue to take the drama and its implications very seriously: for the substantial majority the religious significance of Easter informs every action during Holy Week. Even those who make a conscious effort to live outside the influence of the Church are drawn into the spirit of things, for it is also in some mysterious way a time of patriotism – a time to take pride in traditions that are quintessentially Greek.

In Loutses all the culinary events of Easter centre around the lamb. Traditionally it was slaughtered at eleven o'clock on Saturday night, when the church bells ring, but these days it is just as likely to be killed in the morning, either by the man of the house, or by a neighbour expert in such things. It will take him about half an hour to kill, eviscerate and skin the lamb. The carcass is taken indoors to a larder or to the *apothiki* to be hung, the fleecy hide is stretched on a cross of two sharpened bamboo sticks and left in the sunshine to dry – it will later be pressed under a mattress and used as a rug – and the entire offal is carried into the kitchen. A little of the lamb's blood is used to paint a cross on the front door of the house.

Almost everyone (except Philip) goes to church on Saturday night, standing packed around the sepulchre that has been decorated by the unmarried girls of the village with gorgeous flowers, and involving themselves in a service that represents Orthodoxy at its most visually dramatic. Just before midnight the lights in the church are extinguished to represent the darkness of the tomb. Then the priest lights his candle from the eternally burning altar flame and announces that Christ is risen – *Christos Anesti*. '*Alithos Anesti*' – 'Truly, He is risen', answers the congregation, then they light their own candles from the priest's and as the bells ring they leave the church. In Corfu Town those who have remained at home throw something breakable out of the highest window of the house to spite Satan and to curse the Jews who crucified Christ; in the village, though, midnight is marked by a procession of the children, all in white and carrying lavishly beribboned candles. While their proud parents look on, they walk down the steep path from the church to the main street of the village. Everyone hugs and kisses everybody else and then the families go home to begin their celebrations.

At the heart of these festivities, in households all over Greece, will be a dish called *mayiritsa*. It is made from the organs of the lamb that was slaughtered that morning (except for the kidneys which are considered to have an unpleasant flavour) and technically it is the first meat anyone will have eaten since the Carnival week before Lent, a month and a half before.

In other parts of the country, *mayiritsa* is made with so much liquid that it amounts to being a soup, or in some homes the ever-popular *avgolemono* sauce is added at the end of cooking, but the Loutsiotes prefer to reduce the liquid in the recipe to a thick gravy and to finish with the addition of lemon juice. This, with the plentiful amounts of herbs in the recipe, helps to conceal any bitterness inherent in the offal. To foreign eyes, the intestines, so apparent on the plate, can be somewhat disconcerting, but those with the courage to taste will be pleasantly surprised.

To make **Mayiritsa** you will need the liver, heart, spleen, stomach and intestines of 2 milk-lambs, a kilo (2 lbs 2 oz) of onions, 5 garlic bulbs or 3 cloves of garlic, 3 heaped tablespoons of a mixture of fresh fennel leaves, dill weed, mint, parsley and *rigani*, 4 tablespoons of oil, salt and white pepper, 2 lemons and water.

First clean the intestines. Cut them into two or three long pieces and, holding a piece tightly at one end, squeeze out whatever may be inside by pulling the intestine through two fingers. Hold the intestine under a tap and run first cold then warm water through it. Cut it into two inch lengths. Chop the other organs into small pieces. Grate the onions and chop the garlic finely then fry them in the oil until they are golden. Chop the herbs and add them to the onions with the offal and the seasoning. Let everything fry for a few minutes until it threatens to stick, then add 400 ml (14 fl oz, 1¾ cups) of water and let it stew for about an hour and a quarter until the liquid has reduced to a thick gravy. Squeeze the lemons over everything and serve it at once.

A good *mayiritsa* is an unforgettable experience, especially in the excited atmosphere of a Greek kitchen so late at night, surrounded by cheese, salad, bread and wine, but it is not the only recipe known to the villagers when it comes to the offal of their lambs. The countryman's disinclination to waste anything from the sacrifice has produced other traditions. A taste still remains amongst the older villagers, for example, for *horthi* – sausages that are made entirely from the peritoneum and large and small intestines of the lamb, seasoned with salt and white pepper, and grilled on Sunday as an appetiser to the lamb itself. For those intending to enjoy *horthi* next day a *mayiritsa* is out of the question, since it uses up the intestines, so in its place a different dish is made for the midnight feast, a pie (made without pastry) of herbs and the chopped lamb's liver and lungs, all bound together by eggs, rice and cheese.

A third alternative are *hgardoubes*. Though they are not really sausages, since the contents are whole pieces of offal, *hgardoubes* look as if they are as they emerge golden and sizzling from the oven.

 To make **Hgardoubes** all the lights of a lamb are cut into finger-sized pieces, two or three of which are then laid side by side with a whole spring onion, and the little parcel is bound tightly with the rinsed intestines. The outside of each is seasoned with herbs and lemon juice and they are roasted in a moderate oven for an hour.

To a few old men in the village these dishes have remained the indispensible highlights of Easter, but in most homes, particularly if the family has been swelled by visiting relatives, the offal of the Easter lambs will be made into *kokoretsi*. *Kokoretsi* can only be cooked on a spit and is therefore grilled simultaneously with the main roast and eaten as an hors-d'œuvre, though since its salty, spicy flavour encourages drinking, it is also a regular *meze* in the tavernas, and in the few remaining restaurants on the island that offer traditional dishes.

Greek butchers sell the still-connected innards of lambs as a complete item, hanging them from large hooks in the windows of their shops around Eastertime, so that city-dwellers can make *mayiritsa* and *kokoretsi* without buying a whole lamb. In other countries where the more esoteric organs of the animal are harder to come by or not eaten at all, one could barbecue a sort of *kokoretsi* using just the lamb's pluck (the heart, liver and lungs) and the kidneys, though some Greeks find them unpalatable, and intestines.

 To make a traditional **Kokoretsi** you will need 1½ kilos (3¾ lbs) of the liver, lungs, heart, spleen and thyroid of a lamb (or a calf), 1 kilo (2 lbs 2 oz) of intestines, plenty of salt, mild paprika and *rigani*, and at least 3 lemons. If using calves' lights, which are less fatty than lamb, local cooks include a little of the white fat from inside the animal, wedged between the pieces of offal.

Clean the intestines as for *mayiritsa* and set them aside. Cut the other offal into large pieces as thick as a man's wrist. Thread them compactly on to a spit, alternating them as much as possible. Rub the *rigani* to a powder in a bowl and mix it well with the salt and paprika. Sprinkle the spitted offal generously with this mixture, saving a little for the outside of the *kokoretsi*, then bind the whole thing twice with the intestines, as if cross-gartering, knotting the intestines at both ends to secure the construction. Set the spit over the charcoal and grill it for two and a half hours if it is thin, or for up to four hours if its diameter approaches four inches (10 cm), starting at a comparatively cool position high up on the *rôtisserie*, then gradually bringing it down to where the heat is stronger. The outside of the *kokoretsi* must be brown and well-done by the time it is eaten, the inside must also be thoroughly cooked. Slip the *kokoretsi* off the spit, and cut it into thin slices. Squeeze plenty of lemon juice over each slice and serve it with fresh white bread.

Easter is better in the countryside. Whether or not this is an unconscious return to the most ancient pre-Christian festivities – for the seasons are changing and the island is at its most beautiful – or just that a Greek party belongs out of doors, Easter is the time for relatives living in the town or even abroad to make the effort to return to the villages and reaffirm their roots.

On Easter Sunday morning, Loutses seems positively crowded. The lanes and street are blocked by the cars of visiting families. For the devout there is church again and for others there are the shops and the bar where friendships can be renewed and old jokes reiterated. Swarms of children scamper everywhere, ignoring warnings to keep their best clothes clean.

In the houses the kitchens are hives of industry as the women get the great meal ready for the afternoon. Some of it has been prepared beforehand – plates of *koulouria Paschalina*, Easter biscuits, stand next to pinnacles of eggs, hard-boiled on Good Friday and dyed the darkest of crimsons in memory of Christ's blood – but there are still salads, especially lettuce salads, to make, chips to cut and pilafs to season.

The centrepiece of the day, the lamb itself, is not in the kitchen but outside in the garden with the man of the house. The traditional way of roasting a whole lamb at home, as opposed to on the enormous brazier in a taverna, was to dig a pit on a sheltered piece of land near the house. Very early on Sunday morning, the host of the Easter gathering would kindle a fire of olive boughs in the pit. After a couple of hours the embers, fortified by the addition of charcoal, were raked together and the lamb, impaled on the long spit called a *souvla*, was set above them. The family and guests would remain close to the fire, picking at *kokoretsi* and *hgardoubes* and turning the spit, their arms strengthened by copious amounts of wine and much singing. As the lamb cooked, it too was sampled until there was nothing left but bones.

Many families still follow the tradition though the meal itself has become more formal. Down in Koulouri, the small valley at the end of Zervou, Spiros Vlahos and his son have invited friends, neighbours and relatives from Peritheia and Akharavi up for the day and have dug their pit into the hillside behind the kitchen window. Spiro keeps no lambs himself, so he bought two from a neighbour and killed them himself the day before. This morning he washed the carcasses thoroughly and prepared the two other ingredients: a bowl of salt, black pepper and *rigani* rubbed to powder, and a bowl of oil and lemon juice, diluted with a little water. Before the lambs were spitted he rubbed them inside and out with lemon juice and the seasoning, then he sewed up the neat incision he had made in the belly of the animals with butcher's thread, doing the same for the cut in the back from where the kidneys were taken. Each spit passes right through the lamb, emerging through the head, and the forelegs are bound to the torso. The hind legs are brought up behind and secured around the spit by forcing one of them between the bone and tendon of the other. Four hours before a roughly estimated lunchtime, Spiro mounts the lambs and a plump *kokoretsi* above the glowing charcoal.

They begin their cooking about two feet above the embers – far enough to allow the heat to penetrate the lamb without scorching it. A sheet of metal has been propped up behind the pit to direct the heat upwards and to block the light morning breeze, but almost immediately the air is suffused with the marvellous aroma of roasting meat and herbs. After an hour or so Spiro moves the spits down to a lower support on the stanchions. By the end of the morning the lambs have descended to no more than a foot above the charcoal which has been raked into piles below the rump and shoulders, for the head and torso are thin and need less cooking. The whole point of the exercise is to roast them very slowly but thoroughly, until the meat shrinks and threatens to separate from the bones; frequent basting with a bunch of *rigani* dipped into the oil and lemon juice mixture and the natural fattiness of the meat keeps the skin from burning.

All morning long the party has been quietly gathering momentum under the influence of Spiro's dry, golden wine and the sheer pleasure of the bright spring weather. Tables have been pushed together and covered with dazzling white cloths on the broad veranda outside the house, and Spiro's elderly relatives are already sitting there, watching their grandchildren tear about the property. Beyond the fence, the hills cascade down to the sea which glitters the deepest of blues in the clear air, and across the water the mountains of godless, Marxist Albania seem close enough to touch.

At last the lambs are ready and the party gathers to the table. The *kokoretsi* appears, sliced on to three large platters and already moist with lemon juice, closely followed by the lamb, cut roughly into large pieces that are piled on trenchers in the middle. Fragrant with *rigani* and its own natural perfume, the meat is still succulent despite its long cooking. Spiro has split the lamb's heads neatly down the middle and the four senior guests are each given half, but they are as enthused with the holiday spirit as any of the children and share the tastiest morsels with everyone. Plates of bread, lettuce salad, sliced cucumber and tomatoes, *feta* and fried potatoes are passed around and there is Spiro's own wine to drink. The meal will last for hours in the carefree, informal atmosphere of the warm afternoon. Only when the day begins to fade and the air to grow cool will the family carry the party indoors, leaving the evening to the swallows.

🍇THE TAVERNAS

It was Erakles who came to the door, and from the look on his face it was clear that I was not expected. A week before, he had met me wandering about the remote hamlet above Peritheia where he lives with his wife Sofia and his mother, and had asked me, a stranger, into his home for coffee. There had been talk of a house he had for sale and later in the conversation he suggested this dinner. Perhaps the invitation had been rhetorical – certainly he now seemed bemused by the fact that I had taken him literally – but in seconds he recovered his *élan*. Grinning and slapping my back, he led me into the parlour.

It was not the formal sitting-room of the house, but a part of the kitchen, separated from the actual cooking area by an open archway. A man from another village who was introduced as Sofia's brother was sitting at the large round table in the centre, while his wife and three-year-old son sat on a sofa, shelling almonds with the help of Erakles' mother. The old lady at least remembered the invitation and beamed reassuringly whenever I looked at her. I was given a chair at the table and a beaker of brandy and, while his brother-in-law engaged me in polite conversation, Erakles returned to his cooking.

Dominating the room was an enormous half-domed fireplace sunk deep into a wall and raised a foot and a half from the floor, and it was there that Erakles was preparing the evening meal. An olive root so big that my arms could not have reached around it was burning in the centre of the flagstone hearth and Erakles had to sprinkle it with water whenever the flames became too ferocious. He had raked some of the embers from the root to the front of the fireplace and had set a small and very old, four-legged grill over them upon which were sizzling four steaks and two tiny birds – a thrush and a sparrow-hawk – that his brother-in-law had shot that morning. On the table lay half a dozen wild *stefanitis* mushrooms, the biggest the size of a side-plate, that Sofia had found while working in the olive groves.

I had already been there half an hour when Sofia herself came in. She had just finished tidying the olive nets she would lay next day and was not expecting company. Her hand went to her hair and she listened to my muddled apologies: the telephone lines had been down for a week following a storm and I had been unable to confirm my invitation. Later I heard her remonstrating in the kitchen with a merry Erakles – not about my being there, but because no one had warned her in advance so that she could provide the hospitality she thought appropriate. She came back in and looked me in the eye. 'I didn't know you were coming, you know. This is not the meal I would normally like to offer to a stranger.'

Erakles was sent out into the night and returned with a bunch of carrots, just pulled from the wet, red soil, and a small, firm cabbage. While he shredded them into a salad the family photographs were brought out for my inspection and I was given a bowl of almonds and another brandy. Little Yorgo romped on the sofa to the delight of his old *yiayia*.

Soon Erakles judged the steaks to be ready. He took a lemon of the year's first crop from a basket that stood on the windowsill, and squeezed it into a bowl. Into this he stirred a generous measure of oil, a dash of water, some salt and pepper and a three-fingered pinch of *rigani*, then he dipped each sizzling steak into the liquid, put them all into the bowl and set it on the table. Sofia brought in the salad on a fine china platter, garnished with a sliced green pepper and plenty of soft, black olives and dressed with oil, salt and a few drops of vinegar. She returned for the mushrooms which she had sliced, rolled in salted flour and fried in oil and which now lay carefully arranged, golden and grey, on another china serving plate. A tin of anchovy fillets was opened, dressed with oil on a plate and put beside two plates of fried eggs – two for me, four between everybody else. The meal was completed with bread – a new loaf that Sofia held in the crook of her arm and cut into doorsteps, and one from the day before that Erakles sliced and grilled over the embers, making toast that was smoky, rock-hard and absolutely delicious. Erakles distributed the meat. There was steak for everyone, he took the hawk, and the thrush was given to me, with a hearty – and Italian – '*Buon' appetito*'.

Muscular and youthful, with a debonair moustache, Erakles led the evening's conversation from start to finish, laughing and joking and helping me out with my Greek. Just before the meal he had peeled a head of garlic and arranged the cloves on a plate with half a dozen fiery pickled chillies. Between each mouthful he popped one or other into his mouth, chasing them down with the new home-made wine – his sure-fire remedy against winter colds. The hawk he ate whole, crunching and swallowing the tiny bones, but not before he had given me some of the breast. It was delicious, with the gamey taste of pheasant and the firm texture of grouse. The steaks too were very good – stone cold but tender and infused with the flavour of the fire. Only the anchovies had tempted no one and lay untouched amongst the empty dishes.

Sofia and her sister-in-law cleared the table and then brought in bowls of hot chestnuts which they had roasted on a tin plate over the gas stove. The women sat on the sofa with Yorgo while we three men remained at the table, eating the nuts and drinking the purple wine; then the television was switched on for the news, each item of which inspired vigorous conversation. I asked Sofia if she wouldn't like some nuts herself. She laughed, stood up and joined us at the table – though whether her 'Thank you very much' was delighted or ironical I could not tell.

At around ten Yorgo was led away to a bedroom to rest, but he soon returned, worried about vampires. His *yiayia* took him on her knee, pulled out one of his hairs and made him hold it, then made the sign of the cross with his hand. Now he would be safe. Soon afterwards the party broke up. Erakles walked me out to my car and stood smiling in the rain until the tail-lights disappeared amongst the trees.

> Alkinoos: 'I confess we are not great fighters with our fists . . . but we love eating and harp-playing and dancing and changes of clothes: and hot baths and our beds.'
>
> from the *Odyssey*.

Older than the vampire, invisible and vague even in the bedtime stories the *yiayia* tells her grandchildren, is a spirit called the *Moro*. Every mountain village on the island has a *Moro*, and though the adults of Loutses dismiss the whole idea as nonsense, there are many who will nonetheless shy away from discussing it, lest in doing so they summon the ghost. Lights are left on all night, and radios play non-stop in the bedrooms of some who live alone, because of the *Moro*. It has no shape or form, but it haunts lonely places and preys upon the solitary, driving them mad.

There is something in the Greek character that abhors solitude. In folklore, where such traits are refined to specifics, this anxiety created the *Moro* as a warning; in their language the Greeks express their distrust of deliberately antisocial behaviour by labelling the notion of 'privacy' as either *idiotikos* or *mystikos*. Sociability is a national characteristic, and the intrusion of the modern world into communities like Loutses has barely changed the old traditions. The *kafeneion* and *kafepantopoleion* flourish, the love of parties and of party politics is as strong as ever, and no one is alone on a summer night.

That food should be a part of the conviviality is scarcely surprising. Greeks together must drink, and when drinking they must eat. In traditional households, however, this rarely means sharing a formal meal. There are exceptions: at christenings and weddings the guests will sit down for a real feast; but at a lesser celebration such as the name day of a family member, the food provided will be an impressive selection of *mezethes*, dainties and delicacies that may involve just as much work as a full meal, but which are eaten informally. At lunchtime, trays of them will be set out on the table for the gathered relatives and close friends, while well-wishers passing by later can expect *kourabiethes* and a liqueur.

At other times, any visitor – whether a friend, a stranger or even a casual employee hired to mend a broken fence – will be offered a drink and something to eat with it as a matter of course, but in the most old-fashioned homes only relatives will share the family meal.

Thirty years ago the distinction was clearer, and its economic origins more obvious. In those days, too, a visitor was greeted with a coffee or a drink and a small plate of something sweet or savoury to eat. A *meze* could be accepted with gratitude and a clear conscience, but it was beyond the budget of most households to feed chance guests, let alone a gathering of any size. For weddings and christenings, therefore, and even for the small parties that Philip remembers taking place continually in the summers of his childhood, those who had been invited would bring food and drink by way of gifts, and would help with their preparation and cooking. Today, families take over the taverna to celebrate important occasions, and the guests leave envelopes of money with the host as their contribution.

There is another reason for the distinction between *mezethes* and the family meal: the disinclination of the men and women to socialize together. Men rarely visit one another at home. It is as if they feel uncomfortable in the company of their wives and mothers. They relax in the masculine atmosphere of the *kafeneion* or the taverna; they drink and they eat *mezethes*, and then they go home where their wives are waiting with their suppers. The men are mobile, they have their cars or scooters, and their memories of bachelor days – often in the summer they leave the house again after dinner for the night clubs of Kassiopi and Rodas – but their wives do not go with them. The women's place is firmly in the home and it is there that they meet, sitting outside on summer nights, discussing the meals they have cooked for their husbands and joking about the indignities inflicted upon them by their parents-in-law, who seem always critical, never satisfied that they are sufficiently conscientious homemakers.

At the root of their predicament are the old proprieties that pertain to married women, for as single girls they felt less restricted in their socializing. In their brief adolescence they had their *volta* on a summer Saturday night, the Greek version of the Italian *fa niente*. Dressed in their best, arms linked, they would stroll up and down the main street of Loutses from six o'clock until dusk, laughing and smiling and of course entirely oblivious to the boys, also in their smartest clothes, who sat outside the bar or freewheeled down the hill on their motor-bikes.

The boys had their own code of behaviour, known as *kamaki*, a word which refers to the activities of young men who go out specifically to meet girls, and which was all to do with the games of flirtation, conversation and dancing, executed with as much gallantry as they could muster, and technically devoid of any predatory sexual motive.

These days *kamaki* has faded away, a casualty of tourism, for the young men have work down at the resorts in the summer and the female tourists are not interested in long courtships, but the Saturday night *volta* still takes place. Also, today's generation of single girls has its own ideas about what they want to do. Unlike their mothers, they complete their education in the secondary school in Kassiopi and then at high school in Corfu Town. Their lives are not limited to the village and its valley; one or two of them are even prepared to go out and enjoy themselves in the company of liberated friends like Philip. Traditionally, all but a few well-defined excursions ended when a girl married, but today some of the most modern and sophisticated couples go out to dinner together, though the men are branded as unnaturally uxorious by less enlightened acquaintances.

Such behaviour is still exceptional in Loutses. For most of the married women, their only outing in the week is on a summer Sunday night, and the occasion has a pattern that rarely changes. It begins with a family *volta*. Pushing a pram, or leading toddlers and small children by the hand, husbands and wives walk at a leisurely pace up and down the main road of the village. The women are wearing their best dresses with a light cardigan as a token against an imaginary cold, their children are scrubbed and tidied. Couples pause and talk together, admiring babies and exchanging news, and then as dusk falls grandparents take the infants home while the adults and older children repair to the taverna. Tonight, for once, the women will not have to cook a meal. While their children run between the tables or organize their own games in the darkness beyond the lights of the taverna, the men and their wives sit with friends and eat together.

In a village like Loutses, the taverna fulfills many functions. It is open only in the evening and only in the summer, and has always been distinct from the *kafeneion* and the *kafepantopoleion* in that it provides food as well as a place to drink. During the week this means *mezethes* for the men to eat with their beer and ouzo, but on Sunday the kitchen and the grill, the *psistaria*, are a great deal busier.

It is a universal complaint of visitors to the island that the food they are offered in the tavernas is dull, and numbingly limited to a choice that even a fortnight's holiday can exhaust. Part of the responsibility for this must lie with the restaurateurs, who as businessmen cater to the tastes of their clientele, but there is another, less commercial reason for the monotony of the menus that has to do with the attitude of the Greeks themselves.

When the Loutsiotes go out for a meal on a Sunday evening it is a social rather than a culinary event and the fact that they will encounter basically the same food wherever they go is not a cause for dismay. They are not looking for any startlingly creative cooking. They demand freshness and within each narrow recipe there is enough room for the chef to fail or to do well – but not to experiment. The food they want will be happily familiar, and prepared in ways that they – or at any rate their mothers – understand. The preponderance of grills and stews on the menu is a legitimate reflection of traditional home-cooking from the days when the kitchen consisted of a charcoal range and a wood-fuelled stove and oven, and just as the kitchen was and is the central social room of a rural Greek household, so the taverna is a place both to meet and to entertain friends, an extension of one's own kitchen at home, but better equipped and with room for more people to sit down. This is particularly obvious when it comes to large gatherings such as bouzouki nights, wedding feasts or christening celebrations. Sometime after the War the habit of throwing such parties at home began to fade: the taverna was more convenient and gave an impression of grandeur, and it also allowed the festivities to be restricted to a single banquet.

Until quite recently, the taverna in Loutses was run by a man called Georgie and was a place of considerable charm. Inside, there were two small rooms. One was the kitchen where Georgie's wife prepared salads, fried chips and did any other cooking that needed the stove; the other was bare except for the refrigerated cabinet where drinks were kept, and an enormous sky-blue and chrome juke-box, a vintage masterpiece from the late '50s with a repertoire of Greek ballads and bouzouki and a few bizarre but popular exceptions such as 'Viva España' and the Tony Christie hit 'Don't go down to Reno'. Sometimes, at the end of the summer, when the weather began to cool, Georgie would move one or two tables inside, but from May to September the real life of the taverna went on in the garden, shaded by trees and separated from the road by a low wall called the *pezouli*.

Leaning up against the building, then as now, was a ramshackle construction that housed the charcoal brazier, and it was inside this tiny space, a smoky inferno on an already sweltering August night, that Georgie spent his evenings, grilling the great Greek *meze, souvlakia*.

Souvlakia are simply small kebabs of cubed meat that are cooked over a charcoal grill. In the chic Athenian restaurants they are made with lamb, but almost everywhere else these days pork is used, and on a good night Georgie could turn them into little miracles of flavour. First thing in the morning, he would trim most of the fat off three kilos of pork, cut from the leg in thick slices. To clean the meat he would leave it to soak in cold water until the late afternoon, then he would drain it and lie the slices one on top of another in a special box used by all *souvlaki*-makers, a plastic cuboid with nine vertical slits on each of the four sides. He screwed down the lid of the box and then pushed bamboo spears, as long and thin as pencil-leads, down through each of the hundred perforations in the lid, through the meat and into corresponding holes in the box's base. Then he slipped a long, razor-sharp knife through each of the slits in the side, like a conjuror sawing his assistant in half, and thereby cut the pork into a hundred *souvlakia*. These he would keep in his fridge until the evening, when the charcoal was hot and the first customers were sitting with their ouzo or beer.

Before he actually grilled the *souvlakia*, Georgie would dust them with a little salt, black pepper and *rigani*, then he would set them low over the embers, turning them continuously, until the outside of the meat was dark and crisp, the inside well-cooked but still tender and moist. He cooked them as the orders came in, either from his wife or daughter-in-law who waited on the tables, or from the queue of children, peering up at the window in the side of the booth with the twelve drachmas they needed to buy a single *souvlaki*. When they were done he dipped each one into a tray of lemon juice, oil, water, salt, pepper and *rigani*, stuck a doorstep of bread on the end of each skewer and handed them out.

Except on Sundays, Georgie's *souvlakia* were eaten as a *meze* by the men who spent their evenings there. A single *souvlaki* could be stretched out over twenty minutes or so, or if something else was needed Georgie's wife would put together a small plate of morsels of tomato, cucumber, *feta* and chips, each one pierced with a toothpick. If the fish-seller had been up to the village that morning, there would be other *mezethes* such as whole sardines, rolled in flour and salt and shallow-fried until they were crisp on the outside and juicy within, and sometimes, on busy Saturday evenings, Georgie would set a *rolo* or a rack of spare ribs over the charcoal.

On the rare occasions strangers passed by and stopped, attracted by the lights, the laughter and the music, this small variety could be easily amplified into a meal. If given fair warning by any of the handful of tourists who were staying in Loutses, Georgie would also grill succulent chickens, octopus, *kokoretsi*, or even a whole lamb, and there were always *brizzoles*, kept in the ice-cream freezer and ready to be grilled as soon as they had thawed.

Brizzoles are steaks of any kind, but in the vernacular of tourism the word has come to refer to pork chops. Because they freeze well and are always popular, they appear on the menu of every taverna, but they are also great favourites with the villagers and are often barbecued at home.

To prepare **Brizzoles tou hirinou** (pork chops) in the way the villagers do you will need 4 large pork chops, on or off the bone, the juice of ½ a large lemon, 150 ml (¼ pint, ⅔ cup) of oil, 1 teaspoon of salt, 1 teaspoon of *rigani* and ½ teaspoon of black pepper.

Pummel the chops to tenderize them. Mix the other ingredients together in a bowl and cover the chops with this marinade, leaving them for three or four hours, or better still overnight, in the refrigerator. Take the meat out and let it drain on a plate for ten minutes. Grill them on a barbecue, in the oven, or under the grill, basting them occasionally with the marinade and turning them once.

Georgie is a very good cook, but the prices he charged were unrealistically low, a third of those down on the coast, and despite the extremely unpretentious surroundings and the long hours he and his family put into the taverna, he gradually lost control of the financial side of things. The rent on the place and the bills from the butcher in Kassiopi and the drivers who delivered beer and soft drinks became too much for him. During the winter of 1983, when the taverna was closed for the season, he relinquished the lease and went back to looking after his garden.

The last policeman to be stationed in Loutses left in the same year. He had been a regular customer of Georgie's – indeed closing time at the taverna had always been signalled by his finishing his final beer of the night – but his term of duty was up and his superiors had decided that a policeman would be more centrally placed down in Peritheia than in Loutses.

So the police station next to Stamati's shop was put up for sale, to the delight of two men from the village: Tasso, Philip's cousin and a master electrician and plumber, and Christos, a chef who had worked as a cook in the merchant navy and then as a caterer in Athens. They had decided to pool their savings and open a restaurant in the village – a taverna where the locals could eat and also, hopefully, somewhere that would bring tourists up from the coast. They bought the police station and, working hard through the winter, had turned it into a smart new restaurant by the following May, just as the tourist season was beginning.

Meanwhile, Georgie's taverna had reopened. Spiro Parginos was also a ship's cook and had spent many long seasons at sea, but he had decided to come home to spend more time with his wife and young family. When Georgie retired he took over the lease on the taverna, then he repainted the building, laid cement over the old dirt garden where the tables were, and replaced the juke-box with a powerful stereo system.

Those who were interested were now able to witness a new competition in the village. At first it seemed as though Spiro would keep the custom of Georgie's patrons, but then some of them began to wander up the street to Tasso's. At the same time some of the tourists whom Tasso's contacts on the coast had brought up to Loutses would return the following night and out of curiosity would try Spiro's. The rather more genteel ambience of Tasso's restaurant, with its checked tablecloths and imported liqueurs was evenly matched against the noisy exuberance of Spiro's and by the end of the summer the contest was generally conceded to be a draw.

In keeping with its traditional atmosphere, Spiro's menu remained very similar to Georgie's but Tasso and Christos had wanted something more sophisticated. Since most of their weekday customers were men needing something to eat with their drinks, all of whom would return to their homes for a meal later in the evening, Christos turned his expertise towards *mezethes*.

Almost anything can be called a *meze*, from a simple bowl of nuts or olives to a small portion of the most elaborate entrée. Expanded into a mixed hors-d'œuvre, a plate of various *mezethes* becomes a *pikilia*, and the standard of such an offering is an accurate gauge of the quality of a restaurant or taverna. Some establishments go no further than a few pieces of pickled octopus but Christos's *pikilia* have always been exceptional. The *mezethes* he includes are all traditional – fresh salad vegetables, olives and cheese, arranged around two or three central creations of either fish or meat and small mounds of *taramasalata, melitzanosalata* and *tsatsiki*. Sometimes there is fried squid or fried sardines, or morsels of *rolo*, but there are always *tyropittakia*, very small cheese pies wrapped in *fyllo* pastry and shallow fried in oil. *Tyropittakia* are just as popular in Greek homes as they are in the restaurants and there are many different recipes for the filling. Tassò's wife Dimita makes them for the Loutses taverna. Because she uses evaporated milk, they have been criticized by some of the men who drink there as being too sweet, but this is how Dimita likes them. The sweetness is complimented by the salty tang of the *feta* as one bites into the warm, crisp pastry.

 To make about 36 **Tyropittakia** you will need 300 g (10½ oz) of *feta*, 100 g (3½ oz) of grated *kephalotyri*, 3 tablespoons of evaporated milk, 3 eggs, 2 tablespoons of fresh, chopped parsley, 2 teaspoons of fresh, chopped mint, black pepper, about 200 g (7 oz – nine leaves) of frozen *fyllo* pastry, 2 or 3 tablespoons of butter or margarine, and olive oil for shallow frying.

Crumble the *feta* and then mash it with a fork. Beat the eggs well and put them in a bowl with the *feta*, the *kephalotyri*, the milk, herbs and pepper, and mash them all together to make a smooth paste. Melt the butter in a pan without allowing it to brown. Thaw and unfold the *fyllo* as described on p. 35, then take a sharp knife and cut the stack of pastry leaves lengthways three times to make four stacks of strips each 8 cm wide. Cover three of these stacks with a damp cloth to prevent their drying and start work on the fourth. Brush the top strip with melted butter. Put a generous teaspoon of filling close to the buttered end and fold one corner of the strip over it to make a triangle flush with the longest side of the strip. Take the new point of the strip and fold it up along the strip. Fold it again, over the hypotenuse of the triangle, and carry on until the whole strip has been used up and you are left with a single, triangular *tyropittaki*. Technically, the amounts given above should produce thirty-six of them. *Tyropittakia* can be brushed with melted butter and baked in a moderate oven for half an hour, but Dimita prefers to shallow fry them in very hot oil, turning them once, until they are golden brown. They must be eaten warm and with one's fingers.

The other great cheese *meze* served at Christos's taverna and everywhere else in Greece is *saganaki*. A *saganaki* is really the name of a pan, the smallest size of *rihia*, the round, flat-bottomed pan made of thin aluminium, with two looped metal handles, that can be used equally successfully in the oven or on top of the stove. The *saganaki* has always been useful for cooking *mezethes*, especially since it is relatively elegant and handy enough to be carried from the stove to the table. There is a restaurant in Mandouki that offers marvellous chicken livers, quickly fried in a *saganaki* with oil and herbs and eaten from the pan with fresh bread and a squeeze of lemon juice. Over the years, however, a different *meze* has become so firmly associated with the *saganaki* that it has taken the name for itself: to talk about *saganaki* today is to talk about fried cheese, or more precisely, slices of fried *kephalotyri*.

Tart, firm and very salty, *kephalotyri* is perfectly suited to the recipe and there is really no true alternative – though *graviera* (Greek

Gruyère) or Parmesan would almost do. On the mainland it is fried as it is, in butter; on Corfu it is cut into slices a centimetre thick, dipped into beaten egg, rolled in flour and then slipped into half a centimetre of hot oil. It must be fried quickly until it is golden brown, soft but not melting, and then served immediately, very hot, with a quartered lemon to squeeze all over it and a knife and fork to eat it with.

The centrepiece of his *pikilia* on the night Christos's restaurant opened was a *meze* of chicken giblets braised in a dark gravy, one of the few *mezethes* that is claimed by Corfiots as their own. In private kitchens the recipe is often prepared from the giblets of a bird that will appear later in the meal, but it is also a favourite hors-d'œuvre in its own right, though considered too pungent and rich to appear as a main course. Greeks enjoy all the giblets of a chicken and they also often include the wings in the recipe; one could use only chicken livers but to do so would be to sacrifice the variety of textures and flavours of the original.

To make **Endostia poulerikon** (braised chicken giblets) you will need 500 g (1 lb 1 oz) of chicken giblets, 1 small onion, 2 tablespoons of wine vinegar, 1 tablespoon of tomato paste, 3 tablespoons of brandy, 2 cloves of garlic, flour, 120 ml (4 fl oz, ½ cup) of water, a pinch of *rigani* and of freshly chopped parsley, 2 cloves, 1 or 2 bay leaves, salt and pepper, and 3 tablespoons of oil.

Grate the onion and chop the garlic. Wash the giblets well and cut them into pieces, halving the livers and dividing the stomachs into four. Roll them in the flour then shallow fry them in the oil with the onion, garlic and *rigani*, moving them about in the pan, until they are brown. Pour on the vinegar, stirring well, and let it bubble for a minute before adding the tomato paste, brandy, water, cloves, bay leaves, parsley and seasoning. Let it stew gently for fifteen to twenty minutes until the sauce is thick, remove the cloves, and serve it as a *meze* on a small plate with bread.

Dominating Christos's kitchen is a huge charcoal brazier, the *psistaria*. He fires it every evening to grill *souvlakia* and *brizzoles* and its ten automated *rôtisseries* can accommodate whole lambs or kids on special occasions, as well as providing many different degrees of heat for everyday roasts that require the spit. Of these by far the most popular is *rolo*, a traditional speciality of the Corfiot taverna that can also be bought from enlightened butchers, ready-bound and sized for a family barbecue or grill, though one has to accept the butcher's stuffing.

Rolo is stuffed, rolled pork belly, and both Christos and Spiro prepare it as a matter of course when they are expecting a good night's custom. They begin to grill it about an hour and a half before the tavernas open, and are still cutting helpings off it three hours later. The *rolo* has been turning slowly on its spit all the while, but on a level far enough above the charcoal to merely keep it warm, and it is still succulent and marvellous at the end of the evening.

The day's *rolo* is always the first thing Christos makes when he arrives at the taverna in the late afternoon, and he begins by preparing the stuffing of herbs, salt and mild paprika and a little onion and garlic. This he smooths over the inside of a three-foot piece of lean pork belly, then he brings the two sides of the meat together and sews them to one another, tightly, with a length of copper wire he keeps for the purpose. Five feet more of the wire sticks out of one end. He dusts the outside of the meat with a mixture of salt, red pepper and *rigani*, then he scrubs clean one of his five-foot steel spits and pushes it lengthways down the centre of the *rolo*. He mounts the spit above the bed of glowing charcoal, and sets it turning, using the strength and motion of the machine to help him bind the meat tightly with the protruding copper wire. Then he binds it again, at a finer angle, with a length of butcher's string.

The pork is, of course, very fat, but the long, slow grilling reduces it, and the melting fat keeps the string from burning. The flavours of the stuffing permeate the meat and the fat in particular. Christos serves it cut into thin slices on a plate with chips and a garnish of tomatoes, olives and cucumber, and small pieces of it often feature in his *pikilia*.

It is difficult to be didactic about making *rolo* on the smaller scale of an ordinary kitchen. The ventilation, the one-directional heat source and, most importantly, the imparted flavour of a large charcoal barbecue are hard to simulate. Even with a *rôtisserie* grill, temperatures and therefore cooking time vary considerably. Cooked too quickly, a *rolo* can be too fatty inside and overdone on the surface. Also, the belly meat of English pigs is often less lean than the equivalent cut in Greece. Nevertheless, it is worth the effort, particularly for cooks experienced in spit-roasting. The recipe below is for a *rolo* Christos makes occasionally with the addition of *feta* cheese in the stuffing. It must be roasted even more gently than usually, or the *feta* may melt and seep out of the meat.

 To make **Rolo** you will need a cut of pork belly of about 2 kilos (4¼ lbs), 1 small onion, 3 cloves of garlic, 2 tablespoons of fresh, chopped parsley, 2 tablespoons of *selino* (coriander leaves might be an interesting alternative), 1 tablespoon of *rigani*, 1 tablespoon of salt and 1 tablespoon of mild red pepper, and about 100 g (3½ oz) of *feta* cheese.

Mix the salt, pepper and *rigani* in a bowl. Take half of it and mix it with the finely chopped parsley and *selino*, the crushed garlic and the finely chopped onion. Crumble the *feta* and add it to the mixture. Lie the pork belly flat with its inside upwards and spread the stuffing evenly over the meat. Bring the two long sides of the meat together around the stuffing, bind it securely, and rub its outside with the rest of the salt, pepper and *rigani* mixture. Spit the joint and roast it in a *rôtisserie* for at least three hours at a relatively low temperature.

The mixture of salt, red pepper and *rigani* stands ready in its bowl in Christos's kitchen for other pork dishes as well as for *rolo*. When he grills spare ribs over his charcoal brazier he first of all rubs the mixture into them, and he does the same thing to his large *souvlakia*, made with the best cuts from a leg of pork. The lean, moist meat is diced into four-centimetre cubes, twice as large as for a regular *souvlaki*, and six of them are threaded on to each flat skewer, separated by small pieces of onion and green pepper, before being set over the glowing charcoal. Like the smaller variety, they are dipped into a bowl of lemon juice, oil, water, salt, pepper and *rigani* and are then served.

Because of the long dry summers and the parching winds of August, the hills around Loutses have always been susceptible to fires, but in the last few years their number has increased to such an extent that Prime Minister Papandreou himself has promised a large reward for any information about the arsonists. The locals have their own ideas about who is responsible. Some blame the shepherds because the grass is always sweeter and easier for the sheep to crop on a hillside where a fire has been the year before. Others murmur of darker motives. No one can suggest why, but it always seems to be the case that a fire in Albania, glowing far away in the darkness like a dull red horseshoe, will kindle another in the north-eastern mountains of Corfu on the following night.

Usually the fires threaten no one and the villagers, roused from their beds by the clamour of the two church bells, have been known to turn the occasion into an impromptu party, sitting out for the rest of the night under the olive trees with a bottle of wine, smoking and watching the display. Last year, however, a more serious fire broke out on the hills around Ano Peritheia.

In the small hours of the night the bells in Loutses once again rang the alarm and the villagers came out into the street to see what was happening. The sky above the high escarpments to the south was glowing a dull orange and the moon looked brown through the distant pall of smoke. Soon the men had climbed into cars and trucks and were driving off into the darkness of the mountains, blaring their horns as they went, to alert anyone who might still be sleeping.

By the following morning the fire had burned itself out and the men had succeeded in saving the old, abandoned town, but only just. The natural firebreak of the pathway that winds down one side of the steep valley and up the other had stopped the flames within a metre of the nearest buildings. The sharp declivity in between had been overgrown with blackberry bushes and arbutus; now it was a moonscape of warm, grey ash through which multitudes of ants made their way, looking for their vanished burrows. All around the town the surrounding hills had been scorched, but the fire had moved quickly and only the bottom of the trees had been touched by it. The groves of laurel, cypress and wild olive stood out as splashes of dark green against the black ground. Through the efforts of the men and a degree of luck the town, with its fifteen empty churches, had been untouched.

Long ago, when the church in Loutses was nothing more than a private chapel with a single monk's cell, the villagers used their church in Ano Peritheia for their regular worship. It is built into a steep hillside above the abandoned town, commanding the deep valley and closer to God, say the Loutsiotes, than any of the other, larger churches below – a place of extraordinary serenity. Small and white with thick, rough-plastered stone walls, it now stands empty through the changing seasons, hidden by fog in the winter but seeming to live and breathe in the summer as the warm breezes of August pass in and out of its broken windows.

The church is dedicated to the Panayia, the Virgin Mary, and every year on 15 August, the devout of Loutses come here to pay Her homage. On this clear, hot morning, they climb up the path from the road through a thicket of twenty-foot bramble bushes, the children unsnagging their grandmothers' shawls, and congregate in the cleared area around the church. Everyone is in merry spirits, laughing and talking quietly in the bright air, and admiring the view beneath them. The church has no campanile so the bell has been hung from a dead apple tree close by and some of the older men sit down beneath it, calling the day's greeting to friends as they appear.

Inside the church the tabernacle stands in the centre of the room and the old stone floor has been strewn with leaves of bay and basil. Andrei the shop-keeper, who is a church warden, has carried the ornate brass candle-holder up from Loutses, and everybody lights a long pencil-thin candle of caramel-coloured wax from it. Children play tag between the legs of the standing adults and improvize another game with their candles, blowing them out and lighting them again a hundred times. Their fun and some of the murmured conversations of their parents continue even after the priest has emerged through the door in the iconostasis, flanked by the Loutses altar-boys with their silver censers. He begins to chant and the sombre cantor intones the responses; the congregation sing their part with an honest satisfaction, devoid of pomp.

At one point in the service, everyone leaves the church. Four men carry the wooden tabernacle out into the sunlight and process three times around the church, led by a man carrying a heavy silver crosier staff, and another holding a fifteen-foot banner of purple silk, embroidered with gold stars and tassels and a painted medallion of the Virgin. The priest follows, reading from his Bible, and the congregation follows him. As they walk they crush the wild mint and *rigani* that grows around the church and a sharp, invigorating aroma spreads through the warm air.

The herb basil is said to have grown beneath the cross on Calvary; as the service ends a sprig of it is handed to each person as they leave, along with a piece of the holiday bread, a dark-crusted sweet loaf, covered with sesame seeds.

Perhaps fifty of the villagers have come to the church on this beautiful morning. There was not enough room inside for everyone and some of the men have stayed out in the sun, sitting on the wall and smoking cigarettes. The breeze so high in the mountains, the heat and the silence and sense of space around them induce a profound tranquility. For many of the people of Loutses and lower Peritheia, Ano Peritheia is a place of retreat. There are even individuals who come up here during the summer when the heat on the coast becomes too uncomfortable, to spend the day or a night in an old family home.

By some miracle, the town has escaped the notice of the guide books of the island, and even in the height of the season only two or three tourists a day venture so far inland. Apart from the few who have been told about the matchless Corfiot-Venetian architecture, they are all victims of a certain map, which shows a road leading through the town and down to the other side of the island. The road was planned, it is true, but work on it was never begun. The jagged track that winds up from Loutses ends in the old *foro*, the town square – a dusty, unpaved *piazetta* surrounded by empty houses and on one side by the Taverna Capricorn, the tiny restaurant run by a man from Loutses called Kosta and his Chilean wife Lydia.

Kosta's clientele consists largely of chance arrivals. Parched, confused, often on the verge of sunstroke, the Capricorn appears to them as a wonderful oasis, but it is only when their food finally arrives that they realize they have also stumbled upon some of the best cooking on the island. Because of the nature of his business, Kosta's menu is limited. There are fresh, crisp salads and chips, substantial omelettes made with cheese and ham, very small, spicy *keftedakia*, grilled chicken and pork chops, and *souvlakia*, all of which are prepared from scratch when ordered, as both the time one has to wait and the high quality of the food can testify.

Something Kosta does prepare in advance is the famous salad, *tsatsiki*. The combination of yoghurt and cucumber is found in most cuisines east of Italy and west of Bangladesh: *tsatsiki* is its Greek incarnation. On Corfu it was always prepared with the rich, firm yoghurt made from sheep's milk, since it was more readily available and also because natural cow's milk yoghurt can be too thin, or if strained, a little too sweet. Kosta follows the tradition and his *tsatsiki* has a thick, creamy texture within which the cool of the yoghurt and the cucumber and the heat of the garlic unite to marvellous effect.

 To make **Tsatsiki** you will need about 250 g (about 9 oz) of plain full-fat yoghurt, 2 cloves of garlic, and 1 large cucumber.
Peel the garlic and crush it thoroughly, then stir it into the yoghurt. Peel the cucumber and grate it finely. Many English and American graters have holes that are larger than the average Greek grater, so it may be necessary to chop the cucumber further. To get rid of as much water as possible from the grated cucumber, squeeze it as hard as you can between your hands and then let it sit in a colander for ten minutes. Mix the cucumber well into the yoghurt. At this point many people add something else to their *tsatsiki* – a small pinch of salt, perhaps, or a teaspoon of very finely chopped mint or dill weed – but with or without these things, the *tsatsiki* should be allowed to sit for at least an hour before it is served.

Tsatsiki is eaten as a dip, with hunks of white bread, preferably baked the day before. It keeps for a day or two in the fridge, but should be covered as the garlic seems to draw encouragement from the yoghurt and can flavour other foods.

On weekends and on days like a Panayia when he can be sure of a certain custom, Kosta adds to his menu one of the best and simplest of all the excellent things he cooks in his kitchen behind the bar: fried calves' liver. Sometimes a *meze*, surrounded by slivers of cheese, pork, tomato and cucumber, sometimes a main course, the rich and salty flavour of the liver is an inspired match to a cold beer or a bottle of retsina. Kosta marinates thin slices of it in his own red wine for three or four hours, then fires it quickly in a small amount of very hot oil so that the outside is seared the darkest of browns, while the inside remains tender. He serves it immediately, but as he lifts it out of the pan he dips each piece into the ubiquitous mixture of lemon juice, oil, salt, pepper, *rigani* and a little water.

When cooking at home, Kosta sometimes takes this recipe a little further by making a thick, pungent *marinato* sauce for the liver, similar to the *marinato* more frequently used to prepare fish.

 To make **Sikoto marinato** (calves' liver in *marinato* sauce) you will need 1 kilo (2 lbs 2 oz) of calves' liver cut into thin slices, 10 tablespoons of flour, salt and pepper, 200 ml (7 fl oz, a generous ¾ cup) of oil, 4 cloves of garlic, 3 tablespoons of wine vinegar, a sprig of rosemary, a pinch of *rigani*, 3 bay leaves, 350 g (12 oz) of ripe tomatoes, about 180 ml (⅓ pint, ¾ cup) of water, and some chopped parsley to garnish. Season the flour with salt and pepper and roll the slices of liver in it before frying them quickly in the hot oil. Set them aside in a warm pan. Strain the oil and return it to the pan. Fry a heaped tablespoon of the seasoned flour on a medium heat for at least a minute, beating it with a whisk to avoid lumpiness, then add the chopped garlic, the peeled and mashed tomatoes and all the other ingredients except the parsley. Stew them for six or seven minutes, stirring continuously, then pour this sauce over the liver. Sprinkle it with parsley and serve immediately with rice or chips.

Another of Kosta's most popular offerings are *biftekia*, the Greek equivalent of hamburgers, which he makes with plenty of *rigani*, parsley and dill weed, beaten eggs, grated onion and finely chopped, peeled tomatoes in the minced beef and breadcrumb mixture. Either fried or grilled they are excellent, but they pale beside the glories of his *soutsoukakia*. Small, soft sausages cooked in a sauce of tomatoes and wine, *soutsoukakia* came originally from Smyrna, where they were probably made with minced lamb rather than beef. Their unique flavour is due to the cumin in the recipe, a spice that is otherwise never found in Corfiot cooking.

 To make Kosta's **Soutsoukakia** ('Smyrna sausages') you will need 500 g (1 lb 1 oz) of minced beef (or lamb), 2 thick slices of almost stale bread, 3 or 4 cloves of garlic, salt and pepper, a good pinch of ground cumin, 1 egg, 200 ml (7 fl oz, a generous ¾ cup) of oil, 4 or 5 ripe tomatoes, 120 ml (4 fl oz, ½ cup) of red wine, a dozen black olives and ½ teaspoon of sugar. Dip the bread in water and squeeze it dry, then crumble it. Crush the garlic and beat the egg. Mix the breadcrumbs, garlic, egg, meat, cumin, salt and pepper thoroughly together and shape the mixture into rissoles about as long and thick as a man's thumb. This amount of meat should yield between fifteen and twenty *soutsoukakia*. Brown them in half the oil in a frying pan. Now boil the olives for ten minutes, remove their stones and if they are large cut them into quarters. Peel the tomatoes and blend or sieve them. Put them in a saucepan with the rest of the oil, the wine, sugar, olives and some more salt and pepper. Stew this sauce over a very low heat for half an hour. Lay the *soutsoukakia* in a shallow baking pan and pour the sauce over them. Bake them in a preheated moderate oven for a further twenty minutes.
Soutsoukakia are served with rice or macaroni as a main course, or paired on a plate as an extravagant *meze*.

Kosta and his family live in Ano Peritheia during the summer – one of the two families who remain – and the restaurant is open during the evening. On Sunday nights some local families drive up for a meal and to enjoy the unique atmosphere of the deserted town. Draped from the enormous lime tree in the centre of the *foro*, a string of fairy-lights only emphasizes the darkness, while the music from inside the taverna fails to dispel the profound silence beyond the tables. Later, driving back down the mountain track to Loutses, a fox runs suddenly through the beam of the headlights. The steep gradient upsets one's perspective and the lights of Sarranda on the

Albanian mainland seem to glimmer high in the night sky, like a strange new constellation of stars.

The country tavernas of the island have only ever opened in the summer. They were closing in October long before tourism came to Corfu and suggested it as a logical way to maximize profits. They could, after all, expect little winter custom: it was the season of exhausting days spent working in the olive groves, and of rain and cold when people went to bed early, too tired and busy for leisurely evenings out. In the towns, however, there were always a handful of restaurants prepared to open all year round, and for men of Philip's age – the first generation with the money and the motivation to seek entertainment outside the village – they were a welcome sanctuary from the tedium of a winter night.

Today their number has dwindled. Old haunts like Tripas, to the south of Corfu Town, have evolved into restaurants for the tourist trade and are closed between November and May, but there is still a bar in Akharavi (a tourist discothèque in summer, a taverna with Greek folk music in winter), and a grill-room in Karoussades where Philip and his friends can go. Or if they are in a particularly festive mood there are the bouzouki-bars in town, where every night the atmosphere of that quintessential Greek get-together, the bouzouki party, is lovingly recreated.

The word bouzouki has an intricate knot of associated meanings. First and foremost it is the name of the ornate and unmistakable mandolin-like instrument at the heart of Greek folk music. From there it has come to mean the music that is played on the bouzouki – ballads and especially traditional dances like the *syrtaki*. Because such dances require a band and many people to take part and watch, gatherings where bouzouki music is played are also called bouzouki, and the last meaning of the word describes the state of mind induced by such a party with its wine and noise, movement and excitement: in the modern vernacular bouzouki means 'crazy'.

The urban bouzouki-bars are specialized nightclubs, but the tradition of bouzouki parties has always been just as strong in the villages. Thirty years ago, they were a frequent occurrence in Loutses. In the summer they were held outside, starting in the afternoon and carrying on sometimes until dusk, sometimes until deep into the night; in the winter they would take place wherever there was a room big enough to hold the band – in Andrei's shop, in the old taverna, even in someone's home. Musicians would come from all over the area to play. Loutses had no electricity then, so their music was acoustic, and after dark the party was lit by oil lamps and candles. Wine would be jugged from the barrel and to eat there were marvellous *mezethes* that had been prepared beforehand – *keftedakia, tyropittakia*, salami, olives and *feta*, and morsels of grilled pork. Maria Vlahou remembers the bouzouki nights of her girlhood as magical occasions. Women rarely left the village then and diversions were few; there was a romance to these evenings with everyone united in friendship. When the party was over and the revellers had dispersed, she and her girlfriends would go up into the hills and lie in the grass in the darkness, singing the songs they had danced to.

There had been no bouzouki in Loutses for many years, however, when in the second summer of the rivalry between the two tavernas, Spiro decided that he would hold one, to attract business from the coast, and also just for the fun of it. But when he went down to Kassiopi to get police permission to extend his opening hours, he found out that Tasso had had the same idea. The sergeant played Solomon on this occasion: both proprietors could host their bouzouki, but on alternate Saturdays, and Tasso could go first.

Saturday nights at Tasso's had been quiet this season. After the twilight *volta* of the teenagers a few regular customers usually came by to sit out above the street, eating *mezethes* and drinking a little beer. Sometimes a family of tourists would stop and eat, and at ten the priest would walk slowly down from the church in his black hat and grey robe, whistling a tune with his newspaper under his arm and ready for a light supper inside the taverna.

On the night of the first bouzouki, however, the atmosphere was altogether different. The day had been extremely hot even for August and it had been hard work stringing up the lights around the paddock across the road from the restaurant. The week before it had been paved with cement to serve as a dance floor. The musicians Tasso had engaged were a group of teenagers from the village (one of whom was his apprentice) who were about to turn professional under the leadership of their music teacher, the band's singer and bouzouki player. For reasons of dignity and dramatic tension he was delaying his entrance until later, but as the tables around them filled up the boys began to improvize a little simple jazz.

In the kitchen things were chaotic. The resources of the restaurant were stretched to their fullest, with extra tables brought down from Kosta's taverna in Ano Peritheia. Friends of the management had been drafted as waiters and from time to time they would appear in the doorway shouting for bread or a dozen more glasses.

While Dimita frantically tried to keep pace with the orders for *tyropittakia*, Christos was concentrating on the brazier. Turning on one spit was a whole lamb, on another a long *kokoretsi*; above them a third held a *rolo*, and at the back of the *rôtisserie*, a little smaller than the lamb, was a whole kid. Down on the grills, fifty *souvlakia* sizzled away and a hundred more lay ready on the table; the two electric deep-friers were full, one of chips, one of floured and seasoned rings of squid. All this food would be served in the traditional way, not as individual portions, but on large plates set down in the middle of the table for the revellers to dig into as they wished, the *rolo* and *kokoretsi* thinly sliced, the lamb and the sweet pale flesh of the kid cut from the spit in hunks. Beside them would be dishes of *feta*, liberally dressed with oil and *rigani* and decorated with olives and shaved rings of green pepper, and there were platters of salad, cabbage and tomato, onions and more olives, and broad but paper-thin strips of carrots soused in vinegar.

Almost everyone in the village had come to the bouzouki. Stamati and Leonidas were manning their own bars twenty paces up and twenty paces down the street, each bringing drinks to half a dozen elderly friends who preferred to watch the proceedings from a safe distance. Half a mile away up on Zervou, Koula's parents-in-law were sitting as ever on their doorstep, listening to the music, but there were few others who had stayed away.

At ten o'clock the music teacher appeared in tight black trousers and a crimson shirt and the band began to play bouzouki. A table was moved aside and a man sauntered into the empty space, spread his arms and began to dance a muscular, introverted *syrtaki* appropriate to the familiar rhythm of the song, his face turned down to observe the movements of his feet and legs as he crouched and twisted and paused, a dance that he had learned as a boy from his father. Tourists craned to see and his friends laughed and applauded, watching him intently. When the tempo of the music changed another man rose to join him. This time the dance was more exuberant. The men skipped from table to table, grinning and calling others to join in.

The music grew faster and now fifty people were on their feet, men and women, their arms draped about each others' shoulders, dipping and turning in a great circle. A six-year-old boy stood up on a table to imitate them while his older sisters cheered him on, clapping to the rhythm. The music teacher announced an Italian song and then an English one which turned out to be 'Roll Out The Barrel', then they returned to the bouzouki for a traditional dance for the single girls of the village. Their hands held high above their heads they swayed expertly and alluringly from the hips and belly while the single men clapped and shouted.

By midnight the evening was in full swing. Across the valley the gaunt escarpment of the mountain was on fire – a thin line of orange flames that moved slowly upwards, erupting from time to time in a whoosh of sparks as it reached a wild olive tree. Earlier the fire engine from Kassiopi had crawled through the dancers in the street to investigate, but there was small danger of it spreading to the olive groves so the men had come back, parked and plunged into the party.

The kitchen was empty. Christos had finally run out of food and clean glasses and was somewhere on the dance floor. Streams of children raced around the tables and teenagers who all summer long had tried to look as cool as their favourite movie stars were dancing now in intricate traditional steps. Married couples appeared suddenly romantic, talking and laughing together as they had done when they were courting, while the music filled the valley, echoing off the surrounding hills.

Tasso's bouzouki night lasted until three o'clock in the morning. Next Saturday Spiro will host one with a famous band from Karrousades supplying the music, but now for a few hours Loutses is silent. The fire has died to ashes. The villagers are asleep. The night is nearly over but the moon still casts deep blue shadows between the houses. Among the olive groves the rasp of the crickets and the single repetitive note of the owls are interrupted for an instant by a warm gust of wind, and from a distant hillside comes the faint tinkling of sheep's bells.

As dawn breaks, Maria Parginou rises and quietly opens the door of the shop. The rest of the village is still sleeping. The tables and chairs across the road from Tasso's restaurant stand where they were left, crowded with bottles and ashtrays. A faint smell of scorched vegetation, borne on the breeze from the mountains, lingers in the cool morning air.

🍇 INDEX